Fodor's POCKET 1st edition

bermuda

fodor's travel publications
new york • toronto • london • sydney • auckland
www.fodors.com

contents

On the Road with Fodor's   iv

Don't Forget to Write *v*

📖 **introducing bermuda**   1

👉 **perfect days**   24

✗ **eating out**   30

🛍 **shopping**   64

🏖 **golf**   92

🐚 **beaches, outdoor activities, and sports**   104

🚏 **here and there**   136

🍸 **nightlife**   166

🎭 **cultural activities and events** 176

🏠 **where to stay**   190

🔆 **spas**   228

🎴 **portraits**   234

Journalists **Karen Smith** and **Matt Wescott** are senior reporters at the daily *Royal Gazette* and have also contributed to numerous British papers. Together they updated the Nightlife, Shopping, and Sports chapters.

Bermuda-born **Lilla Zuill** is a news reporter for the *Bermuda Sun*, the island's biweekly newspaper. In addition, Lilla has written widely on the island's arts scene—both for the *Bermuda Sun* and other publications, including *Bermudian Magazine*. She updated the "Here and There" chapter.

Don't Forget to Write

Your experiences—positive and negative—matter to us. If we have missed or misstated something, we want to hear about it. We follow up on all suggestions. Contact the Bermuda editor at editors@fodors.com or c/o Fodor's, 280 Park Avenue, New York, NY 10017. And have a fabulous trip!

Karen Cure

Editorial Director

ON THE ROAD WITH FODOR'S

EVERY VACATION IS IMPORTANT. And here at Fodor's we know there's no substitute for advice from a like-minded friend who has just come back from where you're going, but our writers, having seen all corners of Bermuda, are the next best thing. They're the kind of people you'd poll for tips yourself if you knew them.

Ron Bernthal is a professor of travel and tourism at Sullivan County Community College in upstate New York. His travel features have appeared in numerous publications, including *The New Yorker, Newsday, Chicago Tribune, Toronto Sun,* and the *South China Morning Post.* He also writes travel documentaries for NPR affiliate WJFF, the only hydro-powered public radio station in the country. The Railway Trail, the Bermuda Film Festival, and the Dockyard ferry at sunset keep Ron returning to Bermuda.

From an island herself (Manhattan), **Rachel Christmas Derrick** has been revisiting Bermuda for more than 15 years. Her articles about this Atlantic outpost, as well as the Bahamas, the Caribbean, and many other locales around the globe, have appeared in numerous newspapers and magazines including *The New York Times, The Washington Post, Los Angeles Times, The Boston Globe, Travel & Leisure, Essence,* and *Newsweek.*

Kim Dismont Robinson, formerly a senior reporter at the Bermudian *Royal Gazette* newspaper, has also written for *Bermudian Magazine, RG Magazine,* and the *Bermuda Sun.* She is an active participant in the Bermuda arts community and has performed original poetry both at home and in the States, where she is a doctoral candidate at the University of Miami, specializing in Caribbean literature.

💡 **practical information**   244

📄 **index**   276

maps

bermuda 8–9

hamilton dining 38–39

town of st. george dining 46

dining in the parishes 50–51

beaches, golf courses, and outdoor activities 108–109

hamilton sightseeing 138

town of st. george sightseeing 146

west end sightseeing 152

parishes sightseeing 158–159

bermuda lodging 196–197

paget and pembroke lodging 204

bermuda

With its fabulous beaches and coves, its turquoise waters and coral reefs, and its isolation in the Atlantic, Bermuda has long been a favorite travel destination. And yet, if you ask a friend where Bermuda is, he or she may not be able to reply confidently. Of course, Bermuda has all the draws of the Caribbean—sun, surf, seafood, and sleeping late—so the mistake is forgivable. But the isle is actually hundreds of miles north of the Bahamas, and more than 500 mi from the United States, with Cape Hatteras, North Carolina, the nearest point on the mainland. Bermuda is also Britain's most famous resort island—and its oldest colony, due to the wreck of a New World–bound ship in 1609 ...

In This Chapter

British Influences 7 • Other Historical Highlights 13 • The Bermuda Triangle Demystified 17 • Bermuda Shorts 20 • Geography 101 23

introducing bermuda

BASKING IN THE ATLANTIC, 508 mi due east of Cape Hatteras, North Carolina, restrained, polite Bermuda is a departure from other sunny, beach-strewn isles: you won't find laid-back locals wandering around barefoot proffering piña coladas. Bermuda is somewhat formal, and despite the gorgeous weather, residents wearing stockings and heels or jackets, ties, Bermuda shorts, and knee socks are a common sight, whether on the street by day or in restaurants at night. On Bermuda's 22 square mi, you will find pastel cottages, quaint shops, and manicured gardens betray a more staid, suburban way of life. A British diplomat once said, "Bermuda is terribly middle-aged"—and in many ways he was right. Most of the island is residential, the speed limit is 20 mph (although many drivers go faster), golf and tennis are popular pastimes, and most visitors are over 40 years old. With this brings good things: Bermuda is one of the wealthiest countries in the world—average per capita income is $36,500. It has no income tax, no sales tax, no slums, no unemployment, and no major crime problem. There are also no billboards or neon signs, due to laws that regulate these more gaudy displays of commercialism.

A few Bermudians still speak the Queen's English, but the majority have their own unique accent, which reflects the country's diverse English, American, and African influences. (The population of 58,000 is 61% black and 39% white.) White Bermudians have striven to create a middle-class England of their own. And as in so many other colonies, the Bermudian version is more insular, more conservative, and more English than the original. Pubs, cricket, and an obsession with protocol are reminders of a distant loyalty to Britain and everything it used to represent. A self-governing British colony since 1968, with a parliament that dates from 1620, Bermuda loves pomp and circumstance. But the British apron strings are wearing thin. The first pro-independence government—the Progressive Labour Party (PLP)—was elected in 1998, taking Bermudian identity and autonomy to a new high. Nevertheless, great ceremony still attends the convening of Parliament. Marching bands parade through the capital in honor of the Queen's official birthday, a public holiday. Regimental bands and bagpipers reenact centuries-old ceremonies. And tea is served each afternoon.

Bermuda wears its history like a comfortable old coat. Land is too valuable to permit the island's legacy to be cordoned off for mere display. A traveler need only wander through the 17th-century buildings of St. George, now housing shops and private homes, to realize that Bermudian history remains part of the fabric of life, with each successive generation adding its own thread of achievement and color. Indeed, the island's isolation and diminutive size have forged a continuity of place and tradition almost totally missing in the United States. Walk into Trimingham's or A. S. Cooper & Son department store, and you are likely to be helped by a descendant of the original founders. The same names keep cropping up—Tucker, Carter, Trott—and a single lane in St. George's carries memories and historical meaning of centuries. Even today, the love early 19th-century Irish poet Thomas Moore had for the married Hester Tucker—the "Nea" of the odes in which he immortalized his feelings—is gossiped about with a zeal usually reserved for the transgressions of a current neighbor. Bermuda's attachment to its history is more than a product of its size, however. It is through its past that Bermuda creates its own unique identity, drawing on its British roots 3,500 mi away and mixing those memories with the cultural influences of its giant American neighbor.

Since the very beginning, the fate of this small colony in the Atlantic has been linked to that of the United States. The crew of the *Sea Venture*, whose wreck on Bermuda during a hurricane in 1609 began the settlement of the island, was actually on its way to Jamestown, Virginia. Indeed, the passenger list of the *Sea Venture* reads like a "Who's Who" of early American history. On board were Sir Thomas Gates, deputy governor of Jamestown; Christopher Newport, who had led the first expedition to Jamestown; and John Rolfe, whose second wife was the Native American Pocahontas. In the centuries since, Bermuda has been somewhat of a barometer registering the evolving relationship between the United States and Britain. In 1775, Bermuda was secretly persuaded to give gunpowder to George Washington in return for the lifting of a trade blockade that threatened the island with starvation. In the War of 1812, Bermuda was the staging post for the British fleet's attack on Washington, D.C. When Britain faced a national crisis in 1940, it gave the United States land on Bermuda to build a Naval Air Station in exchange for ships and supplies. In 1990, Prime Minister Thatcher and President Bush Sr. held talks on the island.

The fact that Bermuda—just two hours by air from New York—has maintained some of its English character through the years is obviously part of its appeal for the half million–plus Americans (more than 90% of all visitors) who flock here each year. More important, however, Bermuda means sun, sea, and sand. It has a year-round mild climate, pink beaches, turquoise waters, coral reefs, 17th-century architecture, and splendid golf courses. Indeed, Bermuda has more golf courses per square mile than anywhere else in the world.

Bermuda did not always seem so attractive. After all, more than 300 wrecks lie submerged on the same reefs where divers now frolic. William Strachey, secretary-elect for Virginia and a passenger on the *Sea Venture*, wrote that Bermuda was "a place so terrible to all that ever touched on them. Such tempests, thunders and other fearful objects are seen and heard about those islands that they are called the Devil's Islands, feared and avoided by all sea travelers above any place in the world." For the crew of the *Sea Venture*, however, the 181 small islands that compose Bermuda meant salvation. Contrary to rumor, the islands proved to be unusually fertile and hospitable, supporting the crew during the construction of two new ships, in which they departed for Jamestown on May 10, 1610.

Shakespeare drew on the accounts of these survivors in *The Tempest*, written in 1611. The wreck of the *Sea Venture* on harsh yet beneficent Bermuda—"these infortunate (yet fortunate) islands," as one survivor described them—contained all the elements of Shakespearean tragicomedy: that out of loss something greater is often born. Just as Prospero loses the duchy of Milan only to regain it and secure the kingdom of Naples for his daughter, Admiral Sir George Somers lost a ship but gained an island. Today, Bermuda's motto is *Quo Fata Ferunt* (Whither the Fates Carry Us), an expression of sublime confidence in the same providence that carried the *Sea Venture* safely to shore.

That confidence has largely been justified over the decades. Each year, many of the island's nearly 600,000 visitors, who fuel the economy, are repeat vacationers. However, Bermuda's very popularity has threatened to diminish its appeal. Residents have raised concerns about congestion, overfishing, and reef damage. Some of the government's steps to preserve Bermuda's trademark beauty, civility, and elbowroom have been more successful than others.

Traffic jams leading into Hamilton, the island's capital, are no longer uncommon, despite the facts that each resident family can have only one car, and automobile rentals are prohibited. In 1990, the government restricted the number of cruise-ship visits to four a week, citing the large numbers of passengers who add to crowding but contribute little to the island's coffers.

When all is said and done, however, whatever problems Bermuda has stem from a surfeit of advantages, and almost any island nation would gladly inherit them. The "still-vexed Bermoothes" is how Shakespeare described this Atlantic pearl, but he might have changed his tune had he found a chance to swim at Horseshoe Bay, or hit a mashie-niblick to the 15th green at Port Royal. Who knows? Instead of a reference to a storm-wracked island, *The Tempest* might have been Shakespeare's reaction to a missed putt on the 18th.

—Rachel Christmas Derrick

BRITISH INFLUENCES

Bermuda is like England but with perpetual sunshine, it is sometimes said. But, of course, in Bermuda you do not have to contend with ghastly British traffic, endless gossip about the Royal Family, or stiff Anglo-Saxon formality. Still, Bermuda certainly has a British feel to it. After all, it has been a crown colony for more than 300 years and soundly rejected independence in a 1995 referendum. But, with its own constitution and elected officials, Bermuda is truly self-governing as well, and its proximity to both the United States and the Caribbean has allowed for a melding of cultures and influences.

Although British visitors to Bermuda tend to notice the island's American influences, tourists from other countries, especially visiting Americans, are impressed by the subtle images of old England, a result of Bermuda's long history with that country. Bermuda's name comes from a Spanish sea captain, Juan de Bermudez, the first white European to visit the islands around 1503, but it was the British admiral, Sir George Somers, and later the British Virginia Company that really established Bermuda as a colony of Great Britain in the 1600s.

In fact, the first Englishmen to land on Bermuda came quite by accident when their ship, the *Sea Venture*, ran aground on June 23,

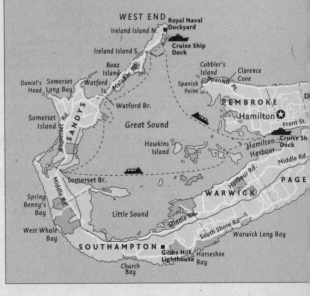

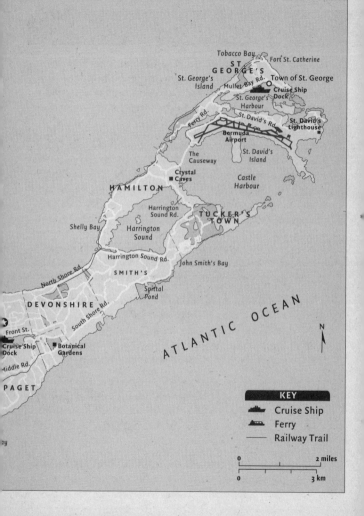

Tobacco Bay

Fort St. Catherine

ST. GEORGE'S

St. George's Island

Town of St. George

Mullet Bay Rd.

Cruise Ship Dock

St. George's Harbour

St. David's Rd.

St. David's lighthouse

Ferry Rd.

Bermuda Airport

The Causeway

St. David's Island

Crystal Caves

Castle Harbour

HAMILTON

Harrington Sound Rd.

TUCKER'S TOWN

Shelly Bay

Harrington Sound

Harrington Sound Rd.

John Smith's Bay

SMITH'S

Spittal Pond

North Shore Rd.

South Shore Rd.

DEVONSHIRE

ATLANTIC OCEAN

Front St.

N

Cruise Ship Dock

Botanical Gardens

Middle Rd.

PAGET

ay

KEY

Cruise Ship

Ferry

Railway Trail

0   2 miles

0   3 km

Weddings and Honeymoons

With moonlit beaches, amazingly vibrant flowers, and an honest-to-goodness Lover's Lane, it's no wonder so many people want to exchange their vows in this romantic paradise. If you're looking for an unforgettably beautiful spot to tie the knot, a wedding or honeymoon in Bermuda could be a fairy tale come true.

There are a few local traditions you may want to include in your special day. Bermudians serve two cakes at their weddings. The groom's cake is plain, wrapped in gold leaf to symbolize wealth. The multitiered bride's cake is a fruitcake for blessings of fertility and is wrapped in silver leaf, symbolizing purity. A cedar seedling usually adorns one of the cakes and is planted to mirror the strength and growth of the couple's love. And it is said that the bride and groom who walk under a Bermuda Moongate—an archway made of limestone and coral usually found at the entrance to gardens—will be assured good luck. The happy couple then travel to their local honeymoon destination on a traditional horse-and-carriage ride.

Although Christianity is the dominant religion in Bermuda, there are more than 100 places of worship on the island where you can exchange your vows. In the event that you prefer to marry in a natural setting, there are many beautiful outdoor locations to choose from—many overlooking the ocean—including Astwood Cove and Sonesta Beach Resort (☞ Where to Stay).

If you want to have a full-service wedding, it's a good idea to contact local wedding coordinators such as Shelly Hamil, who also publishes an annual magazine called Bermuda Weddings, at Bermuda Weddings and Special Events (tel. 441/293–4033). The Bridal Suite (tel. 441/292–2025) staff can also assist with all the details.

To get married in Bermuda, you can request a "Notice of Intended Marriage" form from the Registrar General's Office (tel. 441/297–7709 or 441/297–7707). Your license will be valid for three months.

1609, as it was en route to deliver supplies to the English settlement in Virginia. While on the island for several years, rebuilding the *Sea Venture* and starting construction of another ship to take them back to England, the colonists reported favorable conditions on the island, including the availability of large catches of fish. The Virginia Company, hearing of these positive reports, established an offshoot colony on Bermuda, called the Somers Island Company, and a variety of crops, including tobacco, were soon planted on the island. Thus, Bermuda was settled as an English colony at about the same time as Virginia and the Plymouth Colony in Massachusetts. Unlike the American colonies, however, Bermuda has never claimed independence, and its British roots remain a source of deep pride.

Today's visitor would be hard pressed to travel anywhere in Bermuda without coming across British names, customs, and histories. Its capital city, Hamilton, is named after Sir Henry Hamilton, an Englishman sent to govern Bermuda in the late 1700s, and its second-largest city and first capital, St. George, was named after the English king.

As you walk around Hamilton and cross King, Victoria, or Queen Street, it is obvious the quaint capital city was laid out by British city planners. The city was established in a gridlike pattern, with many "roundabouts" (traffic circles) at intersecting streets, as found in most British cities. Public gardens are scattered throughout the town, and the spire of the Cathedral of the Most Holy Trinity is a wonderful mix of Gothic and Middle English architecture.

A few cultural English traditions continue to be observed here, as well: Bermudians love their afternoon tea, and they mind the very British tradition of dressing up for dinner, school, and most social functions. In fact, Bermudians would never think of walking into town or local restaurants in their "balin," or bathing suits. Shorts of the proper length, however, can be worn with suit jackets and ties, a British tradition that began in the early 1900s when British soldiers stationed on Bermuda were given shorts as part of their tropical military kits. The idea of wearing shorts for leisure, as well as for business, eventually became popular on Bermuda, and Bermuda shorts would soon be purchased by visiting Americans, taken back to New York or Boston or Topeka and, well, the rest is history.

The British influence is also clearly visible within the island's tourism industry. One of its leading hotels, the Hamilton Princess, was constructed in 1884 and named after England's Princess Louise, daughter of Queen Victoria, who visited Bermuda during the winter of 1883. When news spread of the princess's visit to this little gem in the Atlantic, the upper classes of Britain and America soon followed suit, and Bermuda's gracious hospitality shortly became its leading money earner. Today, tourists stay in accommodations like Cambridge Beaches, St. George's Club, Astwood Cove, Oxford House, and, of course, the Royal Palms, all names that would not be out of place anywhere in the British Isles.

The Brits also brought cricket to the island, which is considered the national sport. The first match in Bermuda was played in 1844 among British troops stationed here. A year later the Bermuda Cricket Club was formed, and local men teamed up with the British soldiers for weekend matches. From April through the end of August cricket results fill the sports pages of the local papers, and Cup Match, an annual event played between the St. George's and Somerset clubs, usually played over two days in late July or early August, draws many spectators to the stands at the Somerset Cricket Club.

After the season ends with the cricket Cup Finals in late summer, it is time for football (soccer), another British import. During a long stretch of eight months, in which the many "pitches" (playing fields) of Bermuda are filled day and night with footballers, local teams battle it out for league honors. Occasionally, foreign teams show up to play a match, and if the visitors happen to be from Manchester or Birmingham, the crowds are intense as the rivalry between the colony and her Mother Country is played out between goal nets.

While the British sporting legacy on Bermudian is still quite evident, it's not the only area of island life to be so Anglicized. The English also introduced many food tastes to Bermuda, of course, including the ubiquitous codfish cakes, fish chowder, scones and clotted cream, steak-and-kidney pies, and lots of tea and beer. British-style pubs, like the Hog Penny in Hamilton and the Wharf Tavern in St. George, keep the tradition alive and well.

The most famous British-inspired food product is undoubtedly the distinctively sweet Bermuda onion. The original seeds were shipped from England in the early 1600s, and soon thereafter Bermuda supplied onions to the Caribbean islands; by the mid-1800s the Bermuda onion was finding its way into New York vegetable markets, solidifying the colony's reputation as the "onion patch of the Atlantic." Although the seeds are now imported from countries other than England, and the industry is nowhere near as large as it once was, it was the inventiveness of the early British colonists, combined with the rich soil and perfect climate of Bermuda, that created the very special Bermuda onion.

Of course, the constant presence of these English traditions adds a European flavor to the quiet Caribbean culture of the island. With its lush looks of a Caribbean isle, with the good graces of a British lady, Bermuda's a place in which you'll feel transported—and this will always be on the left side of the road, thank you very much.

—Ron Bernthal

OTHER HISTORICAL HIGHLIGHTS

1503 Juan de Bermudez discovers the islands while searching for the New World. They are eventually named after him.

1609 An English fleet of nine ships, under the command of Admiral Sir George Somers, sets sail for Jamestown, Virginia, with supplies for the starving colony. Struck by a hurricane, the fleet is scattered, and the admiral's ship, the *Sea Venture*, runs aground on the reefs of Bermuda. The colonization of Bermuda begins.

1610 After building two ships, *Deliverance* and *Patience*, from the island's cedar trees, the survivors depart for Jamestown, leaving behind a small party of men. Admiral Sir George Somers returns to Bermuda a few weeks later but dies soon afterward, having requested that his heart be buried on the island.

1612 Asserting ownership of the islands, the Virginia Company sends 60 settlers to Bermuda under the command of Richard Moore, the colony's first governor. The Virginia Company sells its rights to the islands to the newly formed Bermuda Company for £2,000.

1616 The islands are surveyed and divided into shares (25 acres) and tribes (50 shares per tribe). The first enslaved men and women of African descent are brought here from America and the West Indies to dive for pearls and to harvest tobacco and sugarcane.

1620 The Bermuda Parliament meets for the first time (in St. Peter's Church, in St. George), making it the third-oldest parliament in the world, after those of Iceland and Great Britain.

1684 The Crown takes control of the colony from the Bermuda Company. Sir Robert Robinson is appointed the Crown's first governor.

1780 The "Great Hurricane" hits Bermuda, driving ships ashore and leveling houses and trees.

1804 Irish poet Thomas Moore arrives in Bermuda for a four-month stint as registrar of the admiralty court. His love for the married Hester Tucker was the inspiration for his steamy poems to her (the "Nea" in his odes), which have attained legendary status in Bermuda.

1815 Hamilton becomes the new capital of Bermuda, superseding St. George.

1834 Slavery is abolished.

1846 The first lighthouse in the colony, the 117-ft-high Gibbs Hill Lighthouse, is built at the island's western end in an effort to reduce the number of shipwrecks in the area.

1861 Bermuda enters a period of enormous prosperity with the outbreak of the American Civil War. Sympathetic to the South, Bermudians take up the dangerous and lucrative task of running the Union blockade of southern ports. Sailing in small, fast ships, Bermudians ferry munitions and supplies to the Confederates and return with bales of cotton bound for London.

1883 Princess Louise, daughter of Queen Victoria, visits Bermuda, launching the island as a tourist destination.

1899 Britain establishes POW camps on Bermuda during the Boer War with South Africa. Nearly 5,000 prisoners were detained on the Great Sound islands through 1902.

1931 Built at a cost of $4.5 million, the Bermuda Railway opens years behind schedule. Maintenance problems during World War II cripple train service, and the whole system is sold to British Guiana (now Guyana) in 1948.

1937 Imperial Airways begins the first scheduled air service to Bermuda from Port Washington, New York.

1944 Women landowners are given the vote.

1946 Automobiles are lawfully allowed on Bermuda for the first time.

1953 Winston Churchill, Dwight D. Eisenhower, and Prime Minister Joseph Laniel of France meet on Bermuda for the "Big Three Conference."

1959 A boycott leads to the end of racial segregation in movie theaters, hotels, and restaurants.

1968 The first election is held after the law giving landowners an extra vote is abolished.

1971 Edward Richards becomes Bermuda's first black government leader (a title later changed to "Premier").

1973 Governor Sir Richard Sharples and his aide, Captain Hugh Sayers, are shot dead. In 1976, Erskine "Buck" Burrows is convicted of the murder, as well as several other murders and armed robberies. He is hanged in 1977.

1979 Gina Swainson, Miss Bermuda, wins the Miss World Contest.

1987 Hurricane Emily hits Bermuda, injuring more than 70 people and causing millions of dollars in damage.

1994 Her Royal Highness Queen Elizabeth II and Prince Philip pay an official visit.

1995 The Royal Navy closes its Bermuda headquarters after having maintained a presence on the island for 200 years. The U.S. Naval Air Station base closes, having operated since September 1940.

1996 An attempt by a local company to bring McDonald's restaurants to the island fails when Bermuda's Parliament nixes fast-food franchises.

1997 Bermuda's first female premier, the Honorable Pamela F. Gordon, is appointed.

1998 In a landslide victory, the Progressive Labour Party (PLP) is elected to power, putting an end to 31 years of rule by the United Bermuda Party (UBP). The UBP is dominated by affluent descendants of Bermuda's 17th-century English settlers, while the PLP was formed in 1963 from the ranks of Bermuda's labor and desegregation movements.

2000 The historical town of St. George is awarded World Heritage status, as the fourth-oldest municipality in the Western Hemisphere.

THE BERMUDA TRIANGLE DEMYSTIFIED

Bewitchingly beautiful Bermuda is one of the few places in the modern world that still remain wrapped in an aura of superstitious mystery. The Triangle—also called Devil's Triangle, Limbo of the Lost, the Twilight Zone, and Hoodoo Sea—covers some 500,000 square mi of the Atlantic Ocean. Its apexes are most commonly defined as Bermuda, the southernmost tip of Florida, and San Juan, Puerto Rico, although some place a boundary closer to Chesapeake Bay than to Miami. It seems to have been christened in February 1964, when Vincent Gaddis wrote an article titled "The Deadly Bermuda Triangle" for *Argosy* magazine.

Long before the myth of the Bermuda Triangle became popular, Bermuda had already earned a reputation as an enchanted island. It was nicknamed "The Devil's Islands" by early sea travelers, frightened by the calls of cahow birds and the squeals of wild pigs that could be heard on shore. But perhaps the most damning tales were told by sailors terrified of shipwreck on Bermuda's treacherous stretch of reefs. The island's mystical reputation was perhaps immortalized in Shakespeare's *The Tempest*, a tale of shipwreck and sorcery in "the still-vexed Bermoothes."

The early origin of the Triangle myth stretches as far back as Columbus, who noted in his logbook a haywire compass, strange lights, and a burst of flame falling into the sea. Columbus, as well as other seamen after him, also encountered a harrowing stretch of ocean now known as the Sargasso Sea. Ancient tales tell of sailboats stranded forever in a windless expanse of water, surrounded by seaweed and the remnants of other unfortunate vessels. It is true that relics have been found in the Sargasso Sea—an area of ocean in between Bermuda and the Caribbean—but the deadly calm waters are more likely the

Children in Bermuda

Bermuda is a great place to bring your family—or to ship your kids off to with Grandma and Grandpa. When children need a break from the beach or pool (and when does that ever happen?), there is plenty to see and do. From spelunking the Crystal Caves and scrambling over the walls at Fort Hamilton to experiencing a simulated dive at Bermuda Underwater Exploration Institute and sitting in the dunking stool at Ordnance Island— sights and attractions of particular interest to kids are easily found here. Plus they're identified in this book by a duckie 🦆. Need to fill their days, so they'll sleep at night? Wear them out with a snorkeling trip or by chasing them up the stairs of Gibbs Hill Lighthouse. Then all have tea.

Bermuda has no fast-food chains, except for a lone Kentucky Fried Chicken, but kids will have no trouble finding familiar menu items in welcoming settings, expecially at the more casual restaurants. The Beach, Pasta Basta, Rosa's Cantina, are good lunch and dinner bets—as is Baily's Ice Cream any old time.

For baby-sitters—because you didn't come all this way to not have an adult evening out—check with your hotel desk. The charge is usually about $17 for the first hour and $10 for each additional hour. These rates may go up after midnight and they may vary depending on the number of children. Sitters may expect paid transportation.

Note that if you have a very little one, major American brands of baby formula, disposable diapers, and over-the-counter children's medications are widely available. However, prices are steep.

result of circular ocean currents sweeping through the North Atlantic rather than paranormal activity.

In the past 500 years at least 50 ships and 20 aircraft have vanished in the Triangle, most without a trace—no wreckage, no bodies, no nothing. Many disappeared in reportedly calm waters, without having sent a distress signal. Among the legends is that of the *Mary Celeste*, a 103-ft brigantine found floating and abandoned in 1872—with warm food on the stove, according to some accounts. But the real mystery of the *Mary Celeste* is that she turns up in Triangle tales at all. The ship was actually found off the coast of Portugal.

One of the most famous Triangle cases is that of Flight 19. At 2:10 on the afternoon of December 5, 1945, five TBM Avenger Torpedo Bombers took off from Fort Lauderdale, Florida, on a routine two-hour training mission. Their last radio contact was at 4 PM. The planes and 27 men were never seen or heard from again. The official navy report said the planes disappeared "as if they had flown to Mars."

The bizarre disappearances attributed to the Triangle have been linked to everything from alien abduction to sorcery. As one Bermuda book notes, an English vicar was summoned to the island in 1978 to perform a most unusual exorcism—"the spiritual cleansing by prayer and invocation of the dreaded Bermuda Triangle." Although the mystery has not yet been completely solved, there are explanations for the maritime disasters that are more scientific than supernatural.

The most obvious explanations are linked to extreme weather occurrences with which any Bermudian fisherman would be well acquainted. Ships wrecked by hurricanes would perhaps be the most common reason for disappearance. "White squalls"—intense, unexpected storms that arrive without warning on otherwise clear days—are also probable culprits along with waterspouts, which are the equivalent of sea tornadoes.

The most recent scientific theory on the infamous Triangle suggests that the freakish disappearance of ships and aircraft could be the result of large deposits of methane gas spewing up from the ocean floor. Huge eruptions of methane bubbles may push water away from a ship, causing it to sink. If the highly flammable methane then rises into the air, it could ignite in an airplane's engine—causing it to explode and disappear like the planes of the ill-fated Flight 19.

Fact or fiction, the Bermuda Triangle is a part of local lore that won't disappear anytime soon. But don't let the legend scare you away—the Triangle isn't the only thing that makes this island seem magical.

—Kim Dismont Robinson

BERMUDA SHORTS

However many images of Bermudian businessmen in shorts and long socks the books and brochures depict, nothing quite prepares visitors for the first sighting. Tourists can be spotted sniggering in shop doorways after discovering the bottom half of a blazer-and-tie-clad executive on his cell phone. After all, where else in the world could he walk into the boardroom wearing bright-pink shorts without so much as a batting of an eyelid? Only in Bermuda. These unique, all-purpose garments, however flamboyantly dyed, are worn with complete seriousness and pride. Bermudians would go so far as to say it is the rest of the world that is peculiar, and they have a point—particularly in the steaming humidity of the summer months, when full-length trousers are unthinkable to any self-respecting local.

What is surprising is how the original khaki cutoffs evolved into formal attire. They were introduced to Bermuda in the early 1900s by the British military, who adopted the belted, baggy, cotton-twill version to survive the sweltering outposts of the Empire. By the 1920s Bermudian pragmatism and innovation

What's a Parish?

When the 1610 Bermuda Company divided up the islands of Bermuda among its seven original shareholders, Bermuda's parishes, or districts, were delineated into shares (25 acres) and tribes (50 shares per tribe). The parishes are named after investors in the Bermuda Company. The parish names derive from these early shareholders—Sandys, Southampton, Warwick, Paget, Pembroke, Devonshire, Smith, Hamilton, and St. George—who were, as in "Humpty Dumpty," all the king's men: aristocrats, knights, some members of parliament, who financed or played a role in Bermuda's colonization. Although the names are still used colloquially as a reference point, sometimes indicating where one's family is from (and has been for centuries), the function of these property lines today is mostly historical.

Southampton, Warwick, and Paget comprise the Western Parishes. Southampton is known for it's beautiful pink sand beaches, manicured golf courses, and the big resorts which line them. Warwick's claim to fame is the Warwick Long Bay beach, the island's longest, which is open to the public and has a coral outcrop close to shore. Warwick is somewhat isolated from restaurants and nightlife, however. Like Southampton, Paget's terrific selection of accommodations make it a familiar parish for returning visitors. It's also a stone's throw from Hamilton, the ferries, and lots of restaurants.

The Eastern Parishes—Pembroke, Devonshire, Smith's, Hamilton, and St. George's—are somewhat dominated by the lively city of Hamilton in Pembroke and the traffic and pace the city generates. Because it's a part of the action, Pembroke isn't the best place to stay for R and R. The Ocean View Golf Course, nature reserves, and the arboretum are Devonshire's draws. Historical Flatts Village is the de facto center of Smith's Parish, which borders Harrington Sound and is home to the Bermuda Aquarium, Spittal Pond, and Verdmont, an 18th-century estate. Crystal Caves and Bailey's Bay are the landmarks of Hamilton Parish. Tucker's Town, in St. George's Parish, is an affluent area of residential estates, elsewhere in the parish are plenty of historical sites, like Fort St. Catherine, and St. David's Lighthouse.

were at play as locals started chopping off their trousers at the knees to stay cool. Tailors seized on the trend and started manufacturing a smarter pair of shorts, and men were soon discovering the benefits of a breeze around the knees.

But for an island that has a love affair with rules there was always going to be a right and a wrong way to wear this new uniform. Bermudas had to be worn with knee-high socks, and a jacket and tie were the only acceptable way of dressing them up for business. But it didn't stop there. Obsession with detail prevailed, fueled by gentlemen who were disturbed at the unseemly shortness of other men's shorts. A law was passed to ensure propriety, and the bizarre result was patrolling policemen, armed with tape measures and warning tickets, scouring the capital for men showing too much leg. Officially, shorts could be no more than 6 inches above the knee, while 2 to 4 was preferable.

Other rigid but unwritten rules made it unheard of to wear them in hotel dining rooms after 6 PM or in churches on Sunday mornings, and even to this day they are out of bounds in the Supreme Court, although in 2000, legislation was changed to allow them to be worn, even by ministers, in the House of Assembly. Viewed as conservative and respectable men's wear for almost any occasion, they can be seen paired with tuxedo jackets and are even acceptable (provided they are black) at funerals.

If you're planning on joining in the local tradition, however, play by the rules. Don't expect to be allowed in a restaurant with a pair of check-patterned American interpretations. Real Bermudas are characterized by their fabric and styling—linen or wool blends and a 3-inch hem. The official shorts season is from May to November. Take your cue from the local policemen, who trade in their full-length navy blues at the start of summer.

But if Bermuda shorts are practical, smart dress for men, where does that leave the island's women during the sticky summer months? Wearing brightly colored cotton dresses and skirts, it would seem. Shorts are not considered ideal business wear for women and are only really acceptable on the beach and while shopping (but again, not if they're skimpy). In a country where pink is a man's color and men's bare legs are all but mandatory for six months of the year, perhaps the men feel the need to stamp their masculine pride on their pants. Whatever the motives, men have truly claimed Bermudas as their own and look set to be showing leg well into the 21st century.

—*Vivienne Sheath*

GEOGRAPHY 101

Hamilton, Bermuda's capital since 1815, is the departure point for ferries heading to other parts of the island and one of the island's two cruise-ship ports. Colorful Front Street is the main thoroughfare—a major shopping and dining hub.

The Town of St. George was Bermuda's original capital (from the early 17th century until 1815), settled 1609. It was the second English settlement in the New World (after Jamestown, Virginia). Today small museums and historic sights line its quaint alleys and lanes, the most notable of which is King's Square, where cedar replicas of the stocks, pillory, and dunking stool once used to punish criminals serve as props.

The West End encompasses Somerset and Ireland islands. It's a bucolic area of nature reserves, wooded areas, and beautiful bays and harbors, although the big attraction is the Royal Naval Dockyard, a former bastion of the Royal British Navy. It's now a major shopping center, with a crafts market in the old Cooperage building, a shopping arcade, a maritime museum, and a number of restaurants and pubs. The Bermuda Arts Center and Bermuda Clayworks Pottery are also nearby.

—*Kim Dismont Robinson*

How much better can it get, you will ask yourself, as the warm Bermuda sun shines above the Atlantic, and the scene within the frames of your sunglasses is that of turquoise water and the immense blue sky? How could things be more perfect? The following itineraries highlight the best of the best activities on the island— pick one or two that resonate for you and just see if things can't get better still.

In This Chapter

A Perfect Day at the Beach 25 • A Culture Vulture's Perfect Day, Also a Perfect Rainy Day 26 • A Sport Enthusiast's Perfect Day 27 • A Perfectly Romantic Night 28

By Ron Bernthal.

perfect days

A PERFECT DAY AT THE BEACH

With hundreds of beaches to choose from you could lose the better part of the day running from one to another, being mesmerized at each by the sight of shimmering water, startling cliffs and rock formations, or undulating sand dunes. No, you must choose one and stay put, bringing along some beverages, sunblock, and a few good books. After a satisfying Bermuda breakfast head to Warwick Long Bay (☞ Beaches, Outdoor Activities, and Sports), off South Shore Road in Southampton Parish, or consider traveling north to Shelly Bay Beach (☞ Beaches, Outdoor Activities, and Sports), near Flatts Village.

Shelly Bay has shallow water and great breezes for windsurfing. You can also rent snorkeling equipment here. In the late afternoon, when the sun has moved off, gather your belongings and walk five minutes to Shelly Bay Pizza (Crawl Hill, look for signs on North Shore Rd., tel. 441/293–8465). This popular little place has been serving pizza and sandwiches to locals for years.

Warwick Long Bay (on Bus 7) vies for perfect South Shore beach with ½ mi of beautiful pink-and-white coral sand and a tempting wave-riding surf. Two parking lots above the beach lead down to the sand via footpaths. To end the day on the South Shore, stop in at Paw-Paws (☞ Eating Out), a friendly little bistro on the South Shore Road. Make for the patio, consider a glass of chilled white wine and a plate of grilled shrimp, and try to figure out how you're going to have a more perfect day tomorrow.

A CULTURE VULTURE'S PERFECT DAY, ALSO A PERFECT RAINY DAY

Yes, it does rain in Bermuda. Without it the array of bougainvillea, hibiscus, oleander, and passion flowers would not be so lush and alive with color. But rainy weather makes it dangerous for motor scooters, impractical for beach excursions, and not much fun for ferry rides. To change a gloomy day into a perfect one, take a bus or taxi into Hamilton, where there are lots of indoor activities and the sidewalks along Front Street are protected from the weather by wooden balconies and arcaded buildings.

Have a light breakfast at Paradiso Cafe (☞ Eating Out), a relaxing coffee bar with imported coffee and herbal teas, before walking to the nearby Bermuda Underwater Exploration Institute (☞ Here and There) where multimedia displays, and scale models of sunken ships provide a real sense of Bermuda's underwater environment. There's a great gift shop here, selling all sorts of marine-life souvenirs, and a good cafeteria for lunch. Or walk to the Docksider (☞ Eating Out), on Front Street, for fish-and-chips. After lunch, stroll Front Street, under those wonderful Victorian-style overhanging verandas. Shops here sell everything from perfumes to cameras to local rum (duty free!).

By mid-afternoon the sun will probably begin to poke out of the clouds, and Hamilton will be bathed by a delicate ocean light. In this post-rainy state, head to City Hall (☞ Here and There), which houses the Bermuda National Gallery (☞ Here and There) and its European paintings of the 16th through 19th centuries. In the west wing is the Bermuda Society of Arts Gallery, which exhibits local art and photography. There are no entrance fees.

Taking tea is a perfectly civilized way to end your afternoon. So, walk over to the Fairmont Hamilton Princess (☞ Where to Stay), the eye-catching pink hotel, constructed in 1884, that's been a Hamilton landmark ever since. Sit at the bar overlooking Hamilton Harbour as waiters in formal attire bring tea and scones and watch a rainbow arch across the early evening sky.

A SPORT ENTHUSIAST'S PERFECT DAY

For a small island, somewhat isolated in the North Atlantic, Bermuda has a rather international sports scene. Taking cues from its Britain ancestry, and its close social and commercial ties with the United States, Bermuda's sports activities offer a combination of English traditionalism and more adventurous American imports.

Start the day early with a sunrise horseback ride along the dunes in Warwick Parish. Spicelands Riding Centre (☞ Beaches, Outdoor Activities, and Sports) can arrange one-hour excursions on trails overlooking the beaches or, during the winter, on the beach itself. Later in the morning, after breakfast at Ms. Softy's (235 Middle Rd., Southampton, tel. 441/238–0931), an informal roadside restaurant serving large breakfasts, including eggs, pancakes, and bagels, perhaps, head out to one of Bermuda's public golf courses (☞ Golf) for a leisurely game among some of the world's prettiest greens. The Port Royal course in Southampton, at 6,565 yards, was ranked by Jack Nicklaus as among the world's best, and the Ocean View course, in Devonshire, offers just that, stunning views of the north shore and beaches. Call ahead for green reservations, especially in high season.

For lunch, head to North Rock Brewing Company (☞ Eating Out), on South Shore Road in Smith's Parish, the first and only brewpub on Bermuda. After lunch, you may go it by land or by sea. Landlubbers may visit a bike rental shop, which are in all the towns and at the larger hotels, and cycle the Railway Trail, a mostly paved route through the countryside that follows the former rail beds of the old Bermuda Railway system. If you're starting in Hamilton you can pick up the trail at Palmetto Park and head east towards St. George's.

If it's at sea that you must be, you can charter a 45-ft sailboat, or a 7-ft kayak, and explore the bays and coves in the Great Sound or Hamilton Harbour. Or, consider a snorkeling or scuba diving trip, and investigate some of the more accessible shipwrecks, like the *Constellation*.

Curious about cricket, football (soccer), or rugby? Check the local newspapers for times and locations of schedules. Cricket is the island's big summer sport. Big-deal cup matches are held in late July and early August at the cricket grounds in St. George's and Somerset. Football begins in September, and games are often held weekend afternoons in the National Stadium outside Hamilton. Rugby has a long season (April through October) and matches are usually on weekends at the National Sports Club in Devonshire. Unless it's a professional match, Bermudians will welcome you to join in, so come prepared to run with the locals.

The Beach (☞ Eating Out) on Front Street is a casual place to grab a bite and beer. After dinner, if you're still restless, the courts at the Bermuda Squash & Racquets Association are open until 11 PM, or the popular Warwick Lanes have 16 lanes of bowling seven nights a week (☞ Beaches, Outdoor Activities, and Sports).

A PERFECTLY ROMANTIC NIGHT

Bermuda has all the ingredients for the perfect romantic evening—upscale restaurants, a landscape filled with flowers and sea views, starry skies, and a lovely mixture of British formality and Caribbean charm.

When planning your romantic night out, you might want to check the schedule for City Hall Theatre and the Bermuda Philharmonic Society for current performances. And plan the rest of your evening around one of these events. Otherwise, start the evening off with dinner at the Waterloo House (☞ Eating Out), a small, historic Relais & Château guest house overlooking Hamilton Harbour. Both the outdoor patio and the cozy, European-style dining room have views of the water, and at dusk the lights of passing ferries and fishing boats throw sparkling reflections onto the sea. You can expect a candlelit table, fresh fish and lamb specialties, and thoroughly attentive service.

For dinner outside the capital, reserve a window table at the 300-year-old Waterlot Inn (☞ Eating Out), on Middle Road, just down the hill from the Fairmont Southampton Princess resort. Dating from the 1670s, this former manor house is an ideal spot for a leisurely dinner of Bermudian specialties and a bottle of fine wine—don't miss the sumptuous dessert cart.

After dinner, have a drink at Ascots (☞ Eating Out), in the Royal Palms hotel near Hamilton. The lounge is conducive to quiet conversation, as is the garden-view patio. If you're returning to Hamilton late at night make sure you take the Harbour Road back into the city. It's a beautiful night drive, with the lights of the capital twinkling across the harbor and, hopefully, a moonlit landscape leading you back to your hotel or guest house.

After glancing at the menu for a reference to fresh-caught lobster, the bemused diner flags down her waiter. "When is lobster in season in Bermuda?" she asks, mildly alarmed. "I'm not sure my travel guide covers that." The waiter chuckles and in his answer offers her an easy way to remember: "During any month with an 'R' in its name." The diner thinks for a moment, and then a smile anticipating gustatory pleasure spreads across her face—the current month fits the bill.

In This Chapter

Hamilton and Environs 32 • The Town of St. George 45 • The Parishes 48

Revised by Rachel Christmas Derrick

eating out

WITH ABOUT 150 RESTAURANTS from which to choose—nearly seven per square mile—you'll have little trouble getting your fill in Bermuda. Bermuda's culinary lineup has expanded greatly during the past decade—a steady stream of internationally acclaimed chefs have come to the island, giving way to a medley of global cuisines—Italian, Indian, Caribbean, Chinese, English, French, Japanese, and Mexican. Popular now are sushi bars and menus that combine Asian ingredients in island specialties. However, the island's cuisine truly begins and ends with Bermudian ingredients—with local lobster and fish in the forefront—and therein lies its culinary identity.

PRICES AND DRESS

Much harder to swallow than the average spoonful of Bermuda fish chowder are the prices of dining out. Bermuda has never sought a reputation for affordability, and restaurateurs are no exception. A few greasy spoons serve up standard North American fare (and a few local favorites) at a decent price, but by and large you should prepare for a bit of sticker shock. Don't be surprised if dinner for two with wine at one of the very top places—the Newport Room or Fourways Inn, for example—puts a $200–$300 dent in your pocket. And a 15% service charge is almost always added to the bill "for your convenience." Between the Newport Room and the Kentucky Fried Chicken, however, are myriad dining opportunities and some truly innovative menus.

As with most rituals in Bermuda, dining tends to be rather formal. For men, jackets are rarely out of place. We mention when they're required.

CATEGORY	COST*
$$$$	over $35
$$$	$25–$35
$$	$15–$25
$	under $15

*dinner entrée per person, excluding service (a 15% service charge is sometimes added)

HAMILTON and ENVIRONS

American/Casual

$ **THE BEACH.** Across Front Street from the cruise-ship dock, the Beach is one of just a few of Hamilton's casual dining options. Colorful picnic tables, surfboards, and murals of the sand and sea at this laid-back bar and grill evoke the island's lighter side. Dining is both indoors and out, and the menu is unfussy, with soups, salads, sandwiches, burgers, and pastas. Macaroni-and-cheese and peas and rice are popular side dishes. Among the frozen drinks, the Dark and Stormy (black rum and ginger beer) is a winner, and there's a large selection of draft and bottled beer. 103 Front St., tel. 441/292–0219. MC, V.

$ **PARADISO CAFE.** When you're ready for a break from shopping, a high stool in this coffee bar is a good people-watching perch. Assorted Euro-coffees and herbal teas, served hot or iced, are on the light menu, along with salads (try the Oriental chicken), soups, pasta, quiche, and chichi sandwich wraps. *Washington Mall, 7 Reid St., tel. 441/295–3263. AE, MC, V. Closed Sun. No dinner.*

Bermudian

$–$$ MONTY'S. Breakfast can be hard to find outside a resort. Fortunately here you'll find fluffy omelets, pancakes, and French toast. For lunch the Caesar salad with grilled chicken and the fish-cake sandwich are popular. You might start dinner with mango wrapped in smoked salmon, Portuguese red-bean soup, or Bermuda fish chowder. For an entrée try the grilled local fish in champagne sauce, bangers and mash (sausages and mashed potatoes), or curried chicken. *Pitts Bay Rd., tel. 441/295–5759.* AE, MC, V.

$–$$ THE PICKLED ONION. In an old whiskey warehouse with exposed cedar beams, this lively restaurant serves a variety of familiar Bermudian dishes, some with a Bermudian twist, like flame-seared tuna steak with Bermuda avocado and mango salsa. For dessert go straight for Melanie's Bermuda banana bread with brûléed bananas. (Melanie, by the way, is the wife of owner Phillip Barnett.) A wonderful harbor view makes the patio the most popular dining area. Live musicians (pop, jazz, and blues) entertain evenings from April through November, making the Onion a great nightlife destination, too. *53 Front St., tel. 441/295–2263.* AE, MC, V.

British

$$ COLONY PUB. As the crests of the Bermudian parishes that adorn the walls attest, the Colony is redolent with the histories of both Britain and the island. Black leather chairs and plenty of polished brass give the place a clublike atmosphere. The meat-oriented menu features locker-aged Angus steaks and prime roast rib of beef. The 10-ounce salmon fillet promises to satisfy fish lovers. For lighter fare start with the fresh-fruit plate with sorbet and follow with sea scallops. Nightly entertainment might feature a jazz trio, a pianist, or a singer. *Fairmont Southampton Princess, South Shore Rd., tel. 441/295–3000.* AE, DC, MC, V.

Bermudian Cuisine

Although Bermudian cuisine is seemingly elusive, many restaurants highlight local dishes amid their global offerings. Wanna know what they are?

Formerly reserved for Christmas dinner, cassava pie—a savory blend of cassava, eggs, sugar, and sometimes chicken—can be found along with mussel pie (shelled mussels baked with potatoes, onions, and seasoned with thyme, parsley, and curry). Fish chowder is served at high-end establishments and diners alike, accompanied by the traditional splash of sherry peppers (ripe bell peppers marinated in sherry with herbs and spices) and black rum (rum darkened by molasses and a special barrel aging process). Local fish (often called Bermuda fish)—such as rockfish, wahoo, tuna, and mahimahi—is usually offered. A local preparation involves panfrying and then topping the fish with almonds and a fried banana. Bermuda spiny lobster, seasonally available from September through April, is succulent (though somewhat tougher than Maine lobster) and is dipped in drawn butter with lemon. Shark hash, minced shark meat sautéed with spices, is usually served on toast. Fish also composes the island's traditional weekend brunch: a huge plate of boiled or steamed salt cod, boiled potatoes and onions, and sliced bananas is topped with a hard-boiled egg or tomato sauce, then with avocado slices.

Shark hash and mussel pie are usually available at the **Black Horse Tavern,** an out-of-the-way place on the water in St. David's, where the menu is dictated by what the fishermen catch. You can find the codfish brunch at the **Green Lantern,** just outside town, and **Paw-Paws** in Warwick. Note that such a breakfast will stave off hunger for the better part of the day.

$–$$ HOG PENNY PUB. Veterans of London pub crawls may well feel nostalgic at this atmospheric watering hole off Front Street. Die-hard aficionados of British cooking (if such beings exist) will be rewarded with Yorkshire pudding, shepherd's pie, steak-and-kidney pie, fish-and-chips, and bangers and mash. There's even a small sampling of curries. You'll find good fun as well as good food in this dark, cozy den: live music plays nightly from May through August and on weekends the rest of the year. *Burnaby Hill, tel. 441/292–2534. AE, DC, MC, V.*

$ BOTANIC TEA ROOM. One of Bermuda's most pleasant traditions is afternoon tea at Trimingham's. The department store's tearoom is a good place to escape the shopping scene and observe this very civilized and tasty ritual—even if it falls closer to the hour of noon than the typical 4 PM. Look for home-style soups, salads, large-bun sandwiches, and fruit plates. The tea is served daily except Sunday from 8:30 AM to 4:30 PM. *Trimingham's, Front St., tel. 441/295–1183. No credit cards. Closed Sun. No dinner.*

$ DOCKSIDER. You'll mingle with the locals at this sprawling Front Street sports bar with the island's first video jukebox. If you find things a little hectic at the main bar, try the wine bar, which is quieter and more intimate. Go for the English beef pie, fish-and-chips, and fish sandwiches. Wash them all down with draft or bottled beer. Folks come after dark for live music (everything from jazz trios to rock bands) in the nightclub in the back, and there's also a poolroom. *121 Front St., tel. 441/296–3333. MC, V.*

Caribbean

$–$$ JAMAICAN GRILL. Try this casual, family-run restaurant with the colorful murals for Jamaican cooking. You can order at the take-out counter downstairs or dine upstairs. Either way, treat yourself to coconut or *escovich* (salt-cured) fish, red beans and rice, brown stew chicken, akee and salt fish, beef patties, curried goat, and, of course, peppery jerk chicken or fish. No alcohol is served, but the refreshing pineapple-ginger, carrot, mango, and other natural juices hit the spot. 32 Court St., tel. 441/296–6577. MC, V. Closed Sun.

$–$$ SPRING GARDEN RESTAURANT & BAR. If you've never had Barbadian food, come to Spring Garden, where there's a palm tree growing inside and up through the cedar ceiling, and try panfried flying fish—a delicacy in Barbados. Another good choice is the broiled mahimahi served in creole sauce, with peas and rice. From September to April an additional menu appears, featuring broiled or curried lobster and lobster Thermidor ($28 for the complete lobster dinner). For dessert any time, try the coconut-cream pie or the raspberry mango cheese cake. They're both delicious. 19 Reid St., tel. 441/295–7416. AE, MC, V. Closed Sun. Nov.–Apr. No lunch Sun. May–Oct.

Chinese

$–$$ CHOPSTICKS. Perhaps more Pan-Asian than strictly Chinese, Chopsticks mixes it up with a menu of Szechuan, Hunan, and Cantonese, and Thai favorites. Top Chinese selections include jumbo shrimp with vegetables in black-bean sauce and sweet and spicy hoisin chicken. Got a taste for Thai? Try the *pla pae sa* (boneless, steamed fish fillet on a bed of cabbage and celery with ginger, sweet pepper, scallions, red chilies, and cilantro) or beef *panang* (cooked in coconut sauce, curry paste, and lime leaves). All dishes are made to order, so special diets can be accommodated, and MSG omitted. Takeout is available. 88 Reid St., tel. 441/292–0791. AE, MC, V.

Contemporary

$$–$$$$ THE RED CARPET. This tiny restaurant is very popular at lunch,
★ especially among local politicians and businesspeople, who come for the contemporary yet creatively prepared fare. Among the culinary highlights are the grilled lamb chops with rosemary, the rockfish with fried banana and almonds, and the seafood kettle (mussels, shrimp, fish, scallops, and lobster tail in a creamy white

wine and curry sauce). The clever use of mirrors creates an illusion of space in the dining room—but there are no tricks when it comes to the cooking. *Armoury Bldg., Reid St., tel. 441/292–6195. AE, MC, V. Closed Sun.*

$$–$$$ FRESCO'S WINE BAR & RESTAURANT. Fresco's is known for its homemade pasta, seafood, and vegetarian specialties, dishes that might be best categorized as Mediterranean cuisine, often with a French and Caribbean flair. Consider the *tarte Provençal* (roasted vegetables and caramelized onions in a freshly baked pastry crust), panfried yellowtail snapper with zucchini-lime couscous and sweet red pepper reduction, or the lobster medallions roasted with vanilla. At lunch head outdoors to eat in the courtyard among the fountain, palms, and flowers. Inside there's a wine cellar–like room with a vaulted ceiling. The upstairs wine bar serves some excellent vintages by the glass, along with late-night snacks and desserts. *Chancery La., off Front St., tel. 441/295–5058. Reservations essential. AE, MC, V. No lunch weekends.*

$$–$$$ HARBOURFRONT. ★ Few eateries on Front Street have as much variety as this busy place, where sushi is served alongside Continental and Mediterranean specialties. Sit on the porch or behind the large glass doors and watch the Front Street and harbor action. Come at lunchtime for a good burger or salad; for dinner start with grilled calamari or carpaccio followed by lobster, rack of lamb, or any of the excellent pastas. The small sushi bar is usually packed, but you can order at a table as well. Arrive between 6 and 7:15 PM, and you can benefit from an early-bird dinner ($20–$26), which includes an appetizer, a main course, and coffee. *Front St., tel. 441/295–4207. AE, MC, V. Closed Sun. Nov.–Mar.*

$$–$$$ RISTORANTE PRIMAVERA AND OMAKASE SUSHI BAR. ★ A cleverly designed ceiling of grape vines and lattice creates a mood of Mediterranean elegance. The extensive menu yields such spectacular starters as carpaccio primavera (thin slices of beef tenderloin with Parmesan cheese and olive oil on arugula); scampi

N

Serpentine Rd.

Dundonald Street

Park Road

VICTORIA PARK

Richmond Road

Par-La-Ville Road

Wesley Street

Washington St.

Washington Street

Burnaby Street

Church Street

Woodbourne Avenue

7 Rd.

Bermudiana Rd.

9

10

8

7

Queen St.

11

Washington Lane

18

12

BARR'S BAY PARK

PAR-LA-VILLE PARK

6

15

13

16

14

Pitts Bay Road

1

3

4

2

Point Pleasant Rd.

5

17

Front Street

The Birdcage

Ferry Terminal

Hamilton Harbour

0   100 yards
0   100 meters

The Beach, 24

Blue Juice, 22

The Bombay, 30

Botanic
Tea Room, 17

Chopsticks, 28

Coconut Rock
and Yashi
Sushi Bar, 15

Colony Pub, 1

Docksider, 30

Fisherman's
Reef, 14

Fresco's
Wine Bar
& Restaurant, 20

Harbourfront, 5

Harley's Bistro, 1

Hog Penny
Pub, 13

House of
India, 26

Jamaican Grill, 25

La Coquille, 31

La Trattoria, 11

Le Figaro
Bistro & Bar, 27

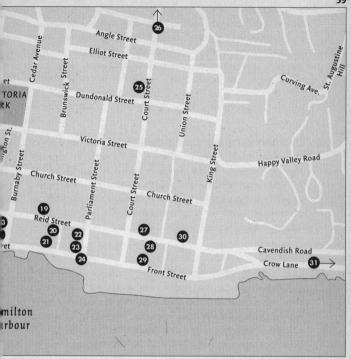

↑
26

Angle Street

Elliot Street

Cedar Avenue

Brunswick Street

25

Dundonald Street

Court Street

Union Street

Curving Ave.

St. Augustine Hill

et

TORIA
RK

ton St.

Victoria Street

King Street

Happy Valley Road

Burnaby Street

Church Street

Parliament Street

Court Street

Church Street

19

Reid Street

20

22

27

30

21

23

28

Cavendish Road

24

29

Crow Lane

31 →

Front Street

milton
rbour

Little Venice, **7**

Lobster Pot, **8**

Monte Carlo, **10**

Monty's, **4**

Paradiso Cafe, **18**

Pasta Basta, **9**

The Pickled
Onion, **16**

Port O' Call, **21**

Portofino, **6**

The Red
Carpet, **19**

Ristorante
Primavera and
Omakase
Sushi Bar, **3**

Rosa's
Cantina, **30**

Spring Garden
Restaurant
& Bar, **12**

Tuscany, **23**

Waterloo
House, **2**

and scallops *innamorati* (sautéed in cognac, paprika, and shallots); and a savory *zuppa di pesce* (fish soup). You can also choose from a variety of consistently good pastas. Upstairs, the popular sushi bar, Omakase, serves creative seafood delicacies, many with telling names: the "Jurassic Maki"—a roll of salmon skin and soft-shell crab with flying-fish roe and smoked eel—is definitely enough for two. *Pitts Bay Rd., tel. 441/295-2167. AE, MC, V. No lunch weekends.*

$–$$ COCONUT ROCK AND YASHI SUSHI BAR. Are you in the mood for sashimi or shrimp tempura served in a quiet room beneath paper lanterns? Or would you rather have fried tiger shrimp, a seafood crepe, or barbecued beef ribs, accompanied by music videos on multiple screens? Either way, the food at these adjoining yet separate restaurants is consistently good. *Williams House (downstairs), Reid St., tel. 441/292-1043. AE, MC, V. No lunch Sun.*

French

$$$ LA COQUILLE. Some diners sail right up to the dock for the delicious Provençal-style food at this restaurant overlooking Hamilton Harbour. The decor, fish and shells painted on the walls highlights the house specialty—seafood. From tables outside or in an enclosed veranda, consider sampling the tiger prawns with caviar and asparagus in a cream sauce, panfried local fish, or chicken stuffed with sun-dried tomatoes. Complement your meal with a selection from the extensive wine list. *40 Crow La. (Bermuda Underwater Exploration Institute), tel. 441/292-6122. AE, MC, V.*

$$$ WATERLOO HOUSE. This restaurant and small Relais & Château
★ hotel in a former private house on Hamilton Harbour serves Bermudian and Continental cuisine. You can dine either on the waterside patio (in summer) or in the more formal dining room, where deep-raspberry walls, rich chintzes, and attractive sconces set the elegant mood. Enticing daily specials may make perusing the menu somewhat difficult, but do consider the Bermuda fish chowder; giant tiger prawns grilled with a garlic, white wine, and

tomato essence; and the tender seared loin of lamb. The service is outstanding. *Pitts Bay Rd., tel. 441/295–4480. Jacket required. AE, MC, V.*

$$–$$$ **LE FIGARO BISTRO & BAR.** Oversize posters adorn the walls of
★ this attractive French bistro. An archway separates the two dining areas, which are often filled with in-the-know locals, from bank tellers to businesspeople. If you sit in the section known as the Wine Shop, you can buy your wine retail and sip it with your meal. Among the most popular dinner selections are the peppered tuna with garlic mashed potatoes, the cassoulet, and the filet mignon with green peppercorn sauce. *63 Reid St., tel. 441/296–4991. Reservations essential. AE, MC, V.*

$$–$$$ **MONTE CARLO.** Some of Bermuda's best meals are served in this
★ cheerful Mediterranean restaurant behind Hamilton's City Hall. Choose an outdoor table or people-watch from the indoor dining room, with its exposed old Bermuda cedar beams and copies of impressionist works painted directly on the walls. At lunch consider the fresh tuna marinated in Provençal oil, herbs, and served with a caper sauce, or the sautéed scallops over a zucchini-crab pancake. For dinner, try the bouillabaisse Marseillaise—fish and shellfish in a delicious broth. An additional lighter menu (with lighter prices) includes a variety of crepes. No matter what you order, save room for the white-chocolate crème brûlée or a homemade pastry from the dessert trolley. *Victoria St., tel. 441/295–5453. AE, MC, V.*

Indian

$–$$ **THE BOMBAY.** The Bombay captures the flavors of the subcontinent without becoming a caricature of the typical British-colony curry house. All the traditional favorites are prepared remarkably well: the *peeaz pakora* (onion fritters) and mulligatawny soup are excellent starters. Then opt for the *jhinga vindaloo* (shrimp in hot curry), lamb *saagwala* (braised lamb in creamy spinach), or anything from the clay tandoor oven. Ask about the discounted dinner menus (November–March), or stop by on a weekday for the buffet lunch ($12). Takeout is available. *Reid St., tel. 441/292–0048 or 441/292–8865. AE, MC, V. Closed Sun. No lunch Sat.*

$–$$ HOUSE OF INDIA. ★ The north side of Hamilton, across from a homeless shelter, isn't exactly the best location, but the food here is well worth a taxi ride. The dishes are bursting with flavor and include offerings from across the subcontinent. Start with vegetable *samosas* (small deep-fried turnovers). Prawns in cashew-nut curry is also a good choice, but any entrée you choose—meat, fish, or vegetarian—will be memorable. All the breads are freshly made in the tandoor, and the *lassi* (sweetened yogurt) drinks, particularly the mango, are excellent and refreshing. A filling weekday lunch buffet is worth every penny ($12). *57 North St., tel. 441/295–6450. MC, V. No lunch weekends.*

Italian

$$$ LITTLE VENICE. Bermudians head for this trattoria when they want more from Italian cooking than pizza. Little Venice can be expensive, but it's worth it and the service is expert. Try an abundant plate of antipasto, with calamari, mozzarella, and salami. Salads are first-rate, particularly those topped with Gorgonzola croutons. Good choices for main courses include linguine with shellfish and calamari in a tomato sauce; the thinly sliced grilled veal; and the duck with smoked bacon. Save room for the delicious tiramisu. *Bermudiana Rd., tel. 441/295–3503. Reservations essential. AE, MC, V.*

$$–$$$ HARLEY'S BISTRO. Popular with Hamilton businesspeople, this poolside eatery overlooking Hamilton Harbour serves up Asian and Italian fare either indoors or alfresco. Pizzas with standard toppings and the usual lineup of pasta dishes are offered alongside Asian-inspired choices like wok-charred rockfish with curried sticky rice and peanut sauce. *76 Pitts Bay Rd., at the Fairmont Hamilton Princess, tel. 441/295–3000. AE, DC, MC, V.*

$$–$$$ TUSCANY. The breezy balcony of this owner-run spot overlooks Front Street and has a great view of Hamilton Harbour—when no cruise ships are in, of course. Inside the spacious dining room are attractive frescoes and a Bermuda beam-and-slate ceiling. Representative dishes include the crepe *alla marinara* (filled with baby shrimp, scallops, and fish, baked and served with lobster sauce); rockfish with fried bananas and pine nuts; and veal sautéed in white wine, with fresh tomato, olives, capers, and fresh spinach. The pizzas—served for both lunch and dinner—are also good, especially the "4 Stagioni" (four seasons), with tomato, mozzarella, artichoke hearts, and asparagus. *Front St., off Bermuda House La., tel. 441/292–4507. AE, MC, V.*

$–$$$ PORTOFINO. This popular Italian indoor-outdoor restaurant is often busy and noisy. If pizza's your game, you'll appreciate the wide array of toppings available (phone 15 minutes ahead if you want a pie to go). The sirloin steak *pizzaiola* (with olives, anchovies, capers, and tomato sauce) is also good, as is calamari fried in a delicate batter. For something more adventurous, consider octopus cooked in red sauce with olives and capers and served over risotto. Homemade pasta and other risotto specials are excellent. *Bermudiana Rd., off Front St., tel. 441/292–2375 or 441/295–6090. AE, MC, V. No lunch weekends.*

$$ LA TRATTORIA. Tucked away in a Hamilton alley, this no-nonsense trattoria has red-and-white tablecloths and a familiar mom-and-pop feel. Recommended entrées are cheese ravioli in a pink sauce and fillet of fish sautéed in white wine with oregano, garlic, and olives. The pizzas are cooked in Bermuda's only brick wood-burning pizza oven. Some 17 creative toppings (such as arugula and prosciutto) are listed on the menu, but the chef will put together any combination a customer wants, no matter how unusual. One recent patron requested, received, and raved about a pizza dressed with shrimp and bananas. *Washington La., tel. 441/295–1877. AE, MC, V.*

$ BLUE JUICE. Upstairs from its sister restaurant, Tuscany, this nightlife hot spot serves late-night snacks (until 3 AM) and dessert year-round and, most of the year, lunch as well. The color of the signature Blue Juice cocktail, made with blue curaçao, vodka, fresh lime, and Triple Sec, matches the modern decor. If you're here for lunch, try the lobster and avocado salad, followed by the fusilli with fresh vegetables. Dine inside or outside on the patio, where music videos are projected on the courtyard walls after dark. At night, Blue Juice transforms into a disco open until 3 AM. The dance floor, it seems, is anywhere you want it to be. *Bermuda House La., tel. 441/292–4507. AE, MC, V. No lunch Jan.–Feb.*

$ PASTA BASTA. This small restaurant is a local favorite, with colorful tables and chairs and widely circulated photos of Italian scenery and food. The dishes here are tasty and thoughtfully prepared, and the ever-changing menu of simple northern Italian dishes keeps things interesting. Try the fettuccine alfredo, classic or spinach lasagna, *orecchiette* (a tiny disk-shape pasta literally translated as "little ears") with pesto and potato, Caesar salad, or any of the daily specials. No liquor is served, nor is smoking allowed. *1 Elliot St. W, Hamilton, tel. 441/295–9785. No credit cards.*

Mexican

$–$$ ROSA'S CANTINA. Despite its monopoly on the island's Mexican cuisine, the food here is consistently good. Popular favorites include "Nachos Unbelievable" (melted cheese, refried beans, beef, onions, tomatoes, peppers, jalapeños, and guacamole), fajitas, and burritos. Any item can be made as mild or as spicy as you like. Along with Mexican fare, the menu includes hearty Texas-style steaks, chicken, and seafood. Rosa's has a loyal local following and is always busy. On balmy evenings it's fun to sit on the balcony overlooking Front Street. *121 Front St., tel. 441/295–1912. AE, MC, V.*

Seafood

$$$–$$$$ FISHERMAN'S REEF. Above the Hog Penny Pub, this upscale seafood spot draws a crowd for seafood and steak. Start with one of the chowders—fish chowder or St. David's conch chowder. Of the wide selection of seafood entrées, the popular picks are the Bermuda lobster (in season); rare-grilled tuna over Thai noodles and steamed Asian vegetables; and the catch of the day, whether blackened, baked, or panfried. *Burnaby Hill, off Front St., tel. 441/292–1609. AE, DC, MC, V. No lunch weekends.*

$$–$$$ LOBSTER POT. Bermudians swear by this place, with the maritime decor—yes, that's brass nautical gear and sun-bleached rope. Local conviction comes from the cooking, no doubt, which turns out excellent versions of island standards, including local lobster (from September through April) and yellowtail or rockfish with bananas and almonds. You might also want to consider the delicious Lobster Pot snails in their buttery garlic-curry sauce. *Bermudiana Rd., tel. 441/292–6898. AE, MC, V. Closed Sun.*

$$–$$$ PORT O' CALL. Resembling the interior of a yacht, this popular yet intimate restaurant is one of the few ground-level dining spots on Front Street, which is a good thing: the outdoor dining area has the feel of a European café. Fresh local fish—such as wahoo, tuna, grouper, and snapper—is cooked perfectly, and the preparations are creative without missing the mark. Consider the pan-roasted snapper with sweet potato puree or the sesame-crusted tuna with Thai curried noodles. *87 Front St., tel. 441/295–5373. AE, MC, V. No lunch weekends.*

THE TOWN OF ST. GEORGE

British

$$$ CARRIAGE HOUSE. Hearty British fare is the daily bread at the Carriage House, an attractive slice of the restored Somers Wharf area. Try to secure a patio table or inside by a window so you can watch the action on the harbor. This is the place to tuck into roast prime rib, cut to order tableside, or roast leg of lamb with rosemary. But don't overlook the fresh Bermuda fish (whatever's fresh-

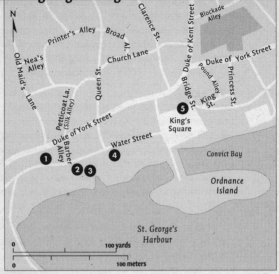

Carriage House, **3**

Pasta Pasta, **1**

San Giorgio, **4**

T.G.I. Freddie's, **5**

The Waterfront Tavern Bar and Restaurant, **2**

caught), like panfried wahoo in lemon-butter sauce. Sundays the Carriage House lays out a generous buffet brunch that includes champagne, and a pianist plays background music. Afternoon tea with all the trimmings is served daily except Sunday. On Friday and Saturday nights, a jazz combo entertains. *Somers Wharf, tel. 441/297–1270. AE, DC, MC, V.*

$–$$ T.G.I. FREDDIE'S. With a quiet, bright restaurant upstairs and a loud, somewhat dim English-style pub downstairs, T.G.I. Freddie's has a split personality, and two respective menus. Sit upstairs on the balcony, overlooking King's Square and St. George's Harbour, for seafood, pasta, chicken, and steak. During the summer, live music from steel pan to Top 40, accompanies dinner. After the upstairs section closes at midnight, you can head down to the pub, which is open until 3 AM. Here you'll find the usual fish-and-chips, bangers and mash, and sandwiches, plus a jukebox (and sometimes a DJ), which attracts a party crowd. A few hours later, Freddie's is up serving breakfast. The Belgian waffles are a hit. *3 King's Sq., tel. 441/297–1717. MC, V.*

$–$$ THE WATER FRONT TAVERN BAR AND RESTAURANT. For many years this establishment was known as Wharf Tavern, but its former dark-hued setting has been spruced up and brightened. Its prime harborside location draws a lively, young, sports-loving crowd, who also come for the wide-screen television, long cedar bar, daily happy hour, and (during the summer season) live music several nights a week. An eclectic menu lets you choose from nachos and conch fritters to Hungarian goulash and fish-and-chips. A children's menu makes this a popular haunt for families. *14 Water St., tel. 441/297–3305. AE, MC, V.*

Contemporary

$–$$$ SAN GIORGIO. The waterside terrace on St. George's Harbour makes this restaurant one of the island's most romantic settings. Owners Nick and Ginny Brown are dedicated to serving a variety of good food. Daily Italian and Asian-inspired specials and fresh local fish and island produce draw a faithful following. The Italian creations—like penne Gorgonzola with spinach and pine nuts— are consistently good. Dinner antipasti are for the most part traditional, but the spring rolls of chicken, shrimp, and sun-dried tomato with a chipotle plum sauce are a decidedly eclectic menu offering. *36 Water St., tel. 441/297–1307. MC, V.*

Italian

$ PASTA PASTA. A brightly painted interior, a lively (if slightly institutional) atmosphere, and plentiful portions of home-style northern Italian cooking quickly turn first-time customers into

What's Missing Here?

Notice anything missing? No McDonald's, Burger King, or any of their ilk? Apart from a lone Kentucky Fried Chicken, which snuck in sometime during 1970 (and a McDonald's on the old U.S. military base, which closed when the U.S. military left in 1998), fast-food chains have since been barred by Bermuda's government. When the island's premier Sir John Swan (who served from 1982 to 1995) saw his plans for British independence rejected in a referendum, he resigned and instead promptly applied for permission to open a McDonald's but was opposed by Parliament in 1996. After several appeals, the highest court—the London-based Privy Council—declared that no new fast-food franchises would be permitted on the island. The Government, and the majority of residents, strongly believed that allowing American franchises in would dilute Bermuda's distinctive foreign (and rather upscale) appeal, eventually leading to the island's resembling Anyplace, USA. So, most Bermudians breathed a sigh of relief when Swan's McDonaldland dream was smashed in the '80s, even if these same folk head straight for the drive-through when off the island themselves.

repeat diners. The pizza as well as the pastas, such as penne with chicken-and-pepper sauce, are sound choices. No liquor is served, and smoking is not allowed. York St., tel. 441/297–2927. *Reservations not accepted. No credit cards.*

THE PARISHES

THE WEST END
Bermudian

$$ FREEPORT GARDENS. If it's good, locally caught fish you want, this is the place. The fish platter and the combination seafood platter with scallops, shrimp, and wahoo or snapper are not presented with great flair, but they're delicious. The fish-and-chips and the fish sandwiches are unforgettable. If you don't fancy fruits of the sea, choose from a range of pizzas, hamburgers, and sandwiches. For dessert you might be offered freshly baked apple or lemon meringue pie. *Pender Rd., Dockyard, Sandys, tel. 441/234–1692. AE, MC, V.*

British

$$–$$$ **SOMERSET COUNTRY SQUIRE.** Overlooking Mangrove Bay, this typically English tavern is all dark wood and good cheer, with a great deal of malt and hops in between. Much of the food isn't good enough to warrant a special trip across the island, but some of it is: the Bermuda fish chowder, the panfried mahimahi, and the steak-and-kidney pie are all delicious choices. *Mangrove Bay, Somerset, Sandys, tel. 441/234–0105. AE, MC, V.*

$–$$ **FROG & ONION PUB.** With its vaulted limestone ceilings and thick walls, the former Royal Naval Dockyard warehouse is a fitting place for this nautically decorated pub and its large poolroom. The food caters to every taste, running the gamut from hearty English pub fare to delicious European dishes to a selection of fresh local fish plates. Pub favorites are bangers and mash, the Argus Bank fish sandwich, panfried local rockfish or tuna, and the Frog & Onion burger, which is topped with fried onions and bacon. A children's menu is available. *The Cooperage, Dockyard, Sandys, tel. 441/234–2900. MC, V.*

Italian

$$–$$$ **IL PALIO.** A ship's spiral staircase ascends from the bar to the dining
★ room, where you'll find some of the island's best pasta and specialty dishes from several Italian regions. Spinach-and-potato gnocchi with herbed tomato or meat sauce is a winner. The veal scallopini and the panfried wahoo with balsamic jus are other treats garnering praise. For dessert try a scoop of one of the assorted Italian ice creams and tiramisu. *Main Rd., Somerset, Sandys, tel. 441/234–1049 or 441/234–2323. DC, MC, V. Closed Mon.*

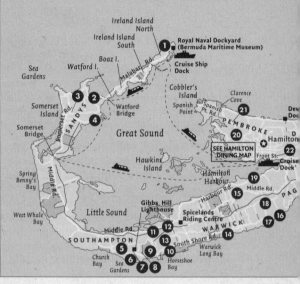

ATLANTIC OCEAN

Royal Naval Dockyard (Bermuda Maritime Museum)

Ireland Island North
Ireland Island South
Boaz I.
Watford I.
Cruise Ship Dock
Cobbler's Island
Clarence Cove
Sea Gardens
Spanish Point Rd.
Spanish Point
PEMBROKE
Somerset Island
Watford Bridge
SEE HAMILTON DINING MAP
Somerset Bridge
Great Sound
Hamilton
Dev Doc
Spring Benny's Bay
Hawkins Island
Hamilton Harbour
Front St.
Cruise Dock
Middle Rd.
Harbour Rd.
PAG
West Whale Bay
Little Sound
Gibbs Hill Lighthouse
Spicelands Riding Centre
WARWICK
Middle Rd.
SOUTHAMPTON
South Shore Rd.
Warwick Long Bay
Church Bay
Sea Gardens
Horseshoe Bay

Ascots, 20	Freeport Gardens, 4	La Coquille, 22	Norwood Room, 17
Black Horse Tavern, 28	Frog & Onion Pub, 1	Lighthouse Tea Room, 7	Paw-Paws, 14
Cafe Lido, 16	Green Lantern, 21	Lillian's, 6	Rib Room, 9
Coconuts, 5	Henry VIII, 8	Newport Room, 12	Rockfish Grill, 19
Dennis's Hideaway, 29	Horizons, 18	North Rock Brewing Company, 24	Rustico Restaurant & Pizzeria, 25
Fourways Inn, 15	Il Palio, 3		

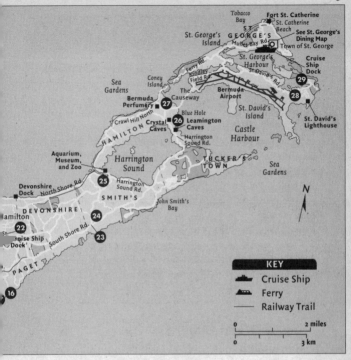

KEY

Cruise Ship

Ferry

Railway Trail

0   2 miles

0   3 km

Seahorse Grill, 16

Somerset
Country Squire, 2

Specialty Inn, 23

Swizzle Inn, 27

Tio Pepe, 13

Tom Moore's
Tavern, 26

Waterlot Inn, 11

Whaler Inn, 10

Wickets
Brasserie, 12

Divine Picnic Spots

Sure, Bermuda is full of pleasant places with forks, knives, and tablecloths. However, the island also has some gorgeous, quiet corners for those times when you'd rather dine closer to nature. **Clearwater Beach** in St. David's is one of Bermuda's nicest—and newest—picnic spots. Since the 1995 closing of the U.S. naval base in St. George's Parish, the large half-moon strand with calm waters has become a favorite, especially for families with children. With verdant open spaces sprinkled with shady poinciana trees, **Arboretum Park,** on Middle Road in Devonshire, makes a peaceful inland setting. Just west of popular Warwick Long Bay, tiny, tranquil **Jobson Cove** beach is backed by the dramatic cliffs and greenery of South Shore Park. Adjacent to a Bermuda Audubon Society nature reserve, **Somerset Long Bay Park** in Sandys has a semicircular beach, fluffy spruce trees, and shallow water. **Lagoon Park,** near Bermuda's northwestern tip, is another placid locale for picnicking and wandering. You won't miss your proper place settings one bit.

THE WESTERN PARISHES
Bermudian

$ **GREEN LANTERN.** For a taste of local flavor at breakfast, lunch, or dinner, this casual, friendly spot is a fine choice. Codfish and potatoes, a local weekend breakfast favorite, is on the menu some Saturdays. For lunch or dinner consider the fish chowder, fish-and-chips (the house specialty), or something broiled (chicken, fish, or pork chops) with a side of peas and rice. The Green Lantern is about a 20-minute stroll (or a quick taxi ride) from the ferry dock, just outside Hamilton. Serpentine Rd., between Pitts Bay Rd. and Rosemont Ave., Pembroke, tel. 441/295–6995. MC, V. Closed late Feb.– mid-Mar. No dinner Wed.

British

$$–$$$ **HENRY VIII.** As popular with locals as it is with tourists from nearby Southampton resorts, the lively Henry VIII effects an Old English look that stops just short of "wench" waitresses and Tudor styling. The mix of English and Bermudian menu favorites includes such classics as steak-and-kidney pie. The fish chowder is wonderful, and the rack of lamb is always cooked to perfection. Save room for sticky toffee pudding—it's tops. A strolling singer often serenades during dinner. After dinner you can join the local crowd in the bar to hear calypso singers or other entertainment. *South Shore Rd., Southampton, tel. 441/238–1977. AE, MC, V.*

$ **LIGHTHOUSE TEA ROOM.** At the base of the famous Gibbs Hill Lighthouse, this former home, serving a selection of properly brewed teas (thank goodness) and such English favorites as scones with clotted cream, makes a charming spot to visit (and rest after the big climb up and down the 185 spiraling steps). Teas are specially cut and shipped from the United Kingdom or blended right on the premises. Expect some unusual herbal teas, such as dandelion or apple and juniper berry, are also served iced as well as hot during the summer. Homemade soups, smoked trout, and pork pie with chutney satisfy larger appetites. For dessert, you might find fresh gingerbread with lemon sauce or banana cake. Breakfast (sausage, eggs, and crumpets, anyone?) is also served. Owner Heidi Cowen, who does all her own baking, grew up in this old dwelling. Her grandfather was the last lighthouse keeper before self-maintaining electronic lights did away with the need for keepers in the late 1960s. *Lighthouse Rd., Southampton, tel. 441/238–8679. AE, MC, V. No dinner.*

Caribbean

$$–$$$ **COCONUTS.** Nestled between high cliff rocks and a pristine ★ private beach on the southern coast, this outdoor restaurant is one of the best places to nab that table overlooking the ocean or, by special arrangement, dinner on the beach. The view is made even more dramatic at night by floodlights. Locals and visitors staying elsewhere vie with guests of the resort for an opportunity to eat here. The changing menu includes freshly grown produce prepared with Caribbean stylings, although you'll see evidence of Asian and Latin inspiration, too. The kitchen is obviously competent and creative—behold, for example, the rock lobster tail on chilled tagliatelle with pickled mango and wasabi cream. A fixed price of about $50 (excluding 15% gratuity) includes four courses. If you're on a budget, a simpler lunch menu includes daily specials, burgers, sandwiches, and good salads. *The Reefs, South Shore Rd., Southampton, tel. 441/238–0222. Reservations essential. AE, MC, V. Closed Nov.–Apr.*

Contemporary

$$$–$$$$ **FOURWAYS INN.** Fourways has risen to preeminence as much for its lovely 18th-century surroundings as for anything coming out of the kitchen. The airy interior evokes a wealthy plantation home, with plenty of fine china, crystal, and silver. Order rockfish in a crabmeat crust with crayfish sauce or beef tenderloin on a bed of couscous with morel mushrooms. But leave enough room for a Dark and Stormy (black rum and ginger beer) soufflé for dessert. Try a "Fourways Special" cocktail, made with the juice of Bermuda loquats and other fruits and a dash of bitters. *1 Middle Rd., Paget, tel. 441/236–6517. Jacket required. AE, MC, V.*

$$$–$$$$ **HORIZONS.** The dining room at Horizons cottage colony is one of Bermuda's most elegant, and reservations can be difficult to secure on short notice, especially during May and June. Occupying what once was a private home, this Relais & Châteaux property has an impeccably trained staff who do their best to make your meal a veritable dining experience. The five-course fixed-price dinner menu changes daily and might include mesclun greens with a loquat vinaigrette, a vegetable terrine with basil oil and tomato coulis, and roasted snapper over sun-dried tomato polenta

($55 per person). *Horizons, South Shore Rd., Paget, tel. 441/236–0048. Reservations essential. Jacket and tie. AE, MC, V.*

$$$–$$$$ NORWOOD ROOM. Don't be put off by the fact that this Stonington Beach Hotel restaurant is run by students of the Hospitality and Culinary Institute of Bermuda: under the supervision of their mentors, they produce both superb food and service. The oversize training kitchen uses local ingredients and European culinary techniques to create a range of fresh tastes. Have a preprandial cocktail at the sunken bar overlooking the swimming pool. Then, go for the cold fruit soup (piña colada, strawberry, or watermelon), followed by mahimahi on spinach and roasted garlic or grilled beef tenderloin with red bell pepper pesto. *Stonington Beach Hotel, South Shore Rd., Paget, tel. 441/236–5416. Jacket and tie. AE, MC, V.*

$$$–$$$$ SEAHORSE GRILL. A chic, minimalist manner restaurant, Seahorse is the perfect place for an expense-account meal. And since it's five minutes from Hamilton, the businesspeople seem to know it. A frequently changing menu showcases locally grown produce, much of it pesticide-free. In fact, ingredients are described in rather minute detail, such that their exact geographic origins are named. The service can be slow, so come prepared to linger between courses. Start with cedar-smoked magret duck with cherry compote or the foie gras. The black rum barbecued tuna is outstanding, as is the rack of lamb. A satisfying end is the sticky ginger cake with passion-fruit sauce or the homemade banana ice cream. *Elbow Beach Hotel, off Shore Rd., Paget, tel. 441/236–3535. AE, MC, V.*

$$–$$$$ WATERLOT INN. This Bermudian treasure resides in a graceful, ★ two-story manor house that dates from 1670. Service is impeccable, and the dining-room staff has just enough island exuberance to take the edge off European-style training. The savory fish chowder prevails as one of Bermuda's best, and the panfried Bermuda fish and the rack of lamb are both superb. Another delicious choice is the rosemary-crusted free-range chicken breast. *Middle Rd.,*

Southampton, tel. 441/238–0510. Jacket required. AE, DC, MC, V. Closed Jan.–mid-Mar. No lunch.

$$–$$$ ASCOTS. In an elegant former mansion just outside downtown Hamilton, Ascots gives you a wonderful excuse for leaving the city. When the weather permits, meals are served on the covered terrace, with its stone fountain, or on the front veranda, as well as indoors. You can assemble before and after meals in the cozy lounge, at the handsome cedar bar. At your table, a good starter is the duck carpaccio (pan seared and served on a bed of bok choy with an avocado-and-mango salsa). The unique cold banana soup with black rum and toasted almonds is a savory surprise. Several vegetarian dishes are just as imaginative, such as the ravioli filled with butternut squash and arugula. For dessert, you can't go wrong with the chocolate truffle torte with Grand Marnier. Reservations are recommended. *Royal Palms Hotel, 24 Rosemont Ave., Pembroke, tel. 441/295–9644. AE, MC, V.*

$$–$$$ LILLIAN'S. ★ How could this be? Lillian's is the premier place for northern Italian cuisine on the island, and its sushi bar is also of the same high caliber. True culinary ambidexterity is at work here: on the Italian side, the Gorgonzola whip with roasted snails is unforgettable, and the osso buco is superbly tender. The freshly made pasta is always a sure bet, too. The sushi bar, in a quiet corner of the spacious restaurant, is tiny, and reservations to sit here are essential. But the fresh and innovative sushi, like conch sashimi and seared tuna nigiri with potato and capers, may also be enjoyed at tables, even alongside a plate of pasta. *Sonesta Beach Resort, South Shore Rd., Southampton, tel. 441/238–8122. Reservations essential for sushi bar. AE, MC, V. No lunch.*

$$–$$$ PAW-PAWS. This bistro can seat you on a patio overlooking busy South Shore Road or in a cozy dining room with colorful murals of Italian garden scenes. The varied menu serves Bermudian, European, and North American dishes, and best bets come from all categories: Bermuda fish chowder, homemade ravioli *d'homard et saumon* (with lobster and strips of smoked salmon), and, in a welcome twist on the usual surf and turf, filet mignon with grilled jumbo shrimp stuffed with crabmeat. During Sunday lunch you can order the traditional Bermudian dish of codfish and potatoes with bananas. *South Shore Rd., Warwick, tel. 441/236–7459. MC, V.*

$$–$$$ ROCKFISH GRILL. Position yourself well to savor the exceptional Asian-Caribbean cuisine and try to snag a table by the windows, from which you can look across the harbor to Hamilton. Then go for the sautéed crab cakes with matchstick potatoes and tomato-mango jam or the steamed lobster wontons to start. The salads are knock-out inventive, such as the one fashioned from baby spinach and cumin-seared scallops. Among the entrées the jerked tuna on sugarcane skewers, and the *pad thai* (stir-fried rice noodles) with ginger shrimp satay are standouts. Reservations are recommended. *Harbour Rd., Paget, tel. 441/236–6060. AE, MC, V.*

$ WICKETS BRASSERIE. Prints of the game of cricket decorate Wickets, whose unfussy fare will suit just about any palate. Bermuda fish chowder is a classic starter on the menu of many casual classics: salads, burgers, sandwiches, pizza, pasta, or chicken. Top off the meal with key lime pie or a piece of Oreo chocolate cheesecake. Note that the restaurant typically closes for a few weeks in the winter, so call ahead. *Fairmont Southampton Princess, South Shore Rd., Southampton, tel. 441/238–8000. AE, DC, MC, V. Closed Jan.*

French

$$$–$$$$ ★ NEWPORT ROOM. With its nautical decor—glistening teak and models of victorious America's Cup yachts—this fine restaurant has been adored by the island's elite for years. Each dish is beautifully presented, and the service is exceptional. Salads are a step beyond traditional, with such offerings as a five-leaf salad with citrus, sautéed corn, crab cakes, and champagne grapes. The seafood entrées, such as the Nantucket Bay scallops and Gulf shrimp with truffles, braised coconut pilaf, finished with mango and lime beurre blanc, are especially noteworthy. For dessert, the

Grand Marnier soufflé and crêpes suzette (for two) are great choices. The Newport Room closes some winter months, so call ahead for information. *Fairmont Southampton Princess, South Shore Rd., Southampton, tel. 441/239–6964. Jacket required. AE, DC, MC, V. Closed Jan. No lunch.*

Italian

$$–$$$ **CAFE LIDO.** On the beachfront terrace at the Elbow Beach Hotel,
★ with waves breaking just below, Cafe Lido is often invoked as one of the island's most romantic settings. Signature dishes at this top contemporary Italian-Mediterranean restaurant include the seafood casserole and pastas, most of which are freshly made on the premises. The ever-changing dessert menu might include crème brûlée or Italian gelato. *Elbow Beach Hotel, off Shore Rd., Paget, tel. 441/236–9884. Reservations essential. AE, MC, V.*

$–$$$ **TIO PEPE.** You needn't spend much money for a satisfying meal at this Italian restaurant with a Mexican name. Plus, the easygoing atmosphere makes it an ideal stop for bathers returning from a day at Horseshoe Bay Beach. Try the spicy eggplant baked in tomato sauce and topped with cheese to start, and follow it up with lobster ravioli or seafood linguine. The grilled local tuna and wahoo are sensational. *South Shore Rd., Southampton, tel. 441/ 238–1897 or 441/238–0572. Reservations essential. AE, MC, V.*

Seafood

$$–$$$$ **WHALER INN.** Perched above the rocks and surf at the Southampton Princess, this seafood restaurant has a truly dramatic island setting. You can almost see the fresh-caught seafood being hauled in. Desserts, such as the brownie sundae, are stupendous. *Fairmont Southampton Princess, South Shore Rd., Southampton, tel. 441/238–0076. AE, DC, MC, V. Closed 1 month in winter. No lunch Nov.– Mar.*

Where to Take Tea

When afternoon arrives, Bermuda, like Britain, pauses for tea. You can join residents in this tradition at several hotels (where afternoon tea is often complimentary to guests) and a few restaurants. Usually, tea is served between 3 and 5 PM, but tea time means anything from an urn and cookies sitting on a sideboard to the more authentic presentation where tea, brewed to order in a pot and served with cream and sugar, accompanies finger sandwiches and scones with clotted cream and jam. English high tea is especially pleasant at **Waterloo House** (☞ Where to Sleep) during the summer, when it is served on the harborside terrace ($7 for nonguests). If you're in Hamilton, you can stop for a cup in Trimingham's **Botanic Tea Room** ($5–$7). Tea at **Elbow Beach Hotel** (☞ Where to Sleep) includes everything from sandwiches to cakes ($19). A panoramic view comes with imported and special tea blends at the hilltop **Lighthouse Tea Room,** which also serves breakfast and lunch.

Steak

$$–$$$$ **RIB ROOM.** Hands down, this is the best place on the island for
★ char-grilled steaks and chops and barbecued ribs. The conservative country club–style dining room overlooks the Fairmont Southampton Princess golf course, and the service is superior. The house specialty, prime rib, is perfection in the genre and served in its juices with traditional Yorkshire pudding. The lamb chops are also superlative, as is the rotisserie-cooked half chicken. Bermuda fish chowder is also a sensation. *Fairmont Southampton Princess, South Shore Rd., Southampton, tel. 441/238–8000. AE, MC, V. No lunch.*

THE EASTERN PARISHES
Bermudian

$$ **DENNIS'S HIDEAWAY.** Little more than a pink ramshackle structure
★ with a scattering of homemade picnic tables, Dennis's may be
decidedly grubby, but it serves what many consider Bermuda's
best local food. For more than three decades, starting in 1968,
eccentric owner Dennis Lamb could usually be found hunched over
his pots, discussing everything from plumbing to the fate of man.
These days, however, his son, Sea Egg, does most of the cooking.
Order the "fish dinner with the works"—a feast of shark hash
(minced shark meat with herbs and spices) on toast, conch fritters,
mussel stew, conch stew, fish chowder, fried fish, conch steak,
shark steak, shrimp, and scallops for just over $30. The chef may
even throw in some bread-and-butter pudding for good measure.
Only the most determined diners can partake, though, as hours
are erratic and the place is way off the beaten path. *Cashew City
Rd., St. David's, tel. 441/297–0044. Reservations essential. No credit cards.*

$–$$ **BLACK HORSE TAVERN.** Islanders fill the casual dining room,
★ whose walls bear mounted fish plucked from local waters, and
the outside picnic tables to savor chef Ronald William's culinary
magic. This is a great place for island originals: curried conch stew
with rice is a favorite, as are the straightforward renderings of
amberjack, rockfish, shark, tuna, wahoo, and Bermuda lobster,
in season. For lunch the fish sandwich is a perfect choice. *St.
David's Rd., St. David's, tel. 441/297–1991. AE, MC, V. Closed Mon.*

Contemporary

$$–$$$$ **TOM MOORE'S TAVERN.** In a house that dates from 1652, this place
enjoys a colorful past, thanks to the Irish poet it's named for. Tom
Moore visited friends here frequently in 1804 and caused a scandal
still talked about today by writing odes to the fictional Nea. She
was widely believed to be Hester Tucker, the wife of one of Moore's
business associates. Today fireplaces, casement windows, and

shipbuilders' cedar joinery capture a sense of history that in no way interferes with the fresh, light, and innovative cuisine. Broiled scampi, Bermuda lobster (in season), and sautéed-then-broiled Bermuda fish with pine nuts stand out. The soufflés are always excellent, as is the chef's pastry. Both change daily. Eat in one of five cozy rooms; by special arrangement, groups may dine alfresco on a terrace that overlooks Walsingham Bay. *Walsingham La., Bailey's Bay, Hamilton Parish, tel. 441/293–8020. Jacket and tie required. AE, MC, V. Closed Jan.–mid-Feb. No lunch.*

$$–$$$ NORTH ROCK BREWING COMPANY. The copper and mahogany tones of the handcrafted beers and ales are reflected in the warm decor of this bar and restaurant, Bermuda's first and only brewpub. Seating surrounds the glass-enclosed brewery where David Littlejohn, who runs North Rock with his wife, Heather, tinkers with the gleaming copper kettles. Sit in the dining room or outside on the breezy patio for fish-and-chips, codfish cakes, or prime rib. *10 South Rd., Smith's, tel. 441/236–6633. AE, MC, V.*

$ SWIZZLE INN. People come here as much to drink as to eat. In fact, Swizzle Inn created one of Bermuda's most hallowed (and lethal) drinks—the rum swizzle (amber and black rum, triple sec, orange and pineapple juices, and bitters). Grab a spot in the shadowy bar—plastered with business cards from all over the world—to sip one of these delightful concoctions, or sit on the porch or upstairs balcony and watch the mopeds whiz by. If you get hungry, try a "Swizzleburger" (a hamburger dressed up with bacon and cheese), shepherd's pie, liver and onions, or a delicious Bermuda fish sandwich. The nightly special might include tasty pad thai or fresh fish cooked in the style of your choosing. *Blue Hole Hill, Bailey's Bay, tel. 441/293–1854. AE, MC, V.*

Italian

$–$$ RUSTICO RESTAURANT & PIZZERIA. Owned by Odilio Angeli, the same Italian restaurateur who runs the top-notch Ristorante Primavera in Hamilton, at Rustico you can eat and drink while overlooking boat-filled Flatts Inlet. In fact, the kitchen takes advantage of the seafood for sale right off fishermen's boats each day, hence Bermudian favorites are on the menu along with Italian specialties. The wine list is surprisingly extensive. Families may appreciate the children's menu and the restaurant's proximity to the Bermuda Aquarium and Zoo. *8 North Shore Rd., Flatts Village, Smith's Parish, tel. 441/295-5212. AE, MC, V.*

$ SPECIALITY INN. A favorite with locals, this south-shore restaurant is cheerful and clean, with low prices that seem to explain the sparse decor. The no-frills food is Bermudian with Italian and Portuguese accents. You might find fish chowder or red-bean soup on the menu, along with chicken cacciatore and pizza (vegetarian or pepperoni). Rabbit, prepared Portuguese-style in a red wine sauce and with potatoes, is often served on weekends. *Collectors Hill, Smith's, tel. 441/236-3133. MC, V.*

Light Fare

CAFE ON THE TERRACE. For a simple lunch with a great view of Hamilton Harbour, drop in for a tasty sandwich and salad priced at about $9. It's not a huge place, so come early or you might not get a table. *Front St., above A. S. Cooper & Son, Hamilton, tel. 441/296-5265.*

DOROTHY'S COFFEE SHOP. A popular haunt for locals, Dorothy's is ideal for lunch while out shopping. Try one of the burgers—some say they're among the island's best. They've won *The Bermudian* magazine's Best of Bermuda Gold Award several years running. *Chancery La., off Front St., Hamilton, tel. 441/292-4130.*

FRESCO'S DELI. A gem of a place, Fresco's Deli is always buzzing and offers a great view from its first-floor balcony, from where you can sit and watch the boats and cruise ships go by in Hamilton Harbour. The tasty sandwiches go for about $8. *Front St., next door to A. S. Cooper & Son, Hamilton, tel. 441/295-0449.*

KENTUCKY FRIED CHICKEN. Always busy, and seemingly open all the live-long day, KFC is the island's only fast food chain— hence it warrants mention here. In what might be an unparalleled act of resistance, Bermuda's government has banned international fast-food franchises like McDonald's and shows little signs of caving—except in this one instance. Be prepared to wait in line at peak times. *Queen St., between Front St. and Reid Sts., Hamilton, tel. 441/296–4532.*

TAKE FIVE. Cheap and cheerful and above the shops at Washington Mall is Take Five, a good place to do lunch. Try the burgers (they are particularly good). The staff is friendly. *Washington Mall, Reid St., Hamilton, tel. 441/295–4903.*

Armed with only a purse and pair of sunglasses, the professional shopper emerges from the ferry in the City of Hamilton and peruses the long line of brightly colored canopied stores along Front Street that await her. The atmosphere is relaxed as people amble along the main street in the sunshine, disappearing occasionally into shops or down side streets for shade and curiosity. She knows a busy day is before her, as the sales have begun and there is only so much time to visit all of the department stores and boutiques. Assured of her success, she adjusts her sunglasses, taps her handbag as if to awaken her sleeping credit cards from a deep sleep, and marches purposefully toward Trimingham's.

In This Chapter

When and How 65 • Shopping Districts 65 • Department Stores 67 • Specialty Stores 69

Revised and updated by By Karen Smith

shopping

IF YOU'RE ACCUSTOMED TO SHOPPING in Saks Fifth Avenue, Neiman Marcus, and Bergdorf Goodman, the prices in Bermuda's elegant shops won't come as a surprise. Although the prices on many items are somewhat discounted, a $600 Gucci must-have even discounted by 20% is still a whopping $480. Crystal and china are often less expensive here, too, sometimes on par with American outlet store prices. If you see something cheap, grab it: comparison shopping is a waste of time on Bermuda, as prices are typically fixed island-wide. Best of all, Bermuda has no sales tax, which means that the price on the tag is the price you pay.

WHEN AND HOW

Shops are generally open Monday to Saturday 9–5 and closed on Sunday (although some supermarkets remain open) and public holidays. Between April and October, some of the smaller Front Street shops open on Sunday. The shops in the Clocktower Centre at the Royal Naval Dockyard are usually open Monday–Saturday 10–5 from April through October (11–5 in winter) and Sunday 11–5. Some extend their hours around Christmas. Almost all stores close for public holidays.

Many of Bermuda's more exclusive shops have branches in the larger resort hotels.

SHOPPING DISTRICTS

Hamilton has the greatest concentration of shops in Bermuda, and Front Street is its pièce de résistance. Lined with small,

Bewildered in Hamilton?

Although the numbering of houses is becoming more common—houses have traditionally been known only by their picturesque names rather than numbers—buildings in Hamilton are still numbered rather whimsically. If you check the phone directory for a store address, you may find a listing on Front Street or Water Street, for example, but no street number. In fact, some Front Street buildings have two numbers, one of them an old historic address that has nothing to do with the building's present location. Fortunately, almost all Bermudians, being a friendly and knowledgeable sort, can usually give you precise directions.

pastel-color buildings, this most fashionable of Bermuda's streets houses sedate department stores and snazzy boutiques, with several small arcades and shopping alleys leading off it. A smart canopy shades the entrance to the 55 Front Street Group, which houses several upmarket boutiques. Modern Butterfield Place has galleries and boutiques selling, among other things, Louis Vuitton leather goods. The Emporium, a renovated building with an atrium, has a range of shops, from antiques to souvenirs.

In St. George's, Water Street, Duke of York Street, Hunters Wharf, Penno's Wharf, and Somers Wharf are the sites of numerous renovated buildings that house branches of Front Street stores, as well as studios of local artisans. Historic King's Square offers little more than a couple of T-shirt and souvenir shops.

In the West End, Somerset Village has a few shops, but they hardly merit a special shopping trip. However, the historic Clocktower Centre at Royal Naval Dockyard has a few more shopping opportunities, including branches of Front Street shops and specialty boutiques. The Dockyard is also home to the Craft Market, the Bermuda Arts Centre, and Bermuda Clayworks.

DEPARTMENT STORES

Bermuda's three leading department stores are A. S. Cooper & Son, Trimingham's, and H. A. & E. Smith's, the main branches of which are on Front Street in Hamilton. The third or fourth generations of the families that founded them now run these elegant, venerable institutions, and you stand a good chance of being waited on by a Cooper, a Trimingham, or a Smith. In addition, many of the salespeople have worked at the stores for two or three decades. They tend to be unobtrusive but polite and helpful when you need them.

A. S. COOPER & SON (59 Front St., Hamilton, tel. 441/295–3961; Clocktower Centre, Dockyard; 22 Water St., St. George). With branches in all major hotels, Cooper & Son is best known for its extensive inventory of crystal and china. Here you'll find Waterford and Swarovski crystal; china, including Wedgwood, Royal Doulton, and Royal Copenhagen; and Lladró figurines. A five-piece place setting of the Wedgwood Countryware pattern costs $64.20 (add about 15% for U.S. shipping, with duty, freight, and insurance). Prices on the stock of china and crystal are similarly attractive. The store's private-label collection of clothing can be found in the well-stocked men's, women's, and children's departments. The gift department on the Front Street level carries a large selection of tasteful Bermudian gifts and souvenirs.

GIBBONS CO. (21 Reid St., Hamilton, tel. 441/295–0022). One of Bermuda's oldest stores (still run by the Gibbons family) is also a fairly casual department store that stocks a wide range of men's, women's, and children's clothing, as well as quite a sizable household department rather than china and crystal. It's particularly good for casual designer brands, such as Polo and DKNY. Gibbons also has a large perfume section, a substantial accessories department, and a wide range of quality handbags, purses, and scarves.

H. A. & E. SMITH'S (35 Front St., Hamilton, tel. 441/295–2288; Southampton Princess, Southampton; 18 York St., St. George). Founded in 1889 by Henry Archibald and Edith Smith, this is arguably the best men's store in Bermuda. Men's Burberry raincoats are priced from $495 to $595, and William Lockie cashmeres sell from $248 to $448. Men's 100% cashmere topcoats go for $425, and Italian silk ties for $26 and up. Smith's is also a good place to buy kilts.

Fendi handbags (the only place in Bermuda they're carried) go for about $500 for a medium size. The women's department also has an extensive selection of formal and casual wear. William Lockie cashmere turtleneck sweaters are priced from $278. Burberry raincoats range from $575 to $695. The women's shoe department offers a broad choice of fine Italian styles, both classic and contemporary.

The Front Street–level china department carries a large selection of patterns from Royal Doulton to Rosenthal, and crystal of all types is sold. French perfume sells for 20%–30% less than in the States. As with many of the island's older buildings, the store has a confusing layout that makes it easy to get lost. The staff here is especially genteel, however, and will help orient you.

MARKS & SPENCER (18 Reid St., Hamilton, tel. 441/295–0031). A franchise of the large British chain, Marks and Sparks (as it's called by everyone in Bermuda and England) is usually filled with locals attracted by its moderate prices for men's, women's, and children's clothing. Summer wear, including swimsuits, cotton jerseys, and polo shirts, is a good buy, as is underwear.

High-quality men's and women's cashmere and woolen sweaters are also sold at substantial discounts.

TRIMINGHAM'S (37 Front St., Hamilton, tel. 441/295–1183). Bermuda's largest department store has been a Hamilton fixture since 1842. It's the home of Daks Bermuda shorts ($47.50) and tailored-for-Trimingham's sportswear. Women's designers, such as Liz Claiborne, Tommy Hilfiger, and Calvin Klein, have complete lines here, and fine tableware by Mikasa, Spode, and others is sold for up to 25%–40% less than in the United States. The store has an impressive display of perfumes and cosmetics, and it's Bermuda's exclusive distributor of Christian Dior, Estée Lauder, and Yves St-Laurent. You'll also find a potpourri of fine leather, jewelry, children's fashions, and gift items. Trimingham branches—10 in all—can be found all over, including at Somers Wharf in St. George's, South Shore Road in Paget, and in Somerset Village.

SPECIALTY STORES
Antiques

THE BERMUDA RAILWAY MUSEUM (37 North Shore Rd., Hamilton Parish, tel. 441/293–1774). An extensive collection of historical artifacts from Bermuda's short-lived railway is in the museum. Plus, the museum shop sells photos, maps, books, prints, and antiques as well as collectibles from jewelry and coins to stamps, books, and china. If you take the bus here, get off at the first stop after the Bermuda Aquarium. The shop is open Tuesday to Friday from 10 to 4 or by appointment with Rose Hollis.

PEGASUS (63 Pitts Bay Rd., Hamilton, tel. 441/295–2900). This Dickensian place in an old house with creaky wood floors is a few minutes' walk from downtown Hamilton on Front Street West, near the Princess. The store has bins and bins of antique prints and a small selection of antique maps. Look for the original Leslie Ward (Spy) *Vanity Fair* caricatures that were published between 1869 and 1914 (from $20 and the Curtis botanicals $50). Topographical engravings by Bartlett start at $50. French fashion scenes and early lithographs are priced from $50. You'll also find a huge selection of greeting cards and wrapping paper from England. Popular items are the beautifully crafted ceramic house signs from England, which can be ordered. You can browse here to your heart's content from 10 to 5 Monday through Saturday.

PORTOBELLO (Emporium Bldg., 9 Front St., Hamilton, tel. 441/295–1407). This small, charming shop is tucked away in the modern Emporium Building shopping complex just off Front Street. It's the perfect haunt for stamp and coin collectors with the island's best collection of 19th- and 20th-century stamps. It also sells a small range of antique prints and ornaments.

THISTLE GALLERY (7 Park Rd., Hamilton, tel. 441/292–3839). This is a must for antique-furniture lovers. Porcelain, china, glassware, and silver are also on sale. Hours are 9–5; it's closed Sunday.

Art Galleries

The **ART HOUSE GALLERY** (80 South Rd., Paget, tel. 441/236–6746) has watercolors, oils, and color lithographs by Bermuda artist Joan Forbes.

BERMUDA ARTS CENTRE AT DOCKYARD (Museum Row, Dockyard, tel. 441/234–2809). Sleek and modern, with well-designed displays of local art, this gallery is housed in one of the stone buildings of the former British Naval Dockyard. The walls are adorned with paintings and photographs, and glass display cases contain exquisitely crafted quilts as well as costume dolls, jewelry, and wood sculpture. Exhibits change frequently. Several artists' studios inside the gallery are open to the public. The center is open daily from 10 to 5.

BERMUDA SOCIETY OF ARTS (Church St., West Wing, City Hall, Hamilton, tel. 441/292–3824). Many highly creative Society members sell their work at the perennial members' shows and during a revolving series of special group exhibits. You will find watercolor, oil, and acrylic paintings and pastel and charcoal drawings, as well as occasional photographs, collages, and pieces of sculpture. The Society's second gallery, **Harbour Gallery**, is on Front Street West and is open Monday through Saturday from 10 until 4.

BIRDSEY STUDIO (Rosecote, 5 Stowe Hill, Paget, tel. 441/236–6658). Alfred Birdsey died in 1996, and the island mourned his loss. Mr. Birdsey received the Queen's Certificate of Honour and Medal in recognition of "valuable services given to Her Majesty for more than 40 years as an artist of Bermuda." And thanks to Jo Birdsey Linberg, his daughter, Birdsey's studio remains open and new works continue the tradition admirably. Watercolors cost from $50 and lithographs from $15 at the studio, which is usually open weekdays 10:30 to 1, and by appointment. Call before going, because hours vary.

BRIDGE HOUSE GALLERY (1 Bridge St., St. George's, tel. 441/297–8211). Housed in part of a Bermuda home that dates from 1700, this gallery is of historical and architectural interest in its own right. During the 18th century the two-story white building was the home of Bermuda's governors. Today it's maintained by the Bermuda National Trust. Original works by local artists, inexpensive prints, and souvenirs are for sale.

CAROLE HOLDING PRINT & CRAFT SHOPS (King's Sq., St. George's, tel. 441/297–1373; Clocktower Centre, Dockyard, tel. 441/234–3800; 81 Front St., Hamilton, tel. 441/296–3431 or 800/880–8570). Commercial artist Ms. Holding mass-produces watercolors of Bermuda's scenes and flowers; many of the same works are sold as signed prints and limited editions. Crafts, both imported and by local artists, are also available. Prices range from $15 (small prints) to $200 (framed watercolors).

CLEARVIEW ART GALLERY (Crawl Hill, Hamilton Parish, tel. 441/293–4057) is owned by Otto Trott, a Bermudian artist known for his beautiful oil paintings of landscapes and local characters. His work can be found at other galleries, but often his best pictures are found here. Small watercolors are priced at $50, oils from about $200 to $2,000. Mr. Trott also gives painting lessons.

HERITAGE HOUSE (2 Front St., Hamilton, tel. 441/295–2615). This gallery regularly displays original works by the island's leading artists, including Sheilagh Head, Maria Smith, Kathy Zuill, Diana Amos, and internationally known marine artist Stephen Card. A large selection of local and foreign prints is also available. An on-site framing department has a computerized system that allows for less expensive production. Throughout the store you will find quality reproduction furniture from Great Britain and many interesting and tasteful Bermudian souvenirs.

KAFU HAIR SALON (8 Parliament St., near Victoria, Hamilton, tel. 441/295–5238, fax 441/295–1580). Proving that art can happen anywhere, Glen Wilks' salon also displays contemporary work including paintings and sculpture by local avant-garde artists.

MASTERWORKS FOUNDATION GALLERY (97 Front St., Hamilton, tel. 441/295–5580). Formed in 1987, the foundation exhibits well-known Canadian, British, French, and American artists, including Winslow Homer, whose works were inspired by Bermuda, and Georgia O'Keeffe. The Bermudiana Collection contains more than 400 works in watercolor, oil, pencil, charcoal, and other mediums. The Bermuda National Gallery at City Hall, Camden House, and Waterloo House all display selected pieces from this collection.

The two **MICHAEL SWAN GALLERIES** (Butterfield Pl., Front St., Hamilton, tel. 441/296–5650; Clock Tower Centre, Royal Naval Dockyard, tel. 441/234–3128) are worth noting. Swan uses pastels to capture Bermuda's houses in a very special way. His depiction of the local architecture, in galleries and exhibitions all over the world, has made him one of the island's favorite artists.

OMAX CERAMICS STUDIO (Admiralty House, Pembroke, tel. 441/292–8478) is the best place to peruse ceramic art, much of it Bermuda-inspired.

WINDJAMMER GALLERY (King and Reid Sts., Hamilton, tel. 441/292–7861; 95 Front St., Hamilton, tel. 441/292–5878). The island's largest selection of local and imported art is in a charming four-room cottage whose colorful garden has life-size bronze sculptures. Individual and group shows in painting and photography are held regularly, and work is exported to collectors worldwide. The knowledgeable staff can help with your selection and shipping arrangements. Prints and lithographs are also available. **Prints Plus** (95 Front St.) is Windjammer's print shop, which has an extensive collection of local prints, cards, books, photographs, and art-related gifts as well as wearable art. All purchases may be shipped, and a catalog is available.

Bookstores

BERMUDA BOOK STORE (Queen St., Hamilton, tel. 441/295–3698). Once you set foot inside this musty old place, you'll have a hard time tearing yourself away. Stacked on a long table is a host of books about Bermuda. The proprietor can probably answer any questions you have about Bermuda.

THE BOOK CELLAR (Water St., St. George's, tel. 441/297–0448). This small shop below the National Trust's Tucker House crams in a large selection of books about Bermuda and an interesting assortment of novels by English and American authors beyond the contemporary best-sellers. Coffee-table books and a variety of hard-to-find British children's books are plentiful. Owner Jill White and her well-read staff will be happy to help you search for an obscure title or let you browse at your leisure.

THE BOOKMART (Phoenix Centre, 3 Reid St., Hamilton, tel. 441/295–3838). The island's largest bookstore specializes in best-sellers and paperbacks and has a complete selection of Bermuda titles, as well as a large children's section.

BUDS, BEANS & BOOKS (55 Front St., Hamilton, tel. 441/292–1990). This handy new Front Street store, opened in 2000, is ideal for grabbing a fresh cup of coffee, cut flowers, or the latest best-seller. A plus is the well-stocked selection of magazines and greeting cards.

THE CHILDREN'S BOOKSHOP (International Centre, 26 Bermudiana Rd., Hamilton, tel. 441/292–9078). A wonderful selection of hard-to-find British titles is geared to all ages.

SHIP'S INN BOOK GALLERY (Clocktower Centre, Dockyard, tel. 441/234–2807). Sherlyn Swan carries an ever-changing assortment of used books as well as some rare and antique titles. The only new books are about Bermuda.

WASHINGTON MALL MAGAZINE (Washington Mall, Reid St., Hamilton, tel. 441/292–7420). Come here for Bermuda's best selection of magazines, including hard-to-find periodicals. This is also the place to find a best-seller for the beach or the journey home, children's books, and coffee-table publications about the island.

Cigars

CHATHAM HOUSE (63 Front St., Hamilton, tel. 441/292–8422). Be warned: not only is the air here thick with the aroma of cigar and cigarette smoke, but there is a life-size wooden Indian princess to greet customers. In business since 1895, this shop has the ambience of an old-time country store. It stocks not only top-quality cigars from Cuba (Romeo y Julieta, Bolivar, Partagas, and Punch) but Briar and Meerschaum pipes, Swiss Army knives, Dunhill lighters, sunglasses, gum, and postcards. A sign advises that it's illegal to bring Cuban cigars into the United States.

TIENDA DE TABACS (Emporium Bldg., 69 Front St., Hamilton, tel. 441/295–8475). As sleek as the Chatham House is rustic, this store focuses almost exclusively on cigars, Cuban and otherwise. The hardwood floors are polished to a high sheen, and shelves and glass cases are lined with boxes of stogies. At the rear of the long room three huge soft leather armchairs are grouped around a coffee table, appropriately set with ashtrays. So even if you can't take the Cubans into the States, you're surely invited to smoke 'em right here in the store, along with the sales staff.

Clothing and Accessories

CHILDREN'S CLOTHING

KANGAROO POUCH (Burnaby St.; Hamilton, tel. 441/295–4455). Opened in 2001, this caters to the trend-conscious child, filling every need in his or her wardrobe, along with casual and smart clothes for mothers-to-be. It's a lovely store, but beware—it's not cheap.

MEN'S CLOTHING

ASTON & GUNN (2 Reid St., Hamilton, tel. 441/295–4866). An upmarket member of the island's English Sports Shops, this handsome store carries men's and women's clothing and accessories. Men's European clothing, including Hugo Boss and Van Gils, costs up to 30% less than in the United States. Aston & Gunn cotton dress shirts sell for about $100. Women's wear, including designs by Calvin Klein and Anne Klein, is mainly from the United States, but because there's no sales tax it may be less expensive.

ENGLISH SPORTS SHOP (95 Front St., Hamilton, tel. 441/295–2672; Water St., St. George's, tel. 441/297–0142). This shop specializes in British woolens: Shetland woolen sweaters are priced at around $50. Cashmere sweaters start from $200. The store also sells women's sweaters.

H. A. & E. SMITH'S (☞ Department Stores, *above*).

THE SOURCE (Reid St., Washington Mall, Hamilton, tel. 441/295–0989). Popular with locals, these stores are for the trendy types but are quite reasonably priced.

MEN'S AND WOMEN'S CLOTHING

BANANAS (93 W. Front St., Hamilton, tel. 441/295–1106; 7 E. Front St., Hamilton, tel. 441/292–7264; Princess Hotel, Hamilton, tel. 441/295–3000; 3 King's Sq., St. George's, tel. 441/297–0351; Sonesta Beach Resort, Southampton, tel. 441/238–3409). Sportswear and T-shirts make this store a teenager's dream. Brightly colored Bermuda umbrellas cost about $20.

DAVISON'S OF BERMUDA (73 Front St., Hamilton, tel. 441/292–2083; Water St., St. George's, tel. 441/297–8363; Southampton Princess Hotel, South Shore Rd., Southampton, tel. 441/238–1036; Clocktower Centre, Dockyard, tel. 441/234–0959). The high-quality cotton sportswear items sold here include sweaters and pants, and sportswear for adults and children. They also carry gift packages of Bermuda fish chowder, clam chowder, and sherry peppers, and a collection of deliciously vicious-looking stuffed trolls. In the United States you'll find branches in Baltimore and Myrtle Beach.

UPSTAIRS GOLF & TENNIS SHOP (26 Church St., Hamilton, tel. 441/295–5161). Upstairs stocks clubs and accessories from some of the best brands available, including Ping, Callaway, and Titleist. Tennis players can choose a racket by Yonex or Dunlop. Men's and women's sportswear is also sold.

SHOES AND HANDBAGS

BOYLE, W. J. & SONS LTD. (Queen St., Hamilton, tel. 441/295–1887; Mangrove Bay, Somerset, tel. 441/234–0530; Water St., St. George's, tel. 441/297–1922; Trends, The Walkway, Reid St., Hamilton, tel. 441/295–6420; The Sports Locker, Windsor Place, 18 Queen St., Hamilton, tel. 441/292–3300). Bermuda's leading shoe store chain, Boyle's sells a wide range of men's, women's, and children's shoes. Trends on Reid Street has the most up-to-the-minute foot fashions.

CALYPSO (45 Front St., Hamilton, tel. 441/295–2112; other branches at Princess Hotel, Hamilton; Coral Beach & Tennis Club; Sonesta Beach Resort; Southampton Princess, Southampton;

Clocktower Centre, Dockyard). If you're looking for something a little snazzy and sharp for your feet, then you are bound to find something at this branch. The shoe and bag section is small, but they come in an array of bright colors and wonderful shapes. Items may cost a little more here, but serious bargains can be had during sales.

GUCCI (71 Front St., Hamilton, tel. 441/295–2351). This small designer shop, tucked away at the back of Crisson's jewelry on Front Street, stocks a small range of fabulous women's sandals, shoes, and handbags and some men's shoes, too. Watch for frequent sales that often cut the tag price by as much as half.

LOCOMOTION (Upper Level, Washington Mall, Hamilton, tel. 441/296–4030). A small shop with a modest range of very young, up-to-the-minute, affordable styles for women and children.

LOUIS VUITTON (Butterfield Pl., Front St., Hamilton, tel. 441/296–1940). Come here to find the famous monogram in ladies' handbags, men's and women's briefcases, carry-on luggage, wallets, credit-card cases, and other items. Prices here are the same as in the United States, except there's no tax. Small ladies' handbags start at about $750. Small soft leather monogram carry-ons cost up to $1,000, and natural cowhide briefcases start from $3,000.

THE YANKEE STORE (15 Reid St., Hamilton, tel. 441/295–2570). One of Bermuda's rare low-cost shops has a good range of very reasonably priced women's shoes downstairs, including extra-wide sizes. Quality varies, and some styles may be last season's, but it's one of the best places for a bargain. Upstairs (road level) sells everything from cedarwood ornaments and fashion jewelry to leather wallets and souvenirs.

WOMEN'S CLOTHING

BENETTON (Reid St., Hamilton, tel. 441/295–2112). A big hit with locals, this branch of the international chain has a wide variety of casual and chic men's, women's and children's clothing, in both brash, bright colors and more subdued tones. Prices are reasonable and the store is well laid out and airy, making shopping easy. The children's department is upstairs.

CALYPSO (45 Front St., Hamilton, tel. 441/295–2112; other branches at Princess Hotel, Hamilton; Coral Beach & Tennis Club; Sonesta Beach Resort; Southampton Princess, Southampton; Clocktower Centre, Dockyard). This expensive women's clothing shop carries an array of sophisticated leisure wear, and has the island's largest selection of swimwear. Accessories, including Italian leather shoes and straw hats, are also plentiful. Eclectic novelty items from Europe make great gifts. Calypso's shop in Butterfield Place, **Voila!**, carries Longchamps leather goods, Oscar Leopold leather jackets, and Johnston & Murphy men's shoes.

CECILE (15 Front St., Hamilton, tel. 441/295–1311; Southampton Princess Hotel, South Shore Rd., Southampton, tel. 441/238–1434). Specializing in upscale off-the-rack ladies' fashions, Cecile carries such designer labels as Mondi, Basler, and Louis Feraud of Paris. There's a good selection of swimwear, including swimsuits by Gottex, and of European lingerie, especially La Perla. An expanded accessories department carries shoes as well as scarves, jewelry, handbags, and belts.

COW POLLY (Somers Wharf, St. George's, tel. 441/297–1514). Phoebe Wharton's store brings together expensive hand-painted clothing and attractive accessories from the far corners of the globe. Beautifully crafted straw bags and hats are worth the trip from Hamilton. And you won't find the store's unusual pottery, jewelry, or men's ties sold anywhere else on the island.

CROWN COLONY SHOP (1 Front St., Hamilton, tel. 441/295–3935). This branch of the English Sports Shop sells quality formal and business wear for women. The shop's signature item is a line of Parisian-designed Mayeelok silk dresses and two-piece skirt and pant sets in polyester and silk, which sell for $235 and $295.

FRANGIPANI (Water St., St. George's, tel. 441/297–1357). The colorful women's fashions sold in this little store have an island resort look. Cotton, silk, and rayon leisure wear are the backbone of the stock, but vibrant Caribbean art is also sold. Frangipani also sells a collection of unusual accessories in various styles.

PIRATE'S PORT (Queen St., Hamilton, tel. 441/292–1080). Pirate's is less expensive than the average Bermudian clothing store, with clothing for men, women, and children. It's particularly good for casual and work wear. However, give yourself time to hunt around—the stock can sometimes be a little crammed together.

STEFANEL (12 Walker Arcade, Reid St., Hamilton, tel. 441/295–5698). This small, trendy international boutique is good for simple, stylish, modern women's clothes at reasonable prices. They have lots of cotton and natural fabrics, neutral colors, and delicate small-print fabrics. A good children's section is at the back of the shop.

TRIANGLE'S (Queen St., access next to Bermuda Bookstore, Hamilton, tel. 441/295–5247). This boutique stocks a good range of designer labels and upmarket outfits, some at almost half of what they would cost in the United States.

Crafts

BERMUDA GLASSBLOWING STUDIO & SHOW ROOM (16 Blue Hole Hill, Hamilton Parish, tel. 441/293–2234). A restored village hall in the Bailey's Bay area houses this glassblowing studio, where eight artists have created more than 200 examples of hand-blown glass in vibrant, swirling colors. You can watch glassblowers at work daily in the studio and purchase their work here. Prices range from $10 to $1,600.

CRAFT MARKET (The Cooperage, Dockyard, tel. 441/234–3208). The old cooperage building dates to 1831 and is one of the few places today that sells island-made handicrafts. Anna

Good Buys

If you are the type of person who insists on only buying bargains, then Bermuda is probably not the place for you to spend hours shopping. However, there are bargains to be had, particularly during sale times (which can be any time), when stores reduce their prices (without warning) by 50%. Due to a lack of storage space in Bermuda and the unforgiving humidity, when retailers decide to sell off their goods, they do so fairly quickly, so even the most expensive stores can offer bargains.

There's not much shopping diversity on this tiny island. You'll find that a lot of stores assume crystal and china are your thing. Although European-made crystal and china—Waterford and Wedgwood, to name a few—are available at prices at least 25% lower than those in the United States. Figurines are also sold at significantly discounted prices. European fragrances and cosmetics are priced about 25%–30% less than in the United States, as are Rolex and other watches.

But there are some more mundane objets that you can also buy cheaply here. Perfume and beauty products, such as Clinique and Estée Lauder, tend to be at duty-free prices, often as much as 30% cheaper than in the United States or United Kingdom. Jewelry is also a good buy, as it's tax free, and casual designer wear, particularly Levis and Ralph Lauren brands, tend to be good bargains. Woolens and cashmere are good buys, especially after Christmas and in January when many stores offer substantial discounts. Naturally, Bermuda shorts are hot items, as are kilts, but bargains on these are a rarity.

and Glenn Correia's wooden creations are beautifully executed and reasonably priced. Outstanding is Judith Faram's exquisite—but expensive—handmade jewelry. Celia and Jack Arnell's detailed dollhouse cedar furniture is also popular. A four-poster bed sells for $125, chairs for about $35, depending on the model.

Crystal, China, and Porcelain

BLUCK'S (4 W. Front St., Hamilton, tel. 441/295–5367; Reid and Queen Sts., Hamilton, tel. 441/292–3894; Water St., St. George's, tel. 441/297–0476; Southampton Princess Hotel, South Shore, Southampton, tel. 441/238–0992). A dignified establishment that has been in business for more than 150 years, Bluck's is the island's only store devoted exclusively to the sale of crystal and china. Royal Doulton, Royal Copenhagen, Villeroy & Boch, Herend, Lalique, Minton, Waterford, Baccarat, and others are displayed in its two Front Street stores. A good selection of the popular Kosta Boda Swedish crystal and Limoges boxes can be found here. The courteous staff will provide you price lists upon request.

VERA P. CARD (11 Front St., Hamilton, tel. 441/295–1729; 9 Water St., St. George's, tel. 441/297–1718; Sonesta Beach Resort, South Shore Rd., Southampton, tel. 441/238–8122). Lladró and Swarovski silver crystal figurines are available at almost identical prices elsewhere, but this store has the largest selection, including open-edition and limited-edition gallery pieces. The shop's collection of more than 250 Hummel figurines is one of the world's largest. The impressive selection of Swiss and German watches and clocks includes the Bermuda Time collection; and the stock of fine and costume jewelry includes 14-karat gold earrings, charms, and pendants.

Gifts and Souvenirs

FLYING COLOURS AT RIIHUOLMA'S (5 Queen St., Hamilton, tel. 441/295–0890). This family-owned and -operated shop, established in 1937, has the island's largest selection of T-shirts with creatively designed logos in hundreds of styles. The selection of quality souvenirs and gifts is plentiful, and educational toys are a specialty. The shop also carries everything for the beach—hats, beach towels, toys, and more.

HALL OF NAMES (Butterfield Pl., Hamilton, tel. 441/234–3410). This is a fun place to learn the origins of your family name, or of any nickname. Friendly owner John Doherty punches the pertinent information into a computer and for about $20 per surname gives you a nicely presented document with facts compiled from an extensive bibliography, with your family coat of arms at the top.

HODGE PODGE (3 Point Pleasant Rd., Hamilton, tel. 441/295–0647). Just around the corner from the Ferry Terminal and Visitors Center Service Bureau in Hamilton, this cluttered little shop offers pretty much what its name implies: postcards, sunblock, sunglasses, film, and T-shirts.

PULP & CIRCUMSTANCE (Reid St., Hamilton, tel. 441/292–9586; Old Cellar La., off Front St., Hamilton, tel. 441/292–3224; Queen St., Hamilton, tel. 441/292–9586). If it's an original, quality gift you're after, look no further: exquisite, modern picture frames in all shapes and sizes and from all over the world are a specialty, as are baby gifts, candles, fresh herbs, bath products, and greetings cards.

RISING SUN SHOP (Middle Rd., Southampton, tel. 441/238–2154). This country store is easy to spot: A flag, a horse's head, and other eye-catching inventory usually hang outside the entrance. Owner Anne Powell's warmth and humor infuse her novelty gift items, which may include toilet plungers, a ship's decanter, Portuguese wine coolers, or picnic baskets—though inventory changes frequently. Scads of wicker baskets are usually in stock, as well as more expensive items, such as antique hobby horses starting at $2,000. A large selection of quality tack (stable gear) is always on hand.

SAIL ON (Old Cellar La., off Front St., Hamilton, tel. 441/295–0808). Owned and operated by Hubert Watlington, a former Olympic windsurfer and top local sailor, this must-visit shop is tucked up a quaint alleyway, opposite No. 1 Shed and a cruise-ship dock. It's a top spot for casual clothing and swimwear for adults and children as well as gifts that appeal to those with a wacky sense of humor. Road Toad and Famous Onions clothing are sold here exclusively.

TREATS (Washington Mall, Reid St., Hamilton, tel. 441/296–1123). You'll find bulk candy in just about every flavor here. Plus, you can buy sweets by the piece or the pound. The Candygramme gift box is filled with candy of your choice and decorated with a balloon. Prices start at $15. You will find whimsical gifts here, too.

Grocery Stores

Many of the accommodations on Bermuda allow you to do your own cooking. Considering how expensive Bermuda is, this option has widespread appeal for travelers on a budget. Still, foodstuffs in Bermuda are expensive: A dozen imported large eggs cost about $2.50 (locally raised eggs are even more expensive: about $4 a dozen), a loaf of Bermuda-made bread is $3 (U.S.-made bread is $5), a six-pack of Coke is about $5, and a 13-ounce can of coffee is $8. Unless stated otherwise, grocery stores carry liquor.

A-ONE PAGET (Middle Rd., Paget, tel. 441/236–0351). This grocery is near Barnsdale Guest Apartments and the Sky Top Cottages. Be warned, however, that the route between Sky Top and the store takes in a significant hill, which could make for a difficult hike if you buy a lot.

A-ONE SMITH'S (Middle Rd., Smith's, tel. 441/236–6673). Although part of the Marketplace chain, this store also has a small supply of goods. It's near Angel's Grotto and Brightside Apartments, but not quite within walking distance.

HARRINGTON HUNDREDS GROCERY & LIQUOR STORE
(South Rd., Smith's, tel. 441/293–1635). Harrington is a must for
those observing special diets or seeking out unusual
ingredients. It has the island's best selection of wheat-free
foods, including gluten-free pastas, breads, and cookies. It's
close to Spittal Pond and not far from Angel's Grotto, but it's still
a long walk with bags.

HERON BAY MARKETPLACE (Middle Rd., Southampton, tel.
441/238–1993). One of the island-wide Marketplace chain of
stores, this one has a large selection of fresh vegetables. It's
convenient to Longtail Cliffs and Marley Beach, but not on foot.

LINDO'S FAMILY FOODS, LTD. (Middle Rd., Warwick, tel. 441/
236–1344). A medium-size store with a good selection of quality
and gourmet foods, Lindo's is within walking distance of the
several Warwick accommodations. But when you're heavily
laden with groceries, you'll have to rely on a taxi.

THE MARKETPLACE (Reid St. near Parliament St., Hamilton, tel.
441/292–3163). Marketplace is the island's largest grocery store
and the HQ of the chain. You can take out hot soups, stir-fries,
dinners, salads, and desserts for about $5 a pound. This branch
is also open Sunday 1–5.

MAXIMART (Middle Rd., Sandys, tel. 441/234–1940). Near
Whale Bay Road, this is a good place to stock up on snacks.
There's a good selection of deli meats here, and they deliver.

MILES MARKET (Pitts Bay Rd. near the Hamilton Princess,
Hamilton, tel. 441/295–1234). Miles's is Bermuda's Balducci's,
with a large selection of upscale or hard-to-get specialty food
items and high-quality imported and local meats and fish. Many
items are on the expensive side, but the quality and selection
here are unsurpassed in Bermuda. The market delivers
anywhere on island.

MODERN MART (South Shore Rd., Paget, tel. 441/236–6161).
Part of the Marketplace chain, but smaller than its flagship

Hamilton store this location has all the essentials. It's easily accessible from Sky Top Cottages, Loughlands, and other South Shore hotels.

SHELLY BAY MARKETPLACE (North Shore Rd., Hamilton Parish, tel. 441/293–0966). This Marketplace chain store, the only large grocer on North Shore Road, has a good selection.

SOMERSET MARKETPLACE (Somerset Rd., Sandys, tel. 441/234–0626). The largest grocery store on the island's western end, it's convenient to Whale Bay Inn, but take a moped or taxi.

SOMERS SUPERMARKET (York St., St. George's Parish, tel. 441/297–1177). There's a large selection here despite its small size. Hot items, salads, and sandwiches are available and are made fresh daily. It's within walking distance of the St. George's Club and Aunt Nea's Inn at Hillcrest Guest House.

THE SUPERMART (Front St. near King St., Hamilton, tel. 441/292–2064). In addition to the typical goods, you'll find a well-stocked salad bar, prepackaged sandwiches, and hot coffee. It's a long hike—particularly with heavy bags—from the Ferry Terminal in Hamilton, but once you're aboard it's an easy ride across the harbor to Greenbank Cottages and Salt Kettle House. Fortunately, island-wide deliveries are available.

Jewelry

ASTWOOD DICKINSON (83–85 Front St., Hamilton, tel. 441/292–5805; H. A. & E. Smith's, Front St., Hamilton, tel. 441/296–6664). Established in 1904, this store is the exclusive agent for Colombian Emeralds International. It has an exquisite collection of European jewelry, unmounted stones, and a wide range of Swiss watches. Timepieces by Cartier, Tiffany & Co., Tag Heuer, and others are sold for up to 35% less than in the United States. The shop's exclusively designed gold mementos in the Bermuda Collection sell for $50–$1,000. Created in the store's workshop upstairs, they include a range of 18-karat and bejeweled replicas of the island's flora, fauna, and landmarks available as pins, pendants, and charms.

CRISSON'S (55 and 71 Front St., Hamilton, tel. 441/295–2351; 16 Queen St., Hamilton, tel. 441/295–2351; 20 Reid St., Hamilton, tel. 441/295–2351; Elbow Beach Hotel, South Shore Rd., Paget, tel. 441/236–9928; Sonesta Beach Resort, South Shore Rd., Southampton, ·tel. 441/238–0072; York and Kent Sts., St. George's, tel. 441/297–0672; Water St., St. George's, tel. 441/297–0107). The exclusive Bermuda agent for Rolex, Gucci, Movado, and other famous names, this upscale establishment offers discounts of 20%–25% on expensive merchandise. Earrings are a specialty, and there's a large selection. The gift department carries English flatware, Saint Louis crystal, and imported baubles, bangles, and beads.

JEWELER'S WAREHOUSE (Walker Arcade, Hamilton, tel. 441/292–4247). Astwood Dickinson's bargain jewelry shop offers unbeatable value for the budget-minded shopper. This informal store can give you savings of up to 50% off manufacturer's recommended retail prices. There's a good selection of diamond, sapphire, emerald, ruby, tanzanite, and other gemstone jewelry, as well as watches. With every purchase you can spin the Wheel of Fortune to win a prize.

SOLOMON'S (17 Front St., Hamilton, tel. 441/292–4742 or 441/295–1003). Manager Allan Porter and his skilled staff custom-design one-of-a-kind pieces of genuine stones and minerals. Ranging in price from $70 to upwards of $100,000, the pieces are sometimes whimsical and charming.

VERA P. CARD (☞ Crystal, China, and Porcelain, *above*).

WALKER CHRISTOPHER (9 Front St., Hamilton, tel. 441/295–1466). For the past 10 years *Bermudian* magazine has named this goldsmith the island's best for fine jewelry. Classic pieces include diamond bands, strands of South Sea pearls, and the more contemporary hand-hammered chokers. You can work with the jeweler to design your own exclusive piece. The Walker

Christopher workshop also produces its own line of Bermuda-inspired gold jewelry and sterling silver Christmas ornaments. An excellent collection of rare coins, some salvaged from sunken galleons, are also sold.

Linens

IRISH LINEN SHOP (31 Front St., Hamilton, tel. 441/295–4089). In a cottage that looks as though it belongs in Dublin, this shop is the place for Irish linen tablecloths. Prices range from $10 to more than $3,000. Antique tablecloths can cost nearly $2,000. The best buys are the Irish linen tea towels for around $10. From Madeira come exquisite hand-embroidered handkerchiefs, plus linen sheets and pillowcases, and cotton organdy christening robes with slip and bonnet, hand-embroidered with garlands and tiers of Valenciennes lace (from $220 to more than $800). The store has an exclusive arrangement with Souleiado, maker of the vivid prints from Provence that are available in tablecloths, place mats, and bags, as well as by the yard—the last at a huge savings over U.S. prices.

Liquor Stores

Bermuda liquor stores have a good selection of wines and spirits. Each has branches sprinkled around the island from St. George's to Somerset, and each will allow you to put together your own package of Bermuda liquors at in-bond (duty-free) prices. Be aware that most spirits are sold at identical prices on Bermuda, so comparison shopping is not very fruitful.

BURROWS LIGHTBOURN (Front St., Hamilton, tel. 441/295–0176; Clocktower Centre, Dockyard, tel. 441/234–5078; Harbour Rd., Paget, tel. 441/236–0355; Water St., St. George's, tel. 441/297–0552; Main Rd., Somerset, tel. 441/234–0963).

FRITH'S LIQUORS LTD. (Front St., Hamilton, tel. 441/295–3544; Mangrove Bay, Somerset, tel. 441/234–1740; Sonesta Beach Resort, Southampton, tel. 441/238–8122).

Yo, Ho, Ho and a Bottle of Rum

Just try to visit Bermuda without sampling the rum. Gosling's Black Seal Rum seems to be the local favorite—it's darker and thicker than the regular stuff, with a hint of a caramel flavor—especially when mixed with carbonated ginger beer to make a Dark and Stormy, a famous Bermuda drink that should be treated with respect and caution.

Gosling's is one of Bermuda's oldest companies, and its Hamilton liquor shop was established in 1806. Its most famous product is Gosling's Black Seal Rum, which had been sold in barrels until just after World War I and inherited its name from the black sealing wax that sealed the barrel corks. Black Seal, in its 151 proof variety, will test the strongest drinker, although it can also be purchased in the standard 80 proof.

Bermuda's "rum swizzle," another popular drink, also uses the ubiquitous Black Seal Rum, along with a splash of club soda, lime juice, and sugar. Gosling also produces three liqueurs that are big favorites—Bermuda Gold, Bermuda Banana Liqueur, and Bermuda Coconut Rum. These liqueurs can be ordered everywhere, from poolside bars to late-night jazz clubs. Fear not if rum's not your thing: Guinness and Heineken are widely available imported beers, but be sure to try the local varieties, including Spinnaker and Half-Moon, which are quite good and less expensive.

GOSLING'S (Front St., Hamilton, tel. 441/295–1123; York and Queen Sts., St. George's, tel. 441/298–7339; Main and Cambridge Rds., tel. 441/234–1544).

THE WINE RACK (Emporium Building, 69 Front St., Hamilton, tel. 441/295–1711). This is one of the best places in Bermuda to buy a quality bottle of wine, particularly the top-end California reds and whites, and French Bordeaux, the shop's specialty. There is also a great Italian selection. Free home delivery is offered, but not duty-free service.

Perfume

BERMUDA PERFUMERY (212 North Shore Rd., Bailey's Bay, tel. 441/293–0627 or 800/527–8213). This highly promoted perfumery is on all taxi-tour itineraries. Regularly scheduled guided tours of the facilities include a walk through the ornamental gardens and an exhibit on the distillation of flowers into perfume. At the Calabash gift shop you can purchase the factory's Lili line of fragrances as well as imported soaps and an assortment of fragrances.

PENISTON-BROWN'S PERFUME SHOP (23 W. Front St., Hamilton, tel. 441/295–0570; 6 Water St., St. George's, tel. 441/297–1525; 21 Reid St., Hamilton, tel. 441/295–5535). In addition to being the exclusive agent for Guerlain products, Peniston-Brown's stocks more than 127 lines of French and Italian fragrances, as well as soaps, bath salts, and bubble bath. Makeovers are available at the Front Street shop, where there's an in-store beauty consultant.

PERFUME & GIFT BOUTIQUE (55 Front St., Hamilton, tel. 441/295–1183). Trimingham's fragrance salon carries Chanel No. 5, Laura Ashley No. 1, Elizabeth Taylor's Passion and White Diamonds, and Calvin Klein's Obsession, along with most other leading scents.

Beyond T-Shirts and Key Chains

Baseball caps, refrigerator magnets, T-shirts, and key chains, not your thing? Consider these tips:

BUDGET FOR A MAJOR PURCHASE If souvenirs are all about keeping the memories alive in the long haul, plan ahead to shop for something really special—a work of art, pottery or something else hand-crafted, or a major accessory for your home. One major purchase will stay with you far longer than a dozen tourist trinkets, and you'll have all the wonderful memories associated with shopping for it besides.

ADD TO YOUR COLLECTION Whether antiques, used books, salt and pepper shakers, or ceramic frogs are your thing, start looking in the first day or two. Chances are you'll want to scout around and then go back to some of the first shops you visited before you hand over your credit card.

GET GUARANTEES IN WRITING Is the vendor making promises? Ask him to put them in writing.

ANTICIPATE A SHOPPING SPREE If you think you might buy breakables, include a length of bubble wrap. Pack a large tote bag in your suitcase in case you need extra space. Don't fill your suitcase to bursting before you leave home. Or include some old clothing that you can leave behind to make room for new acquisitions.

KNOW BEFORE YOU GO Study prices at home on items you might consider buying while you're away. Otherwise you won't recognize a bargain when you see one.

PLASTIC, PLEASE Especially if your purchase is pricey and you're looking for authenticity, it's always smart to pay with a credit card. If a problem arises later on and the merchant can't or won't resolve it, the credit-card company may help you out.

When you pack your MCI Calling Card, it's like packing your loved ones along too.

Your MCI Calling Card is the easy way to stay in touch when you travel. Use it to call to and from over 125 countries. Plus, every time you call, you can earn frequent flier miles. So wherever your travels take you, call home with your MCI Calling Card. It's even easy to get one. Just visit **www.mci.com/worldphone**.

EASY TO CALL WORLDWIDE

1. Just enter the WorldPhone® access number of the country you're calling from.

2. Enter or give the operator your MCI Calling Card number.

3. Enter or give the number you're calling.

Argentina	0-800-222-6249
Bermuda ⁕	1-800-888-8000
Brazil	000-8012
United States	1-800-888-8000

⁕ Limited availability.

EARN FREQUENT FLIER MILES

AmericanAirlines®
AAdvantage®

MIDWEST EXPRESS
AIRLINES

PROGRAM PARTNER

///UNITED
Mileage Plus®

US AIRWAYS
DIVIDEND MILES

SEE THE WORLD IN FULL COLOR

Fodor's Exploring Guides bring all the great sights vividly to life with hundreds of photographs, fascinating historical background, and colorful anecdotes. Detailed maps and practical information keep you headed in the right direction.

Pair a Fodor's Exploring Guide with your trusted Fodor's Pocket Guide for a complete planning package.

Fodor's EXPLORING GUIDES

At bookstores everywhere.

Toys

THE ANNEX TOYS (3 Reid St., Hamilton, tel. 441/295–3838). This large toy department in the basement of the Phoenix Centre has one of the best and most up-to-date selections of toys, including Barbie dolls. A "Generation Girl" Barbie, for example, will cost you around $50.

JACK 'N' JILL'S TOY SHOP (7 Park Rd., Hamilton, tel. 441/292–3769). At one of Bermuda's top toy retailers you'll find a good selection of traditional toys as well as more modern merchandise.

TOYS 'N' STUFF (Queen and Church Sts., Hamilton, tel. 441/292–6698). Popular with locals, this huge, centrally located store sells everything from children's furniture and prams (strollers) to the latest toys and games for all ages.

Fore! Distracted by the spectacular view, the errant golfer shouts a word of warning as a hook shot heads for the opposite fairway. Expecting to see people racing for cover, the player, used to the overcrowded courses of home, sighs with relief when the only noises to reach his ears are the lapping of waves and the occasional chorus of birdsong. Collecting his ball, he finishes his round, knowing there will always be another hole and another course where he might just hit a shot as perfect as the surroundings.

In This Chapter

Golf Courses and Clubs 95

By Matt Westcott

golf

BERMUDA IS JUSTIFIABLY RENOWNED for its golf courses. The scenery is spectacular, and the courses are challenging. However, you should not expect the soft, manicured fairways and greens typical of U.S. courses. Just as courses in Scotland have their own character, those in Bermuda are distinguished by plenty of sand, firm fairways and greens, relatively short par fours, and wind—*especially* wind.

Because the island's freshwater supply is limited, irrigation is minimal and the ground around the green tends to be quite hard. Bermudian greens are normally elevated and protected by sand traps rather than thick grass. Most traps are filled with the soft limestone sand and pulverized pieces of pink shell. Such fine sand may be unfamiliar, but it tends to be consistent from trap to trap and from course to course.

Greens are usually seeded with Bermuda grass and then overseeded with rye, which means that you putt on Bermuda grass in warmer months (March through November) and on rye when the weather cools and the Bermuda grass dies out. Greens are reseeded anytime from late September to early November, according to the weather. (The greens at the Castle Harbour Golf Club are reseeded in early January.) Some courses use temporary greens for two to four weeks. Others keep the greens in play while reseeding and resurfacing. Greens in Bermuda tend to be much slower than the bent-grass greens prevalent in the United States, and putts tend to break less.

Golf Tournaments

With eight courses, Bermuda's golf competitions are many and varied and offer something for all categories of player. Overseas entrants are actively encouraged, but you will face stiff competition from the savvy islanders who are used to playing these challenging courses. The last day for entry to most competitions is about a month prior to the event.

Golf season is almost year-round. The Bermuda Golf Association Calendar begins in early March with the Men's Amateur Match Play Championship at the Mid Ocean Club. With a handicap limit of 12, the tournament offers singles match play at scratch in flights. At the same time and venue is the Bermuda Ladies Amateur Match Play Championship. The Bermuda Senior Amateur Championships are staged in early May for men and women at Riddell's Bay. A month later, the Bermuda Men's Amateur Stroke Play Championship is held over 72 holes for men and 54 for women at Port Royal. The Mixed Foursomes Championship is held in mid-September also at Port Royal, while the highlight of the year, the Bermuda Open (for men), takes place in mid-October at the same course. The end of the year sees the Four Ball Stroke Play Amateur Championship for men and women in early November at Port Royal. And December brings the main overseas competition, the Goodwill Tournament.

For more information and entries contact the Secretary, **Bermuda Golf Association** (Box HM 433, Hamilton HM BX, Bermuda, tel. 441/238–0983). Or e-mail for information only.

Another characteristic of Bermudian courses is the preponderance of rolling, hummocky fairways, making a flat lie the exception rather than the rule. Little effort has been made to flatten the fairways, because much of the ground beneath the island's surface is honeycombed with caves. Bulldozer and backhoe operators are understandably uneasy about doing extensive landscaping.

HOW AND WHEN

The ratings of Bermuda's eight golf courses, devised and administered by the United States Golf Association (USGA), "represent the expected score of an expert amateur golfer based upon yardage and other obstacles." For example, a par-72 course with a rating of 68 means that a scratch golfer would hit a four-under-par round, and ordinary hackers would probably score a little better, too. Ratings are given for the blue tees (championship), white tees (men's), and red tees (women's). Tee times are available by calling any of the courses directly.

Lessons, available at all courses, usually cost $40–$60 for a half hour, and club rentals range from $15 to $40. Caddies are a thing of the past, except at the Mid Ocean Club.

GOLF COURSES AND CLUBS

Belmont Golf & Country Club

Length: 5,777 yards from the blue tees. Par: 70. **Rating:** blue tees, 68.9; white tees, 67.9; red tees, 69.1.

Among Bermuda's eight courses, the layout of this public course is perhaps the most maddening. The first two holes, straight par fours, are a false preview of what lies ahead—a series of doglegs and blind tee shots. You may be able to trim six or more shots from a round by playing with an experienced Belmont player who knows where to hit drives on such blind holes as the 6th, 11th, and 16th and how best to play a dogleg hole such as the

8th. Despite the layout, Belmont remains one of Bermuda's easier courses, and it's ideal for inexperienced players. The course is inland, with few ocean panoramas; instead, most holes overlook pastel houses with white roofs, a few of which have taken a beating from errant golf balls. Fairway grass tends to be denser and the rough is generally deeper than other courses. For these reasons, and because Belmont is a short course (only one par four is more than 400 yards), consider using a three or five wood, or even a low iron, from the tee. Belmont's chief drawback, especially on the weekend, is slow play. Weekend rounds of four hours or more are common, although it's possible to get around in three.

Highlight hole: The par-five 11th has a severe dogleg left, with a blind tee shot—Belmont in a nutshell. A short but straight drive is the key. Trying to cut the corner can be disastrous. The approach to the green is straight, although a row of wispy trees on the left awaits hooked or pulled shots. *Belmont Rd., Warwick, tel. 441/236–6400, fax 441/236–6867. Greens fees $86 per person with cart. Shoe rentals $8. Club rentals $28.*

Castle Harbour Golf Club

Length: 6,440 yards from the blue tees. Par: 71. **Rating:** blue tees, 71.3; white tees, 69.2; red tees, 69.2.

The only flat areas on this course seem to be the tees. The first tee, a crow's-nest perch, speaks for all: looking out over the fairway, with the harbor beyond, is like peering onto a golf course from a 20th-story window. Wind can make this course play especially long. Although most par fours have good landing areas despite all the hills, holes such as the 2nd, 16th, and 17th require you to drive over fairway rises. A wind-shortened drive can mean a long, blind shot to the green. Carrying the rise, however, can mean a relatively easy short shot, especially on the 2nd and 17th holes. Elevated greens are a common feature of Castle Harbour. The most extreme example is the 190-yard, par-three 13th, with the green perched atop a steep, 100-ft embankment. Balls short of the green inevitably roll back down into a grassy basin between the tee and the green. Mercifully, sand traps at Castle Harbour are few and far between by Bermudian standards. Ten holes have two or fewer bunkers around the green.

Castle Harbour is one of Bermuda's most expensive courses, but the money is clearly reinvested in the course. Greens are well maintained and generally faster than most here. The course also rewards you with several spectacular views, such as the hilltop panorama from the 14th tee, where blue water stretches into the distance on three sides.

Highlight hole: The 235-yard, par-three 18th is the most difficult finishing hole on Bermuda, especially when the wind is blowing from the northwest. Say a prayer: On the right are jagged coral cliffs rising from the harbor, on the left are a pair of traps, and a flower-lined pond graces the front right of the green. *Paynters Rd., Tucker's Town, tel. 441/293–2040 ext. 6869, fax 441/293–1051. Greens fees $149 per person with cart Mar.–Nov., $99 per person with cart Dec.–Feb. Shoe rentals $8. Club rentals $30.*

Fairmont Princess Golf Club

Length: 2,684 yards from the blue tees. Par: 54. **Rating:** none.

The Princess Golf Club unfolds on the hillside beneath the Fairmont Southampton Princess. The hotel has managed to sculpt a neat little par-three course from the steep terrain, and players who opt to walk around find their mountaineering skills and stamina severely tested. The vertical drop on the first two holes alone is at least 200 ft, and the rise on the fourth hole makes 178 yards play like 220. Kept in excellent shape by an extensive irrigation system, the course is a good warm-up for Bermuda's full-length courses, offering a legitimate test of wind and bunker play with a minimum of obstructions and hazards. Ocean views are a constant feature of the front nine, although the looming presence of the hotel does detract from the scenery.

Highlight hole: The green of the 174-yard 16th hole sits in a cup ringed by pink oleander bushes. The Gibbs Hill Lighthouse, less than a mile away, dominates the backdrop. *Southampton Princess Resort, South Rd., Southampton, tel. 441/238–0446, fax 441/238–8479. Greens fees $66 per person with mandatory cart. Shoe rentals $8. Club rentals $25.*

Mid Ocean Club

Length: 6,512 yards from the blue tees. Par: 71. **Rating:** blue tees, 72; white tees, 70.1; red tees, 72.7

It isn't Bermuda's oldest course—that honor belongs to Riddell's Bay—and other Bermudian courses are equally difficult, but the elite Mid Ocean Club is generally regarded as one of the world's top 50 courses. Quite simply, it has charisma, embodying everything that is golf in Bermuda—tees on coral cliffs above the ocean, rolling fairways lined with palm trees, doglegs around water, and windswept views. It's rich in history, too. At the dogleg 5th hole, for example, Babe Ruth is said to have splashed a dozen balls in Mangrove Lake in a futile effort to drive the green. The course rewards long, straight tee shots and deft play around the green while penalizing—often cruelly—anything less. The 5th and 9th holes, for example, require that tee shots (from the blue tees) carry 180 yards or more over water. And whereas length is not a factor on two fairly short par fives, the 471-yard 2nd and the 487-yard 11th, accuracy is. Tight doglegs ensure that any wayward tee shot ends up in trees, shrubbery, or the rough. However, the course may have mellowed with age. Having lost hundreds of trees to a tornado in 1986, and again to Hurricane Emily in 1987, the tight, tree-lined fairways have since become more open, and the rough, less threatening.

Highlight hole: The 433-yard 5th is a par-four dogleg around Mangrove Lake. The elevated tee overlooks a hillside of flowering shrubbery and the lake, making the fairway seem impossibly far away. Big hitters can take a shortcut over the lake (although the green is unreachable, as the Babe's heroic but unsuccessful efforts attest), but anyone who hits the fairway has scored a major victory. To the left of the green, a steep embankment leads into a bunker that is among the hardest in Bermuda from which to recover. *Mid Ocean Dr., off South Shore Rd., Tucker's Town, tel. 441/ 293–0330, fax 441/293–8837, themidoceanbbermuda.com. Greens fees $190 ($70 when accompanied by a member). Nonmembers must be introduced by a club member; nonmember starting times available Mon., Wed., and Fri., until noon, except holidays. Caddies $35 per bag (tip not included) for Grade A. Cart rental $45.*

Ocean View Golf & Country Club

Length: 2,940 yards (nine holes) from the blue tees. Par: 35. **Rating:** none.

Founded in the 1940s, the Ocean View Golf & Country Club has magnificent views of the island's north shore. The good restaurant and bar and excellent driving range enhance the club's popularity. Call ahead for tee times: this nine-hole course is busy all week long. Several holes challenge and intrigue. The first is a tough par five that is a tight driving hole, with a 40-ft coral wall on one side and views of the north shore on the other. The 6th is a difficult par four because of its elevated green. The 9th is a par three with water guarding the front of the green, so shooting with accuracy is the key.

Highlight hole: The green on the 187-yard, par-three 9th hole is cut out of a coral hillside that's beautifully landscaped with attractive plants. This is a demanding tee shot, and club selection can be tricky, particularly when strong winds are blowing from the north or west. *2 Barker's Hill, off North Shore Rd., Devonshire, tel. 441/295–9092, fax 441/295–9097. Greens fees $48 weekdays, $50 weekends. Three-course five-day package $200. Cart rental $22 per person for 18 holes, $11 for 9 holes; hand cart $8. Club rentals $25.*

Secrets from a Golf Pro

Most golf courses elsewhere are designed with the wind in mind—long downwind holes and short upwind holes. Not so on Bermuda, where the wind is anything but consistent or predictable. Quirky air currents make play on a Bermudian course different every day. Some days a 350-yard par four may be drivable. On other days a solidly hit drive may fall short on a 160-yard par three. Regardless, the wind puts a premium on being able to hit the ball straight and grossly exaggerates any slice or hook.

The hard ground of Bermudian courses means you must adjust your strategy used on lush, well-watered greens. For success in the short game, therefore, you need to run the ball to the hole, rather than relying on high, arcing chips, which require plenty of club face under the ball. It's also helpful to know that Bermudian greens are normally elevated and protected by sand traps rather than thick grass.

So, how should golfers prepare for a Bermuda trip? Answer: anticipate the wind and practice hitting lower shots. Punching the ball or playing it farther back in the stance may be helpful. Working on chip-and-run shots, especially from close-cropped lies, should also help. You can also save yourself some strokes by practicing iron shots from awkward hillside lies. On the greens, a long, firm putting stroke may keep you from the bugaboo that haunts many first-time visitors—gently stroked putts dying short of the hole. As Allan Wilkinson, the former professional at the Princess Golf Club, has said, "In Bermuda, ya gotta slam 'em into the back of the cup."

Port Royal Golf Course

Length: 6,565 yards from the blue tees. Par: men, 71; women, 72. **Rating:** blue tees, 72; white tees, 69.7; red tees, 72.5.

Such golfing luminaries as Jack Nicklaus rank the Port Royal Golf Course among the world's best public courses. A favorite with Bermudians, too, the course is well laid out, and the greens fees are modest. By Bermudian standards, Port Royal is also relatively flat. Although there are some hills (on the back nine in particular), the course has few of the blind shots and hillside lies that prevail elsewhere, and those holes that do have gradients tend to run either directly uphill or downhill. In other respects, however, Port Royal is classically Bermudian, with close-cropped fairways, numerous elevated tees and greens, and holes raked by the wind, especially the 8th and the 16th. The 16th hole, one of Bermuda's most famous, is often pictured in magazines. The green sits on a treeless promontory overlooking the blue waters and pink-white sands of Whale Bay, a popular boating and fishing area. When the wind is blowing hard onshore, as it frequently does, you may need a driver to reach the green, which is 176 yards away. One complaint often raised about Port Royal is the condition of the course, which sometimes gets chewed up by heavy usage—more than 55,000 rounds a year.

Highlight hole: Like the much-photographed 16th hole, the 387-yard, par-four 15th skirts the cliffs along Whale Bay. In addition to ocean views, remains of Whale Bay Battery, a 19th-century fortification, lie between the fairway and the bay. Only golf balls hooked wildly from the tee have any chance of a direct hit on the fort. The wind can be brutal on this hole. *Off Middle Rd., Southampton, tel. 441/234–0974; 441/295–6500 automated system to reserve golf time 4 days in advance; fax 441/234–3562. Greens fees $85 weekdays, $95 weekends, discount rates after 4. Cart rental $24 per person, hand cart $9. Club rentals $27. Shoe rentals $12.*

Riddell's Bay Golf and Country Club

Length: 5,588 yards from the blue tees. Par: men, 69; women, 71. **Rating:** blue tees, 66.9; white tees, 66.1; red tees, 70.6.

Built in 1922, the Riddell's course is Bermuda's oldest. In design, however, it more nearly approximates a Florida course—relatively flat, with wide, palm-lined fairways. You don't need to be a power hitter to score well here, although the first four holes, including a 427-yard uphill par four and a 244-yard par three, might suggest otherwise. The par fours are mostly in the 360-yard range, and the fairways are generously flat and open. Despite the course's position, on a narrow peninsula between Riddell's Bay and the Great Sound, water comes into play only on holes 8 through 11. With the twin threats of wind and water, these are the most typically Bermudian holes on the course, and accuracy off the tee is important. This is especially true of the par-four 8th, a 360-yard right dogleg around the water. With a tailwind, big hitters might try for the green, but playing around the dogleg on this relatively short hole is the more prudent choice. A few tees are fronted with stone walls—an old-fashioned touch that harks back to the old courses of Great Britain. Like Mid Ocean's, Riddell's is private and opens to the public only at certain times, but the clubby atmosphere is much less pronounced here.

Highlight hole: The tees on the 340-yard, par-four 10th are set on a grass-top quay on the harbor's edge. The fairway narrows severely after about 200 yards, and a drive hit down the right side leaves you no chance to reach the green in two. Two ponds guard the left side of a sloped and elevated green. The hole is rated only the sixth most difficult on the course, but the need for pinpoint accuracy probably makes it the hardest to par. Riddell's Bay Rd., Warwick, tel. 441/238–1060, fax 441/238–8785. Greens fees $70 weekdays, $90 weekends ($40 weekdays, $50 weekends when accompanied by a member). Cart rental $40 (for 2 people), hand cart $5. Club rentals $25.

St. George's Golf Club

Length: 4,043 yards from the blue tees. Par: 63. **Rating:** blue tees, 62.8; white tees, 61.4; red tees, 62.8.

Built in 1985, St. George's Golf Club dominates a secluded headland at the island's northeastern end. The 4,043-yard course is short, but it makes up for its lack of length with sharp teeth. No course in Bermuda is more exposed to wind, and no course has smaller greens. Some are no more than 25 ft across. To make matters trickier, the greens are hard and slick from the wind and salty air. Many of the holes have commanding views of the ocean, particularly the 8th, 9th, 14th, and 15th. Wind—especially from the north—can turn these short holes into club-selection nightmares. Don't let high scores here ruin your enjoyment of some of the finest views on the island. The course's shortness and its relative emptiness midweek make it a good choice for couples or groups of varying ability.

Highlight hole: Pause to admire the view from the par-four 14th hole before you tee off. From the elevated tee area, the 326-yard hole curls around Coot Pond, an ocean-fed cove, to the green on a small, treeless peninsula. Beyond the neighboring 15th hole is old Fort St. Catherine, and beyond it the sea. With a tailwind, it's tempting to hit for the green from the tee, but Coot Pond leaves no room for error. 1 Park Rd., St. George's, tel. 441/297–8067; 441/295–5600 tee times and information; 441/297–8148 pro's office; 441/297–8353 pro shop; fax 441/297–2273. Greens fees $45; $23 after 3 PM Apr.–Oct.; $18 after 2 PM Nov.–Mar. Cart rental $36, hand cart $8.

With his briefcase 600 mi away in Washington, DC, the workaholic lets the soft coral pink sand rise through his toes as he lounges in his beach chair. Without his cell phone, only the clear turquoise waters nudge him from this uncustomary reverie. The only noise is that of children playing, couples splashing around, and the gentle breeze whistling through the trees and shrubs that snake their way along the bays. Cares, worries, and hassles of everyday life seem to disappear into the vastness of the ocean. On this beach he escapes to another world where rest and relaxation are the watchwords.

In This Chapter

Beaches 106 • Participant sports 112 • Spectator Sports 131

Revised by Karen Smith and Matt Wescott

beaches, outdoor activities, and sports

LONG BEFORE YOUR PLANE TOUCHES DOWN in Bermuda, the island's greatest asset becomes breathtakingly obvious—the crystal-clear, aquamarine water that frames the tiny, hook-shape atoll. For this reason exploratory scuba diving and snorkeling, especially among the age-old wrecks off the island, are gorgeous pursuits. The presence of these sunken ships is actually one of Bermuda's ironies—as translucent as the water is, it wasn't quite clear enough to make Bermuda's treacherous reefs visible to the hundreds of ship captains who have smashed their vessels on them through the centuries.

Bermudians take their on-shore sports seriously, too. The daily newspaper's sports section is full of local coverage. Cricket and soccer grab most of the headlines, but road running, golf (☞ Golf), rugby, and a host of other island activities also get their share of space. Tennis is a big deal here, with 70 courts packed into these 22 square mi—it's hard to believe there's room left for other things to do.

HOW AND WHEN

Thanks to Bermuda's position near the Gulf Stream, the water stays warm year-round. In summer the ocean is usually above 80°F, and it's even warmer in the shallows between the reefs and shore. In high season, which runs from April through October, fishing, diving, and yacht charters fill up quickly. Most boats carry fewer than 20 passengers, so it's advisable to sign up as soon as you arrive. There's less call for water sports December through March. Although the water's warm enough, winter does tend to be windier, so conditions can be less than ideal.

BEACHES

Bermuda's south-shore beaches are more scenic than those on the north side—fine, pinkish sand; coral bluffs topped with summer flowers; gentle, pale-blue surf slipping past the barrier reefs offshore. The water at south-shore beaches does get a little rougher when the winds are from the south and southwest, but waves continuously roll in and break on this sandy shoreline even when breezes are gentle. You can join locals in the popular pastime of body surfing, or pick up a body board for as little as $20 from many shops in town. Most Bermudian beaches are relatively small compared with ocean beaches in the United States, ranging from about 15 yards to half a mile or so in length.

The Public Transportation Board publishes "Bermuda's Guide to Beaches and Transportation," available free in all visitor centers and most hotels. A combination map and bus and ferry schedule, the guide shows locations of beaches and how to reach them.

Few Bermudian beaches offer shade, but some have palm trees and thatched shelters. The sun can be intense, so bring a hat and plenty of sunscreen. You can rent umbrellas at some beaches, but food and drink are rare, so pack snacks and lots of water.

NORTH-SHORE BEACHES

SHELLY BAY BEACH. As at Somerset Long Bay, the water at this beach near Flatts is well protected from strong southerly winds. In addition, a sandy bottom and shallow water make this a good place to take small children. Shelly Bay also has shade trees, a rarity at Bermudian beaches. A playground behind the beach

Shocking Pink!

The sands of the world's beaches come in many hues, from basaltic black to gleaming quartz white, with a rainbow of red, green, yellow, and brown thrown in—and yes, even pink. Pink sand is considered choice by many beach connoisseurs, and Bermuda's south shore has plenty of it. You'll find the rosy tint of the island's sand most intense in the bright sun of midday, but in the gentler light of early morning and late afternoon the hue can appear darker, tending toward mauve.

In only a few regions where tropical coral reefs flourish offshore do pink-sand beaches form. What makes the sand pink is an amalgam of calcium-rich shells and fragments of invertebrate sea creatures, from minute, single-cell protozoa to spiny sea urchins. Chiefly responsible are foraminifera ("foram" for short), a type of protozoan that lives in great profusion in reef environments. The microscopic red *Homotrema rubrum* (red foram) variety is numerous both on the reefs and in the ocean sediments that surround Bermuda, and their persistent red pigment remains even in the microscopic "skeletons" these animals leave behind when they die. The red gets mixed in with other (predominantly white) reef debris—broken clam and snail shells, fragments of coral—and, when washed ashore, forms the island's signature pink sand.

The most visited pink sand beaches are Warwick Long Bay Beach and Horseshoe Bay Beach in Southampton. But just about any beach you visit on the South Shore will have the famous sand in abundance.

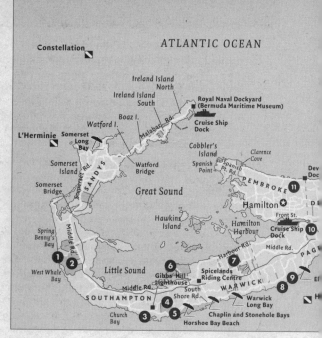

ATLANTIC OCEAN

Constellation

Ireland Island North

Ireland Island South

Royal Naval Dockyard (Bermuda Maritime Museum)

Boaz I.

Cruise Ship Dock

Watford I.

Malabar Rd.

L'Herminie

Somerset Long Bay

Cobbler's Island

Clarence Cove

Spanish Point

Spanish Pt. Rd.

PEMBROKE

Dev Doc

Somerset Island

SANDYS

Watford Bridge

Great Sound

Somerset Bridge

Hamilton

Front St.

Hawkins Island

Hamilton Harbour

Cruise Ship Dock

Middle Rd.

Spring Benny's Bay

Little Sound

Harbour Rd.

PAG

West Whale Bay

Gibbs Hill Lighthouse

Spicelands Riding Centre

WARWICK

Middle Rd.

South Shore Rd.

Warwick Long Bay

SOUTHAMPTON

Church Bay

Chaplin and Stonehole Bays

Horseshoe Bay Beach

Golf Courses	Ocean View Golf & Country Club, 12	Riddell's Bay Golf and Country Club, 6	Tennis and Squash Courts
Belmont Golf & Country Club, 7	Port Royal Golf Course, 2	St. George's Golf Club, 17	Bermuda Squash Club, 13
Castle Harbour Golf Club, 15	Princess Golf Club, 4		Coral Beach & Tennis Club, 8
Mid Ocean Club, 14			Elbow Beach Hotel, 9

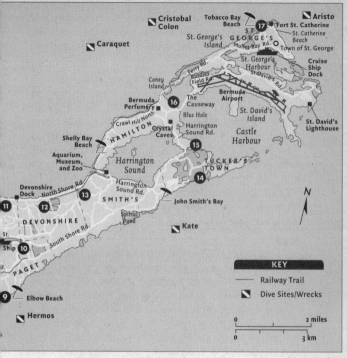

Fairmont
Southampton
Princess Hotel, **5**

Government
Tennis
Stadium, **11**

Grotto Bay
Beach Hotel &
Tennis Club, **16**

Pomander Gate
Tennis Club, **10**

Port Royal
Course, **1**

Sonesta Beach
Hotel & Spa, **3**

attracts hordes of youngsters on weekends and during school holidays. A drawback can be the traffic noise from nearby North Shore Road. *North Shore Rd., Hamilton Parish. Bus 10 or 11 from Hamilton.*

SOMERSET LONG BAY. Popular with Somerset locals, this beach is on the quiet northwestern end of the island, far from the bustle of Hamilton and major tourist hubs. In keeping with the area's rural atmosphere, the beach is low-key. Undeveloped parkland shields the beach from the light traffic on Cambridge Road. The main beach is long by Bermudian standards—nearly ¼ mi from end to end. Although exposed to northerly storm winds, the bay water is normally calm and shallow—ideal for children. The bottom, however, is rocky and uneven. *Cambridge Rd., Sandys. Bus 7 or 8 from Hamilton.*

TOBACCO BAY BEACH. The most popular beach near St. George's—about 15 minutes northwest on foot—this small north-shore strand is huddled in a coral cove. Its beach house has a snack bar, equipment rentals, toilets, showers, and changing rooms. From the bus stop in the town of St. George's, it's a 10-minute hike, or you can flag down one of St. George's Minibus Service's vans and ask to for a lift here ($2 per person). In high season it becomes very busy, especially midweek when the cruise ships are docked. *Coot Pond Rd., St. George's, tel. 441/ 297–8199. Bus 1, 3, 10, or 11 from Hamilton.*

SOUTH-SHORE BEACHES

CHAPLIN AND STONEHOLE BAYS. In a secluded area east of Horseshoe Bay Beach, these tiny adjacent beaches almost disappear at high tide. An unusual high coral wall reaches across the beach to the water, perforated by a 10-ft-high, arrowhead-shape hole. Like Horseshoe Bay, the beach fronts South Shore Park. *Off South Rd., Southampton. Bus 7 from Hamilton.*

ELBOW BEACH. Swimming and body surfing are great at this beach, which lies adjacent to the prime strand of sand reserved for guests of the Elbow Beach Hotel. As pleasant as the setting is, however, it can get very noisy and crowded on summer weekends. A nearby lunch wagon sells fast food and cold soft drinks. *Off South Rd., Paget. Bus 2 or 7 from Hamilton.*

HORSESHOE BAY BEACH. Horseshoe Bay has everything you would expect of a Bermudian beach: clear water, a ½-mi crescent of pink sand, a vibrant social scene, and the uncluttered backdrop of South Shore Park—hence it's one of the island's most popular beaches. Lifeguards in summer, a variety of rental facilities, a snack bar, and toilets add to the beach's appeal. In fact, it can become uncomfortably crowded here on summer weekends. Parents should keep a close eye on children in the water, as the undertow can be strong. *Off South Rd., Southampton, tel. 441/238–2651. Bus 7 from Hamilton.*

JOHN SMITH'S BAY. Backed by the odd residence and South Road, this beach consists of a pretty strand of long, flat open sand. The presence of a lifeguard in summer makes it an ideal place to bring children. The only public beach in Smith's Parish, John Smith's Bay is also popular with locals. Groups of young folks like to gather in the park area surrounding the beach for parties, especially on weekends and holidays, so if you're not in the mood for a festive bunch with loud radios, this may not be the place for you. *South Rd., Smith's. Bus 1 from Hamilton.*

WARWICK LONG BAY. Unlike the covelike bay beaches, Warwick Long Bay has about a ½-mi stretch of sand—the longest of any beach here. Its backdrop is a combination of very steep cliffs and low grass- and brush-covered hills. The beach is exposed to some strong southerly winds, but the waves are usually moderate because the inner reef is close to shore. A 20-ft coral outcrop less than 200 ft offshore looks like a sculpted boulder balancing on the water's surface. South Shore Park, which surrounds the bay, is often empty, a fact that only heightens the beach's appealing isolation and serenity. *Off South Rd., Southampton. Bus 7 from Hamilton.*

PARTICIPANT SPORTS

BICYCLING

Bermuda is not the easiest place in the world to bicycle. Steep, narrow, and winding roads, incorrigible traffic, and wind can sap even the strongest rider's strength, especially along South Road in Warwick and Southampton parishes. Island roads are no place for novice riders. Helmets are strongly recommended, and parents should think twice before allowing preteen children to bike. The Railway Trail, on the other hand, requires almost no road riding. Restricted to pedestrian and bicycle traffic, the trail is mostly paved, and it runs intermittently for almost the length of the island along the route of the old Bermuda Railway. The free pamphlet "The Bermuda Railway Trail Guide," published by the Bermuda Department of Tourism, outlines a series of short exploring tours along the trail. Because it's somewhat isolated, it's not advisable to ride or walk the trail after dark.

In Bermuda, bicycles are called pedal or push bikes to distinguish them from the more common, motorized two-wheelers. Some of the cycle liveries around the island also rent pedal bikes. If you can, reserve bikes a few days in advance. Rental rates are around $25 a day (the longer you rent, the more economical your daily rate becomes). You may be charged an additional $15 for a repair waiver and for a refundable deposit.

➤ **BIKE-RENTAL CONTACTS: Eve's Cycle Livery** (Middle Rd., near South Shore Rd., Paget, tel. 441/236–6247). **Oleander Cycles** (Middle Rd., west of firestation, Southampton, tel. 441/234–0629; Middle Rd., at Valley Rd., Paget, tel. 441/236–2453). **Wheels Cycles** (Front St., near the docks, Hamilton, tel. 441/292–2245).

BIRD-WATCHING

Bermuda has a variety of birds living along its shores, or, because it's on a migration path, visiting them. Forty species of warblers have been spotted here, plus the omnipresent kiskadee, swifts, cuckoos, flycatchers, swallows, thrushes, kingbirds, orioles, and others. The largest variety of birds can be spotted during fall migration, when thousands of birds travel south. Shorebirds like semipalmated and the least sandpiper can be seen this time of year, often around Bermuda's ponds: Spittal, Warwick, and Seymour's. During winter herons and egrets visit the ponds. Summer sees the smallest variety, although some of the late migrators, such as the barn swallow, may still pass through the area and the cliff-dwelling longtails (white-tailed tropic bird) are easily spotted, circling out to the water and back.

Bird conservation is a big deal on Bermuda. Now on every island golf course you'll see bluebird boxes, which act as safe nesting sites for this jeopardized species, threatened by development and the invasive sparrow, which colonize the bluebird nests. Birders may be interested in David Wingate's efforts to repopulate the native cahow bird (Bermuda petrel) population via artificial burrows and other means on Non Such Island. Tours with Wingate ($75) can be arranged via the Bermuda Biological Institute and last three to four hours. A variety of birding events are also hosted by the Bermuda Audubon Society throughout the year. Its Web site has a wealth of information plus a bird-watching checklist.

➤ **BIRD-WATCHING CONTACTS: Bermuda Audubon Society** (Box HM 1328, Hamilton HM FX, tel. 441/292–1920, www.audubon.bm). **Bermuda Biological Institute** (17 Biological La., Ferry Reach, St. George's Parish, tel. 441/297–1880).

BOATING AND SAILING

You can either rent your own boat or charter one with a skipper. Rental boats, which are 18 ft at most, range from sailboats (typically tiny Sunfish) to motorboats (13-ft Boston Whalers), in addition to kayaks and pedal boats. Some of these vessels are ideal for exploring the coves and harbors of the sounds, or, in the case of motorboats, dropping anchor and snorkeling around the shorelines, which teem with various coral and colorful fish.

In Great Sound, several small islands, such as Hawkins Island and Darrell's Island, have tiny secluded beaches and coves that are usually empty during the week. If the wind is blowing in the right direction, the islands are about half an hour's sail from Hamilton Harbour or Salt Kettle. The beaches are wonderful places to picnic, although some are privately owned and don't always welcome visitors. Check with the boat-rental operator before planning an island trip.

The trade winds pass well to the south of Bermuda, so the island does not have predictable air currents. To the casual sailor, wind changes can be troublesome. Mangrove Bay, often protected, is the ideal place for novice sailors and pedal boaters. The average summer breeze is 7–10 knots, often out of the south or southwest.

Boat Rentals

Sailboats and powerboats are available for rent at Blue Hole Water Sports, in the Grotto Bay Beach Hotel & Tennis Club. If you want a taste of open water in summer, head for Pompano Beach Club Watersports Centre, on the western ocean shore. A range of boats is available at Somerset Bridge Watersports. For Great Sound and Somerset shoreline boating, go to Windjammer Water Sports at the Dockyard.

Rates for small powerboats start at about $65 for two hours and go up to $185 for a full day. Sailboat rentals begin at $60 for four hours and go up to $170 for a full day. A credit card number is usually required.

➤ BOAT-RENTAL CONTACTS: **Blue Hole Water Sports** (Grotto Bay Beach Hotel & Tennis Club, 11 Blue Hole Hill, Hamilton Parish, tel. 441/293–2915 or 441/293–8333 ext. 37). **Pompano Beach Club** (36 Pompano Rd., Southampton, tel. 441/234–0222).

Salt Kettle Yacht Charters (off Harbour Rd., Salt Kettle Rd., Paget, tel. 441/236–4863, fax 441/236–2427). **Somerset Bridge Watersports** (Somerset Bridge, Sandys, tel. 441/234–0914 or 441/234–3145). **Windjammer Water Sports** (Dockyard Marina, tel. 441/234–3082; Cambridge Beaches, Sandys, tel. 441/234–0250).

Charter Boats

More than 20 large power cruisers and sailing vessels, piloted by local skippers, are available for charter. Ranging from 30 ft to 60 ft long, charter sailboats can carry up to 30 passengers, sometimes overnight. Meals and drinks can be included on request, and a few skippers offer dinner cruises for the romantically inclined. Rates generally range from $300 to $450 for a three-hour cruise, or $650 to $1,500 for a full-day cruise, with additional per-person charges for large groups. Where you go and what you do—exploring, swimming, snorkeling, cruising—is up to you and your skipper. Generally, however, cruises travel to and around the islands of Great Sound. Several charter skippers advertise year-round operations, but the off-season schedule can be haphazard. Skippers devote periods of the off-season to maintenance and repairs or close altogether if bookings lag. Be sure to book well in advance; in the high season do so before you arrive on the island.

➤ **POWERBOAT CHARTER CONTACTS: Bermuda Barefoot Cruises** (tel. 441/236–3498). **Salt Kettle Yacht Charters** (tel. 441/236–4863). **Tam Marina** (tel./fax 441/236–0127).

➤ **SAILBOAT CHARTER CONTACTS: Adventure Enterprises** (tel. 441/297–1459). **"Restless Native" Tours** (tel. 441/297–1459, 441/234–8149, or 441/234–1434). **Salt Kettle Yacht Charters** (tel. 441/236–4863). **Starlight Sailing Cruises** (tel. 441/292–1834). **Wind Sail Charters** (tel. 441/238–0825 or 441/234–8547, fax 441/238–1614).

Boat Tours

Two-hour tours of the Sea Gardens (around $35) in glass-bottom boats leave year-round from the ferry terminal in Hamilton. Departures are 10 AM and 1:30 PM all days except Thursday and Sunday, when there's just one trip. On Thursday the tour leaves at 2 PM and on Sunday at 1:30 PM.

A six-hour island cruise (around $65–$70) runs on Wednesday year-round. The boat leaves Hamilton at 8:15 AM, cruises to Dockyard to gather more passengers at 9, then travels to St. George's and Hawkins Island.

COCKTAIL CRUISES

Not exactly tours per se, these cruises do leave the dock and are usually only available during the summer months.

"Don't Stop the Carnival Cruise" costs around $79 and includes dinner, drinks, and entertainment. The 200-passenger boat leaves Albuoy's Point in Hamilton at 7 PM daily except Thursday and Sunday.

A three-hour "Calypso Cruise" runs Tuesday and Thursday afternoons, with rum swizzles, live entertainment, and a Hawkins Island swim. The cost of the cruise is $52 for adults. It leaves Albuoy's Point in Hamilton at 2 PM.

➤ BOAT-TOUR CONTACTS: Bermuda Island Cruises (tel. 441/292–8652, fax 441/292–5193, www.bicbda.com).

Kayaks

Good kayaking areas in Bermuda range from protected coves to open ocean. Hourly rates begin at about $10 for a single kayak for one hour and $25 for two hours, or about $18 for a double. For a full day, plan to spend about $75 for a single and $80 for a double.

➤ KAYAK-RENTAL CONTACTS: Blue Hole Water Sports (Grotto Bay Beach Hotel & Tennis Club, 11 Blue Hole Hill, Hamilton

Parish, tel. 441/293–2915 or 441/293–8333 ext. 37). **Somerset Bridge Watersports** (Somerset Bridge, Sandys, tel. 441/234–0914). **Windjammer Water Sports** (Dockyard Marina, Sandys, tel. 441/234–0250; Cambridge Beaches, Sandys, tel. 441/234–3082).

BOWLING

WARWICK LANES (Middle Rd., near St. Mary's, tel. 441/236–5290) is open nightly Monday–Saturday 6–11 and Sunday 3–11. Adults pay $4 per game, plus $1.25 for shoes. The place can fill up, so it's best to reserve a lane.

DIVING

Bermuda has all the ingredients for classic scuba diving—reefs, wrecks, underwater caves, a variety of coral and marine life, and clear, warm water. Although you can dive year-round (you will have to bring your own gear in winter, when dive shops are closed), the best months are May through October, when the water is calmest and warmest. No prior certification is necessary. Novices can learn the basics and dive in water up to 25 ft deep on the same day.

Three-hour resort courses ($95–$110) teach the basics in a pool, on the beach, or off a dive boat and culminate in a reef or wreck dive.

The easiest day trips, offered by Nautilus Diving, involve exploring the south-shore reefs that lie inshore. These reefs may be the most dramatic in Bermuda. The ocean-side drop-off exceeds 60 ft in some places, and the coral is so honeycombed with caves, ledges, and holes that opportunities for discovery are pretty much infinite. Despite concerns about dying coral and dwindling fish populations, most of Bermuda's reefs are still in good health. No one eager to swim with multicolored schools of fish or the occasional barracuda will be disappointed. In the interest of preservation, however, the removal of coral is illegal.

Dive shops around Bermuda prominently display a map of the outlying reef system and its wreck sites. Only 38 of the wrecks from the past three centuries are marked. They are the larger wrecks that are still in good condition. The nautical carnage includes some 300 wreck sites in all—an astonishing number—many of which are well preserved. As a general rule, the more recent the wreck or the more deeply submerged it is, the better its condition. Most of the well-preserved wrecks are to the north and east, and dive depths range between 25 ft and 80 ft. Several wrecks off the western end of the island are in relatively shallow water, 30 ft or less, making them accessible to novice divers and even snorkelers.

The major dive operator for wrecks on the western side of the island is Blue Water Divers at Somerset Bridge. From this company's Elbow Beach Hotel location, in Paget, you can ride a diver propulsion vehicle (DPV), which is like an underwater scooter, past a wreck and through caves and canyons. A one-tank dive costs $40–$55; for introductory divers the price range is $95–$110. Two-tank dives for experienced divers cost $75–$80. With two tanks you can explore two or more wrecks in one four-hour outing. For all necessary equipment—mask, fins, snorkel, scuba apparatus, and wet suit (if needed)—plan to spend about $40 more. Some operators also offer night dives.

➤ **DIVING CONTACTS: Blue Water Divers Ltd.** (Elbow Beach Hotel, Paget, tel. 441/232–2909, fax 441/234–3561; Robinson's Marina, Somerset Bridge, Sandys, tel. 441/234–1034, fax 441/234–3561). **Fantasea** (Sonesta Beach Hotel, Southampton, tel. 441/238–1833, fax 441/236–0394). **Fantasea Diving** (Darrell's Wharf, Harbour Rd., Paget, tel. 441/236–6339). **Nautilus Diving** (Princess Hotel, Hamilton, tel. 441/295–9485, fax 441/296–4006; Southampton Princess Hotel, off South Rd., Southampton, tel. 441/238–2332, fax 441/234–5180). **Scuba Look** (Grotto Bay Beach Hotel, 11 Blue Hole Hill, Hamilton Parish, tel. 441/293–7319, fax 441/295–2421).

Helmet Diving

A different, less technical type of diving popular in Bermuda is "helmet diving," offered between April and mid-November. Although helmet-diving cruises last three hours or more, the actual time underwater is about 25 minutes, during which time underwater explorers walk along the sandy bottom in about 10–12 ft of water (depending on the tide), wearing helmets that receive air through hoses leading to the surface. Underwater portraits are available for an extra charge. A morning or afternoon tour costs about $50 for adults and includes wet suits when the water temperature is less than 80°F. Note that not all outfitters permit children to helmet dive.

➤ **HELMET DIVING CONTACTS: Adventure Enterprises** (Ordnance Island, St. George's, tel. 441/297–1459). **Bermuda Bell Diving** (Flatts Village, Smith's, tel. 441/292–4434, fax 441/295–7235). **Greg Hartley's Under Sea Adventure** (Watford Bridge, Sandys, tel. 441/234–2861, fax 441/234–3000).

FISHING

Fishing in Bermuda falls into three basic categories: shore or shallow-water fishing, reef fishing, and deep-sea fishing. No license is required, although some restrictions apply, particularly regarding the fish you can keep (for instance, only Bermudians with commercial fishing licenses are allowed to take lobsters). There's also a prohibition against spearguns.

Reef Fishing

Three major reef bands lie at various distances from the island. The first is anywhere from ½ mi to 5 mi offshore. The second, the Challenger Bank, is about 12 mi offshore. The third, the Argus Bank, is about 30 mi offshore. As a rule, the farther out you go, the larger the fish—and the more expensive the charter.

...arter fishing captains go to the reefs and deep water to ...hwest and northwest of the island, where the fishing is ...ches over the reefs include snapper, amberjack, ...er, and barracuda. Of the most sought-after deepwater fish—marlin, tuna, wahoo, and dolphinfish—wahoos are the most common, dolphinfish the least. Trolling is the usual method of deepwater fishing, and charter-boat operators offer various tackle setups, with test-line weights ranging from 20 pounds to 130 pounds. The boats, which range from 31 ft to 55 ft long, are fitted with a wide array of gear and electronics to track fish, including depth sounders, global positioning systems, loran systems, video fish finders, radar, and computer scanners.

Half-day or full-day charters are offered by most operators, but full-day trips offer the best chance for a big catch because the boat has time to reach waters that are less often fished. Rates are about $600 per boat for half a day (four hours), $850 per day (eight hours). Many captains encourage clients to participate in the catch-and-release program to maintain the abundant supply of fish, but successful anglers can certainly keep fish if they like.

The **BERMUDA DEPARTMENT OF TOURISM** (Global House, 43 Church St., Hamilton, tel. 441/292–0023; ferry terminal, Front St., tel. 441/295–1480, www.bermudatourism.com) runs the free **GAME FISHING COMPETITION,** open to all anglers, throughout the year. Catches of any of 26 game varieties can be registered with the department, and prizes are awarded.

In addition to the outfitters we list, several independent charter boats operate out of Hamilton Harbour as well as harbors in Sandys, at the island's western end. For more information about chartering a fishing boat, you can request or pick up a copy of "What to Do: Information and Prices" at the Bermuda Department of Tourism.

➤ **FISHING BOAT CHARTERS: Bermuda Sport Fishing Association** (Creek View House, 8 Tulo La., Pembroke, tel. 441/295–2370). **ST. George's Game Fishing Association** (Box 107GE, St. George's, tel. 441/297–8093 or 441/234–8953, fax 441/297–1455, www.fishandfun.bm).

Shore Fishing

The principal catches for shore fishers are pompano, bonefish, and snapper. Excellent sport for saltwater fly-fishing is the wily and strong bonefish, which hovers in coves, harbors, and bays. Among the more popular spots for bonefish are West Whale Bay and Spring Benny's Bay, which have large expanses of clear, shallow water protected by reefs close to shore. Good fishing holes are plentiful along the south shore, too. Fishing in the Great Sound and St. George's Harbour can be rewarding, but enclosed Harrington Sound is less promising. Ask at local tackle shops about the latest hot spots and the best baits. You can also make rental arrangements through your hotel or contact Windjammer Water Sports.

WINDJAMMER WATER SPORTS (Dockyard Marina, tel. 441/234–3082; Cambridge Beaches, Sandys, tel. 441/234–0250) has rod and reel rentals for shore fishing available for about $15–$20 a day ($20–$30 deposit or credit card required). Rental prices usually include bait and a tackle box.

GOLF
☞ *See* Golf chapter.

HORSEBACK RIDING

Because most of the land on Bermuda is residential, opportunities for riding through the countryside are few. The chief exception is **SOUTH SHORE PARK,** between South Road and the Warwick beaches. Sandy trails, most of which are open only to walkers or riders, wind through stands of dune grass and oleander and over coral bluffs.

SPICELANDS RIDING CENTRE (Middle Rd., Warwick, tel. 441/238–8212 or 441/238–8246) leads riders on trails along the dunes above the south-shore beaches at 7 AM, 10 AM, and 11:30 AM daily. These one-hour jaunts cost $50 per person, with a maximum of 10 people in each group (and no one under age 12). In winter you can ride along the beach. Afternoon rides are also offered on weekdays. Spicelands gives private lessons in its riding ring for $30 per half hour. Beginners are required to take a series of at least three lessons. On Saturday, children ages 12 and under can take 15-minute pony rides for $10.

JET-SKIING

If riding a moped on terra firma isn't enough for you, consider mounting a Jet Ski. In Bermuda you can ride these high-speed aqua-cycles only in the company of a guide.

At **SOMERSET BRIDGE WATERSPORTS** (Somerset Bridge, Sandys, tel. 441/234–0914) you can arrange to take a "speed tour" at the western end of the island, in the Great Sound, Ely's Harbour, Mangrove Bay, and above the visible Sea Gardens coral formations. Groups are kept small—no more than six Jet Skis per guide.

WINDJAMMER WATER SPORTS (Dockyard Marina, Sandys, tel. 441/234–0250; Cambridge Beaches, Sandys, tel. 441/234–3082) has 1¼-hour Jet Ski tours ($95 for a single Jet Ski, $125 for a double) during the summer months.

JOGGING AND RUNNING

Many of the difficulties that cyclists face in Bermuda—hills, traffic, and wind—also confront runners. And the lack of roadside footpaths and sidewalks, except in the city center, makes the problem worse. Take extreme care when walking or running along the twisting, narrow roads.

Runners who like firm pavement are happiest (and perhaps safest) on the Railway Trail or on South Road. For those who like running on sand, the trails through South Shore Park are relatively firm. Horseshoe Bay Beach and Elbow Beach are frequented by a large number of serious runners in the early morning and after 5 PM. Another beach for running is ½-mi Warwick Long Bay, the island's longest uninterrupted stretch of sand. But the sand is softer here than at Horseshoe and Elbow, so it's difficult to get a good footing, particularly at high tide. By using South Shore Park trails to skirt coral bluffs, runners can create a route that connects several beaches, although trails can be winding and uneven in some places.

BERMUDA TRIATHLONS are held about once a month from April to October. The events combine a swim, a cycling leg, and a run. Contact the Bermuda Triathlon Association (48 Par-la-Ville Rd., Suite 547, Hamilton HM 11, tel. 441/293–2765).

Two-mile "fun runs" sponsored by the **MID-ATLANTIC ATHLETIC CLUB** (Box HM 1745, Hamilton HM BX, tel. 441/293–8103, fax 441/293–4089) are held Tuesday evening April through October. Runs begin at 6 PM near the Berry Hill Road entrance to the Botanical Gardens. There is no fee.

PARASAILING

Parasailing outfits operate in the Great Sound and in Castle Harbour from May through October. The cost is about $45 per person for an eight-minute flight. Want to sail through the sky with your significant other under a single parachute? Call Skyrider Bermuda or Adventure Enterprises. A two-person trip costs about $80.

➤ **PARASAILING CONTACTS: Adventure Enterprises** (Ordnance Island, St. George's, tel. 441/297–1459). **Bermuda Island Parasail Co.** (Darrell's Wharf, Paget, tel. 441/232–2871). **Skyrider Bermuda** (Dockyard, Sandys, tel. 441/234–3019).

SNORKELING

The clarity of the water, the stunning array of coral reefs, and the shallow resting places of several wrecks make snorkeling in the waters around Bermuda—both inshore and offshore—

particularly worthwhile. You can snorkel year-round, although a wet suit is advisable for anyone planning to spend a long time in the water in winter, when the water temperature can dip into the 60s. The water also tends to be rougher in winter, often restricting snorkeling to the protected areas of Harrington Sound and Castle Harbour. Underwater caves, grottoes, coral formations, and schools of small fish are the highlights of these areas.

When Bermudians are asked to name a favorite snorkeling spot, they invariably rank Church Bay in Southampton (at the western end of the south-shore beaches) at or near the top of the list. A small cove cut out of the coral cliffs, the bay is full of nooks and crannies, and the reefs are relatively close to shore. Snorkelers should exercise caution here (as you should everywhere along the south shore), as the water can be rough. A small stall often sells snorkeling equipment, underwater cameras, and fish food here. Other popular snorkeling areas close inshore are the beaches of John Smith's and Tobacco bays. Despite its small size, West Whale Bay is also worth a visit.

Some of the best snorkeling sites are accessible only by boat. As the number of wrecks attests, navigating around Bermuda's reef-strewn waters is no simple task, especially for inexperienced boaters. If you rent a boat yourself, stick to the protected waters of the sounds, harbors, and bays, and be sure to ask for an ocean-navigation chart. (These point out shallow waters, rocks, and hidden reefs.)

For trips to the reefs, let someone else do the navigating—a charter-boat skipper or one of the snorkeling-cruise operators. Some of the best reefs for snorkeling, complete with shallow-water wrecks, are to the west, but where the tour guide or skipper goes often depends on the tide, weather, and water conditions. For snorkelers who demand privacy and freedom of movement, a boat charter (complete with captain) is the only answer, but the cost is considerable—$650 a day for a party of 18. By comparison, half a day of snorkeling on regularly scheduled cruises generally costs $45–$65, including equipment and instruction.

Snorkeling equipment is available for rent at most major hotels. The Grotto Bay Beach Hotel & Tennis Club, Sonesta Beach Hotel & Spa, and Southampton Princess have dive operators on site. Rates for mask, flippers, and snorkel are usually $15–$20 a day, with the price per day decreasing when a rental is longer. A deposit or credit card is required. You can also rent equipment, including small boats and underwater cameras, at several marinas.

➤ **SNORKELING CONTACTS: Horseshoe Bay Beach** (off South Rd., Southampton, tel. 441/238–2651). **Pompano Beach Club Watersports Centre** (36 Pompano Rd., Southampton, tel. 441/234–0222). **Salt Kettle Yacht Charters** (off Harbour Rd., Salt Kettle Rd., Paget, tel. 441/236–4863 or 441/236–3612). **Windjammer Water Sports** (Dockyard Marina, Dockyard, tel. 441/234–0250).

Snorkeling Cruises

Snorkeling cruises, offered from April to November, are a less expensive albeit less personal way to experience the underwater world. Some boats carry up to 40 passengers to snorkeling sites but focus mostly on their music and bars (complimentary beverages are usually served on the trip back from the reefs). Smaller boats, which limit capacity to 10–16 passengers, offer more personal attention and focus more on the beautiful snorkeling areas themselves. To make sure you choose a boat that's right for you, ask for details before booking. Many of the boats can easily arrange private charters for groups. Half-day snorkeling tours cost between $45 and $65, including instruction and gear.

Hayward's Snorkeling tours are aboard the 54-ft glass-bottom *Explorer*. From this boat, access into and out of the water is easy. Special excursions are arranged during the spring migration of the humpback whales. Hayward's Snorkeling and Pitman's Boat Tours have half-day snorkeling trips (or longer for special charters). Both relate interesting historical and ecological information about the island in addition to visiting pristine offshore snorkeling areas, often at shipwreck sites. Half-day cruises are also available from Jessie James Cruises, which are aboard the 40-passenger luxury Chris-Craft *Rambler*. Captain Kirk Ward's Native Tours has regularly scheduled sailing-snorkeling trips to the outer reefs on a 38-ft trimaran and a 48-ft catamaran. Salt Kettle Yacht Charters also has half-day tours.

➤ **CRUISE CONTACTS: Hayward's Snorkeling & Glass Bottom Boat Cruises** (dock adjacent to Hamilton Ferry Terminal, tel. 441/236–9894 after hours). **Jessie James Cruises** (47 Front St., Hamilton, tel. 441/296–5801). **"Restless Native" Tours** (Dockyard, Sandys, tel. 441/234–8149 or 441/234–1434). **Pitman's Boat Tours** (Robinson's Marina, Somerset Bridge, tel. 441/234–0700). **Salt Kettle Yacht Charters** (off Harbour Rd., Salt Kettle Rd., Paget, tel. 441/236–4863 or 441/234–8165).

SQUASH

The **BERMUDA SQUASH & RACQUETS ASSOCIATION** (111 Middle Rd., Devonshire, tel. 441/292–6881, www.bermudasquash. com) makes its four courts available to nonmembers between 11 AM and 11 PM by reservation. A $10 per-person fee (plus $5–$7 court fees, depending on the time of day) buys 40 minutes of play, and you can borrow rackets and balls. Temporary memberships are available, if you plan to play a lot.

To play on the two courts at the **CORAL BEACH & TENNIS CLUB** (South Rd., Paget, tel. 441/236–2233), you must be introduced by a member.

TENNIS

Bermuda has one tennis court for every 600 residents, a ratio that even the most tennis-crazed countries would find difficult to match. Many are private, but the public has access to more than 70 courts in 20 locations island-wide. Courts are inexpensive and seldom full. Hourly rates for nonguests are about $10–$16. You might want to consider bringing along a few fresh cans of balls, because balls in Bermuda cost $6–$7 per can—two to three times the rate in the United States. Among the surfaces used in Bermuda are Har-Tru, clay, cork, and hard composites, of which the relatively slow Plexipave composite is the most prevalent. Despite Bermuda's British roots, the island has no grass court.

Wind, heat (in summer), and humidity are the most distinct characteristics of Bermudian tennis. From October through March, when daytime temperatures rarely exceed 80°F, play is comfortable throughout the day. But in summer, the heat radiating from the court (especially hard courts) can make play uncomfortable between 11 and 3, so some clubs take midday break, making this a bad time for scheduling a lesson. Most tennis facilities offer lessons, ranging from $25 to $30 for 30 minutes of instruction, and racket rentals for $4–$6 per hour or per play.

CORAL BEACH & TENNIS CLUB. Introduction by a member is required to play at this exclusive club, which is the site of the annual Bermuda Open tournament in April. Coral Beach has eight clay courts, three of which are floodlit. It's open daily from 8 AM to 8 PM. *Off South Rd., Paget, tel. 441/236–6495 or 441/236–2233.*

ELBOW BEACH HOTEL. This facility is fortunate to have as its Director of Tennis David Lambert, who is also president of the Bermuda Lawn Tennis Association. Serving under Mr. Lambert as a teaching pro is Ricky Mallory, one of the island's top men's players. There are five Plexipave courts on hand, two with lights, and hours of play are 8 AM to 6 PM daily. Courts cost $16 per hour. Lessons and match play can be arranged for hotel guests. *Off South Shore Rd., Paget, tel. 441/236–3535.*

FAIRMONT SOUTHAMPTON PRINCESS HOTEL. Despite their position at the water's edge, the Plexipave hard courts here are reasonably shielded from the wind, although the breeze can be swirling and difficult. Six courts are at hand with fees ranging from $12 per hour to $16 per hour on any of the three courts that have lighting. Hours of service are daily from 8 AM to 6 PM, until 8 PM in summer. *South Rd., Southampton, tel. 441/238–1005.*

GOVERNMENT TENNIS STADIUM. These are the busiest of Bermuda's tennis courts, their inland location ideal for combating strong winds. Of the eight all-weather courts available, five are Plexi-Cushion and three are Har-Tru. Three courts in the main stadium have floodlights. Hours are from 8 AM to 10 PM on weekdays and from 8 AM to 6 PM on weekends. Rates are $8 per hour during the day and $16 per hour at night. *2 Marsh Folly, Pembroke, tel. 441/292–0105.*

GROTTO BAY BEACH HOTEL AND TENNIS CLUB. A little more than a stone's throw from the Bermuda International Airport, Grotto Bay has four Plexipave cork-based courts, two lighted, with an hourly rate of $12. It's open daily, 7–7, with a midday break. Lessons are available upon request. *North Shore Rd., Hamilton Parish, tel. 441/293–8333 ext. 1914.*

POMANDER GATE TENNIS CLUB. There are five hard courts available (four with lighting) at this scenic club located off Hamilton Harbour. Temporary membership is available for $30 per couple per week. Hours of play are 7 AM to 11 PM on weekdays, until 10 PM on weekends. *Pomander Rd., Paget, tel. 441/236–5400.*

PORT ROYAL GOLF COURSE. Port Royal has four hard courts, two of which are floodlit. A host of pros are on hand to offer instruction to juniors and seniors. Rates for court play are $10 per hour in the day and $14 per hour at night until 10 PM. Arrangements can be made through the golf club from 10 AM. *Off Middle Rd., Southampton, tel. 441/238–9430.*

SONESTA BEACH HOTEL & SPA. The Sonesta offers players one of the more spectacular settings on the island, but the courts are exposed to summer winds from the south and southwest. The hotel has six clay courts, two lighted for night play. Rates are $10 per hour (free for guests), with lessons also available from the resident pro between 9 AM to 6 PM. *Off South Rd., Southampton, tel. 441/238–8122.*

WATERSKIING

BLUE HOLE WATER SPORTS (Grotto Bay Beach Hotel & Tennis Club, 11 Blue Hole Hill, Hamilton Parish, tel. 441/293–2915) is your only option unless you know a local with a boat. Prices fluctuate with fuel costs but average $40 for 15 minutes, $60 per half hour, and $100 per hour, instruction included.

WINDSURFING

Elbow Beach, Somerset Long Bay, Shelly Bay, and Harrington Sound are the favorite haunts of Bermuda board sailors. For novices, the often calm waters of Mangrove Bay and Castle Harbour are best. The open bays on the north shore are popular among wave enthusiasts when the northerly storm winds blow. Only experts should consider windsurfing on the south shore. Wind, waves, and reefs make it so dangerous that rental companies are prohibited from renting boards there.

Even the most avid board sailors should rent sailboards rather than bring their own. Transporting a board around Bermuda is a logistical nightmare. There are no rental cars, and few taxi drivers are willing to see their car roofs scoured with scratches in the interest of sport. Rental rates range from $25 to $35 an hour and from $60 to $90 a day. Some shops negotiate special long-term rates.

Experienced board sailors who want to meet local windsurfers can call former Olympic competitor Hubert Watlington at **SAIL**

Cricket

The Oval and Lords are names of English cricket grounds that evoke memories of Britain long ago, a time of cucumber sandwiches and tea poured from china pots—but the atmosphere of cricket on Bermuda is very definitely Caribbean. The thwack of leather on willow is the same, but overcast skies and frequent breaks as the ground staff move quickly to put the rain covers in place are not for these players. The fans, gathered on grassy knolls and open terraces, are also far removed from those back in England where the game first saw the light of day. Polite clapping and hearty hurrahs are not to be heard here. Instead the air is filled with chanting and the structures reverberate to the sound of music. Allegiances are clearly defined though few miles separate the opposing factions— mothers, fathers, sons, and daughters all cheering on their favorites, just as their forefathers in years gone by. As the match comes to a conclusion, the setting sun falls low behind the clubhouse and players and fans mingle as one to await the dawn of another day of runs, catches, and cries of "Howzat."

ON (Old Cellar, off Front St., Hamilton, tel. 441/295–0808). He's an integral part of this sailing circuit.

➤ **WINDSURFING CONTACTS:Blue Hole Water Sports** (Grotto Bay Beach Hotel & Tennis Club, 11 Blue Hole Hill, Hamilton Parish, tel. 441/293–2915). **Pompano Beach Club** (36 Pompano Rd., Southampton, tel. 441/234–0222). **Windjammer Water Sports** (Dockyard Marina, Sandys, tel. 441/234–3082; Cambridge Beaches, Sandys, tel. 441/234–0250).

YOGA
INTEGRAL YOGA CENTRE (Dallas Bldg., 8 Victoria St., Hamilton, tel. 441/295–3355) has classes around the island.

SPECTATOR SPORTS

Bermuda is a great place for sports fans seeking a change of scenery from baseball, football, and basketball—sports that mean little to Bermudians. In addition to golf and tennis, the big spectator sports here are cricket, rugby, soccer, and yacht racing.

The World Rugby Classic, in the fall, brings erstwhile top players, now retired, to the island for a week of top play and parties. At this time of year, the fabled Mid Ocean Club hosts a two-day golf tournament, the Tour Challenge, that has drawn such top names as Corey Pavin, Tom Watson, Ray Floyd, and Se Ri Pak. Top runners flock to the island in January for the Bermuda International Race Weekend, which includes marathon, half-marathon, and 10K events. Prestigious summer and fall sailing events include the Newport-to-Bermuda Race and the Colorcraft Gold Cup. The Bermuda Department of Tourism can provide exact dates and details for all major sporting events.

CRICKET

Cricket is the big team sport in summer, and Cup Match in late July or early August is the summer sporting event played over two days. The top players from around the island compete at the Somerset Cricket Club or the St. George's Cricket Club. Although the cricket is taken very seriously, the event itself is a real festival, attended by thousands of picnickers and partyers. There is an entry fee of $10 per day. The regular cricket season runs from April through September. For more information, contact the Bermuda Cricket Board of Control.

➤ **CRICKET CONTACTS: Bermuda Cricket Board of Control** (tel. 441/292–8958, fax 441/292–8959). **St. George's Cricket Club** (Wellington Slip Rd., tel. 441/297–0374). **Somerset Cricket Club** (Broome St., off Somerset Rd., tel. 441/234–0327).

EQUESTRIAN EVENTS

Events are held most weekends during the season from October to May at the National Equestrian Centre. Some highlights are FEI competition in dressage and show jumping in March and April, and the annual three-day Agricultural Exhibition held in April at the Botanical Gardens. Harness Pony Racing is held Friday or Saturday evenings under lights at the center between October and March. For more information, write to the Bermuda Equestrian Federation.

➤ **EQUESTRIAN EVENTS CONTACTS: Bermuda Equestrian Federation** (Box DV 583, Devonshire DV BX, tel. 441/234–0485). **National Equestrian Centre** (Vesey St., Devonshire, tel. 441/234–0485, fax 441/234–3010).

GOLF

☞ *See* Golf chapter.

RUGBY

Bermuda's rugby season runs from September to April. November brings the World Rugby Classic. The competition attracts teams from the United States, Great Britain, France, New Zealand, South Africa, Argentina, and Australia as well as Bermuda. Tickets cost about $12. During the rest of the season you can watch matches between local teams. For more information, contact the **WORLD RUGBY CLASSIC** (tel. 441/291–1517, www.worldrugby.bm).

RUNNING

The **BERMUDA INTERNATIONAL MARATHON, HALF MARATHON AND 10K RACE (INTERNATIONAL RACE WEEKEND),** held in mid-January, attracts world-class distance runners from several countries, but it's open to everyone. For information, contact the **Race Committee** (Box DV 397, Devonshire DV BX, tel. 441/236–6086).

It may be second to International Race Weekend in worldwide appeal, but the **BERMUDA MARATHON DERBY** captures the imagination of the island like no other race. A public holiday, Bermuda Day, is celebrated with thousands of locals and visitors lining the edges of the 13.3-mi course. The race, which begins in Somerset and finishes near the Government Tennis Stadium, is open to residents only.

SOCCER

Football (soccer) season runs from September through April in Bermuda. You can watch local teams in various age divisions battle it out on fields around the island. For details, contact the **BERMUDA FOOTBALL ASSOCIATION** (Cedar Ave., Hamilton, tel. 441/295–2199).

TENNIS

April's **BERMUDA OPEN,** an ATP Tour, USTA-sanctioned event of the world's top professionals, is played on clay courts at the Coral Beach & Tennis Club (tel. 441/236–2233).

Every November there is back-to-back tournament activity at the Coral Beach & Tennis Club, which attracts numerous visitors and a host of the top local players. The action begins with the Bermuda Lawn Tennis Club Invitational followed by the Coral Beach Club Invitational.

For information about Bermuda's tennis tournaments, contact the **BERMUDA LAWN TENNIS ASSOCIATION** (Box HM 341, Hamilton HM BX, tel. 441/296–0834, fax 441/295–3056).

YACHTING

Bermuda has a worldwide reputation as a center of yacht racing. Spectators, particularly those on land, may find it difficult to follow the intricacies of a race or regatta, but the sight of the racing fleet, with brightly colored spinnakers flying, is always striking. The racing season runs from March to November. Most

Distance Conversion Chart

Kilometers/Miles

To change kilometers (km) to miles (mi), multiply km by .621.
To change mi to km, multiply mi by 1.61.

km to mi	mi to km
1 = .62	1 = 1.6
2 = 1.2	2 = 3.2
3 = 1.9	3 = 4.8
4 = 2.5	4 = 6.4
5 = 3.1	5 = 8.1
6 = 3.7	6 = 9.7
7 = 4.3	7 = 11.3
8 = 5.0	8 = 12.9

Meters/Feet

To change meters (m) to feet (ft), multiply m by 3.28.
To change ft to m, multiply ft by .305.

m to ft	ft to m
1 = 3.3	1 = .30
2 = 6.6	2 = .61
3 = 9.8	3 = .92
4 = 13.1	4 = 1.2
5 = 16.4	5 = 1.5
6 = 19.7	6 = 1.8
7 = 23.0	7 = 2.1
8 = 26.2	8 = 2.4

races are held on weekends in the Great Sound, and several classes of boats usually compete. You can watch from Spanish Point and along the Somerset shoreline. Anyone who wants to get a real sense of the action should be on board a boat near the race course.

In June in alternating years, Bermuda serves as the finish for oceangoing yachts in three major races beginning in the United States: the Newport–Bermuda Ocean Yacht Race, the Marion to Bermuda Race, and the Bermuda Ocean Race from Annapolis, Maryland. Of these, the Newport–Bermuda Race, to be held in 2002, typically attracts the most entries, but all fill the island's harbors and yacht-club docks with yachts, which usually range in length from about 30 ft to 80 ft—a spectacular sight.

For those more interested in racing than gawking at expensive yachts, the Colorcraft Gold Cup International Match Race Tournament is the event of choice. Held in October in Hamilton Harbour, the tournament hosts many of the world's top sailors—some of whom are America's Cup skippers—and includes the elite among the Bermudians in a lucrative chase for thousands in prize money.

Traveling by moped, the island visitor intrepidly navigates the narrow twisting roads. Passing sherbet-color cottages bordered by manicured hedges of hibiscus and oleander, he stops at a "lay-by" on South Shore Road. Deeply breathing in the ocean air, he cannot help but smile. He is thinking it is no wonder, as beautiful as the island is, that Mark Twain should say he wanted to go to Bermuda—rather than Heaven—when he died. Looking down from here, he is mesmerized by an expansive stretch of sandy shoreline and rocky coves embracing sapphire-color waters. He contemplates taking a break from sightseeing, the sun and surf calling him to take the next beach detour. . . .

In This Chapter

Hamilton 136 • St. George 144 • West End 151 • The Parishes 156

Revised and updated by Lilla Zuill

here and there

BERMUDA'S STREETS ARE LINED WITH HEDGES OF HIBISCUS and oleander, and the lovingly maintained limestone buildings set just behind them are painted in pastels with gleaming white roofs— many of which are used for businesses and shops. Touring Bermuda, with sights such as these, is a multisensory pleasure.

Hamilton, the island's capital, is of interest for its harbor and its shops. The town is also the main departure point for sightseeing boats, ferries, and the pink-and-blue buses that ramble all over the island. The island's first capital was the historical town of St. George at the island's northeastern end, which was awarded UNESCO World Heritage Site status in 2000. The West End spots to visit are the sleepy hamlet of Somerset and the Royal Naval Dockyard, a former British naval shipyard, now home to the Maritime Museum and a developing arts, crafts, and shopping center.

Hamilton, St. George's, and Dockyard can all be explored easily on foot. The other parishes, however, are best explored by moped, bicycle, or taxi. The main roads connecting the parishes are self-explanatory: North Shore Road, Middle Road, South Shore Road, and Harbour Road. Almost all traffic traversing the island's 22-mi length uses these roads, although some 1,200 smaller ones crisscross the land.

HAMILTON

Bermuda's capital is a small town, with busy streets lined with shops, on a harbor. (Don't confuse Hamilton, the town, with the

hamilton sightseeing

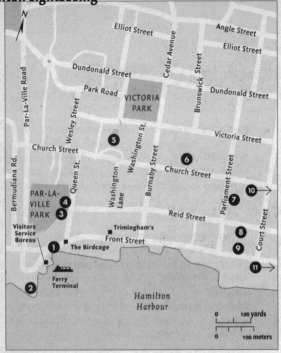

Albuoy's Point, 2

Bermuda
Underwater
Exploration
Institute, 11

Cabinet
Building, 8

Cathedral
of the Most
Holy Trinity, 6

Cenotaph, 9

City Hall, 5

Fort Hamilton, 10

Front Street, 1

Museum of the
Bermuda
Historical
Society/Bermuda
Public Library, 4

Perot Post
Office, 3

Sessions
House, 7

parish of the same name. Hamilton Town is actually a part of Pembroke Parish.) The town has a handful of museums and galleries, though for many its main attractions are the plethora of shops selling discounted woolens, jewelry, and perfumes.

Numbers in the text correspond to numbers in the margin and on the Hamilton, Town of St. George, West End, and Parishes Sightseeing maps.

A Good Walk

Begin on **FRONT STREET** ①, a pretty thoroughfare lined with small, colorful buildings, many with balconies and arcades. The Visitors Service Bureau in the Ferry Terminal Building on Front Street is an appropriate starting point. Turn left after leaving the bureau and follow Point Pleasant Road to the waterside park, for a splendid view of Hamilton Harbour at **ALBUOY'S POINT** ②.

At Front and Queen streets, you'll see the Birdcage, a traffic box named for its designer, Michael "Dickey" Bird, which has been a Hamilton landmark for more than 30 years. Continue up Queen Street to the 19th-century **PEROT POST OFFICE** ③. Just beyond it is the **MUSEUM OF THE BERMUDA HISTORICAL SOCIETY/ BERMUDA PUBLIC LIBRARY** ④. Continue up Queen Street to Church Street to reach **CITY HALL** ⑤, which houses a performing arts theater, the Bermuda National Gallery, and the Bermuda Society of Arts Gallery.

Continue east on Church Street, and one block up on your left you'll see the imposing **CATHEDRAL OF THE MOST HOLY TRINITY** ⑥. Just beyond the cathedral, near the corner of Church and Parliament streets, is **SESSIONS HOUSE** ⑦. Continue down Parliament Street to Front Street to see the **CABINET BUILDING** ⑧ and, in front of it, the **CENOTAPH** ⑨ war memorial. From here, have a leisurely stroll past the Front Street shops and perhaps have tea at Trimingham's (37 Front St.).

Two sights nearby, but not within walking distance, are also worth checking out by taxi or moped: **FORT HAMILTON** ⑩ has a moat, underground passageways, and great views of Hamilton and the harbor. After leaving Fort Hamilton, moped or taxi back down King Street and turn left on Front Street for the **BERMUDA UNDERWATER EXPLORATION INSTITUTE** ⑪, located on East Broadway near the traffic circle, an interactive museum of the sea.

TIMING

You can see Hamilton in less than an hour, but give yourself the better part of a day if you're going to take in some of the museums, Fort Hamilton, and the Bermuda Underwater Exploration Institute. Of course, die-hard shoppers may also want to allow a day or two for browsing the shops alone.

What to See

❷ **ALBUOY'S POINT.** Hamilton Harbour is dotted with islands, and its blue waters are graced with the sails of pleasure craft. Ringside seats for this show are the benches at Albuoy's Point, a small waterside park. Nearby is the **Royal Bermuda Yacht Club,** built in the 1930s. Today international yachting celebrities and the local elite hobnob here, and the club sponsors the Newport–Bermuda Ocean Yacht Race and the Gold Cup International Match Race Tournament.

☝ ⑪ **BERMUDA UNDERWATER EXPLORATION INSTITUTE.** BUEI opened in 1997 and is designed to acquaint you with the vast deep through multimedia and interactive displays. Never heard of a "bathysphere"? Come see a replica of this exploration device, which allowed de facto oceanographer William Beebe and Otis Barton to venture ½ mi down into the deep in 1934. Or consider "conchology," the study of shells, in a whole new light. You can also take a simulated scuba dive in the Dive Capsule—or see some early attempts—or try to identify whales. Located just beyond the traffic circle leading to Hamilton, the modern two-story building also has an auditorium for films and lectures, gift shops, and a French restaurant, La Coquille. E. Broadway, tel. 441/292–7219, fax 441/236–6141. $9.75. Daily 9–5.

8 CABINET BUILDING. Bermuda's Senate, the upper house of Parliament, is best visited amid great ceremony, when the formal opening of Parliament takes place in the Senate Chamber, traditionally on the first Friday of November. His Excellency the Governor, dressed in a plumed hat and full regalia, arrives on the grounds in a landau drawn by magnificent black horses and accompanied by a police escort. A senior police officer, carrying the Black Rod made by the Crown jewelers, then asks the Speaker of the House, elected representatives, and members of the Senate Chamber to convene. The governor makes his Throne Speech (dating from the 1600s) from a tiny cedar throne. Otherwise come on a Wednesday if you want to watch the Senate in action. *Front St., tel. 441/292–5501. Free. Weekdays 9–5.*

★ **6 CATHEDRAL OF THE MOST HOLY TRINITY.** An impressive structure, designed in Early English style with Gothic-revival flourishes, this Anglican church is constructed of Bermuda limestone and imported materials. The tower rises to 143 ft, and the clerestory in the nave is supported by piers of polished Scottish granite. After exploring the interior, climb the 150-odd steps to the tower, at the top of which you'll have spectacular views of Hamilton. *Church St., tel. 441/292–4033. Tower $3. Church daily and for Sun. services, tower weekdays 10–3.*

NEED A BREAK? For more than 50 years, locals have flocked to the **SPOT** (6 Burnaby St., tel. 441/292–6293) for breakfast, lunch, and coffee on the cheap. Sandwiches go for about $5. The Spot is open Monday–Saturday 6:30 AM–7 PM.

9 CENOTAPH. This memorial to Bermuda's war dead stands in front of the Cabinet Building. On Remembrance Day (November 11), the governor and other dignitaries lay wreaths at its base.

★ **5 CITY HALL.** Set back from the street behind a fountain and lily pond, this relatively new building (1960) houses Hamilton's City Hall. Massive cedar doors open into a large lobby with great chandeliers and high ceilings. The City Hall Theatre here often hosts concerts, plays, and dance performances. A handsome cedar staircase leads upstairs to the second-floor art galleries.

On the first landing, the East Exhibition Room houses the **Bermuda National Gallery,** the island's only climate-controlled gallery. Opened in 1992, the gallery has a collection of European paintings from the early 16th to 19th century, including works by Thomas Gainsborough and Sir Joshua Reynolds. The gallery mounts several major exhibits each year, and a selection of paintings from the permanent collection are often exhibited alongside the latest show.

In the West Wing, changing exhibits are displayed in the **Bermuda Society of Arts Gallery.** The juried annual Spring, Summer, Autumn, and Winter Members' Shows attract talented local artists, working in various mediums. *Church St., tel. 441/ 292–1234 City Hall; 441/295–9428 Bermuda National Gallery; 441/ 292–3824 Bermuda Society of Arts Gallery. City Hall free, Bermuda National Gallery $3, Bermuda Society of Arts Gallery free (donations accepted). City Hall weekdays 9–5, Bermuda National Gallery and Bermuda Society of Arts Gallery Mon.–Sat. 10–4.*

NEED A
BREAK?
PARADISO CAFE (7 Reid St., at the entrance to Washington Mall, tel. 441/295–3263) has sandwiches—regular or wraps— and yummy iced coffee. **WINDSOR GARDEN** (Windsor Place Mall, across Queen St. and north of the library, tel. 441/295– 4085) serves light lunch fare and diet-busting pastries.

★ ✋ ❿ **FORT HAMILTON.** On the eastern outskirts of Hamilton is this imposing old fortress, complete with a moat, 18-ton guns, and underground passageways that were cut through solid rock by Royal Engineers in the 1860s. Outdated even before its completion, the fort never fired a shot in aggression, though it continues to yield splendid views of the capital and the harbor. One-way streets make getting here a little circuitous. From downtown

Hamilton head east on Victoria Street, turn left on King Street, and then turn left onto Happy Valley Road. *Happy Valley Rd., Pembroke, no phone. Free. Daily 9:30–5.*

❶ FRONT STREET. Hamilton's main drag runs alongside the harbor. Front Street is lined with colorful little buildings that house shops and boutiques. When cruise ships pull up, the street bustles with shoppers dodging mopeds and darting into department stores in search of deals.

★ **❹ MUSEUM OF THE BERMUDA HISTORICAL SOCIETY/BERMUDA PUBLIC LIBRARY.** Mark Twain admired the giant rubber tree that stands on Queen Street in the front yard of this Georgian house, once the home of Hamilton's first postmaster, William Bennet Perot, and his family. (There's no known connection to former U.S. presidential candidate Ross Perot, although he does have a house here.) Although charmed by the tree, which had been imported from Demerara (now Guyana) in the mid-19th century, Twain lamented that it didn't bear fruit in the form of hot-water bottles and rubber overshoes. The library, upon which Twain had no comment, was founded in 1839 and its reference section has virtually every book ever written about Bermuda, as well as a microfilm collection of Bermudian newspapers dating back to 1784. In the museum's entrance hall are portraits of Sir George Somers and his wife, painted about 1605. Portraits of Postmaster Perot and his wife hang here, too. Ask to see the letter George Washington wrote in 1775 "to the inhabitants of Bermuda," requesting gunpowder. *13 Queen St., tel. 441/295–2905 library; 441/295–2487 museum. Free (donations accepted). Library weekdays 9–6, Sat. 9–5; museum Mon.–Sat. 9:30–3:30. Tours by appointment.*

❸ PEROT POST OFFICE. Bermuda's first postage stamps (1848) originated in this two-story building, which dates from around 1840 and still serves as a small post office. Bermuda's first postmaster, William Bennet Perot, was appointed in 1818. Perot would meet arriving steamers, collect the mail, stash it in his beaver hat, and then stroll around Hamilton to deliver it. To post a letter, residents came and paid Perot, who hand-stamped each one. Queen St., tel. 441/295–5151. Free. Weekdays 9–5.

NEED A BREAK? Next to the Perot Post Office is the Queen Street entrance to **PAR-LA-VILLE PARK** (there's another on Par-la-Ville Road). Paths wind through the luxuriant gardens, and the park benches are ideal for picnicking or enjoying a short rest.

⑦ SESSIONS HOUSE. The eye-catching Italianate edifice called Sessions House now houses the House of Assembly (the lower house of Parliament) and the Supreme Court. The original two-story structure was built in 1819. The Florentine towers and colonnade, decorated with red terra-cotta, were added in 1887 to commemorate Queen Victoria's Golden Jubilee. The Victoria Jubilee Clock Tower made its striking debut at midnight on December 31, 1893. You're welcome to watch the ceremonious and colorful (i.e., robes and full wigs) proceedings inside, but you'll want to call to find out when sessions are scheduled. *Parliament St. between Reid and Church Sts., tel. 441/292–7408. Free. Weekdays 9–12:30 and 2–5.*

ST. GEORGE

The settlement of Bermuda began on what is now St. George nearly 400 years ago, when the *Sea Venture* was wrecked off the coast. Much of the fun of St. George's is exploring the alleys and walled lanes that wind through the town.

A Good Walk

Start your tour in **KING'S SQUARE** ⑫, perhaps stopping in the Visitors Bureau to pick up maps and brochures. Stroll out onto **ORDNANCE ISLAND** ⑬ to see the dunking stool and a replica of the *Deliverance* II. Behind you, just up the street is the **BERMUDA NATIONAL TRUST MUSEUM AT THE GLOBE HOTEL** ⑭, and across the square is the **TOWN HALL** ⑮. Venturing up King

Street, notice the fine Bermudian architecture of **BRIDGE HOUSE** ⑯. At the top of King Street is the **OLD STATE HOUSE** ⑰, the oldest stone house in Bermuda.

Walk up Princess Street and cross Duke of York Street to **SOMERS GARDEN** ⑱ to see the putative burial site of the heart of Sir George Somers. After walking through the garden, ascend the steps to Blockade Alley, where you'll see on a hill ahead the **UNFINISHED CHURCH** ⑲. To your left are Duke of Kent Street, Featherbed Alley, and the **ST. GEORGE'S HISTORICAL SOCIETY MUSEUM** ⑳. Around the corner is the **FEATHERBED ALLEY PRINTERY** ㉑. Cross Clarence Street to Church Street and then turn right on Broad Alley. Straight ahead (as straight as you can go among these twisted alleys) is Printer's Alley, where Joseph Stockdale published Bermuda's first newspaper, on January 17, 1784. The short street connecting Printer's Alley with Old Maid's Lane is **NEA'S ALLEY** ㉒, which looks like something out of a tale retold by the Brothers Grimm.

Return to Church Street and enter the yard of **ST. PETER'S CHURCH** ㉓, an architecturally significant Anglican church (the main entrance is on Duke of York Street). From the church, continue down Duke of York Street to Barber's Alley, turning left to reach **TUCKER HOUSE** ㉔, a historical home and museum filled with antiques.

TIMING

Despite its small size, St. George's encompasses much of historical interest and was recently designated a UNESCO World Heritage Site. Plan to spend a few hours poking around the houses and museums.

What to See

★ ⑭ **BERMUDA NATIONAL TRUST MUSEUM AT THE GLOBE HOTEL.** Governor Samuel Day built this house in 1700, and it served as the Globe Hotel for 150 years and then housed the Confederate Museum until 1995. A video, *Bermuda, Centre of the Atlantic*, and

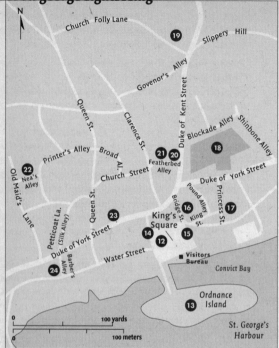

Bermuda National Trust Museum at the Globe Hotel, 14

Bridge House, 16

Featherbed Alley Printery, 21

King's Square, 12

Nea's Alley, 22

Old State House, 17

Ordnance Island, 13

St. George's Historical Society Museum, 20

St. Peter's Church, 23

Somers Garden, 18

Town Hall, 15

Tucker House, 24

Unfinished Church, 19

an exhibit entitled "Rogues and Runners: Bermuda and the American Civil War," tells the complicated story of St. George's career as a port for U.S. Confederate blockade runners. *Duke of York St., tel. 441/297–1423. $4; $5 combination ticket includes admission to Tucker House and Verdmont, in Smith's Parish. Tues.–Sat. 10–4.*

⓰ BRIDGE HOUSE. Named for a bridge that once crossed a small tidal creek nearby, this house was built sometime prior to 1700 and is a fine example of Bermudian architecture.

㉑ FEATHERBED ALLEY PRINTERY. As quaint as its name, the Featherbed Alley Printery is in a little cottage that houses a working printing press of the sort invented by Johannes Gutenberg in the 1450s. *Featherbed Alley, tel. 441/297–0423. $4 (includes admission to St. George's Historical Society Museum). Apr.–Nov., weekdays 10–4.*

⓬ KING'S SQUARE. Now the hub and heartbeat of St. George's, King's Square is actually comparatively new. For 200 years after the town was settled the square was a marshy part of the harbor. It was filled in only in the 1800s.

Prominently displayed in King's Square are cedar replicas of the stocks and pillory originally used to punish criminals. The grisly gizmos now serve as props for photos and for special activities staged here on Wednesday during low season. If you're greeted in the square by the town crier, whose resounding voice is almost enough to wake the dead and who is on hand in full colonial costume, you'll know a walking tour is starting.

㉒ NEA'S ALLEY. The 19th-century Irish poet Tom Moore lived on this street, then known as Cumberland Lane, during his brief tenure as registrar of the admiralty court. Moore, who was endowed with considerable charm, had an impact on the island that endures to this day. His legacy is frankly somewhat small and scandalous: Moore was invited to stay in the home of Admiral Mitchell, the neighbor of Mr. William Tucker and his wife, Hester, who is the "Nea" to whom Moore pours out his heart in several poems.

Moore is thought to have first seen Hester here in Cumberland Lane, which he describes in one of his odes as "the lime-covered alley that leads to thy home."

⓱ OLD STATE HOUSE. A curious ritual takes place every April in King's Square. One peppercorn, regally placed upon a velvet pillow, is presented to the mayor of St. George's amid much pomp and circumstance. The peppercorn is the annual rent paid to the town by the Masonic Lodge St. George No. 200 of the Grand Lodge of Scotland, which has occupied the Old State House ever since the capital moved from St. George's to Hamilton in 1815. The oldest house in Bermuda, it was built in 1620 in what Governor Nathaniel Butler believed was the Italian style. The limestone building used a mixture of turtle oil and lime as mortar and set the style for future Bermudian buildings. *Princess St., tel. 441/292–2480, 441/297–1206 Wed. only. Free. Wed. 10–4.*

★ ✵ ⓭ ORDNANCE ISLAND. *Land Ho!*—a splendid Desmond Fountain statue of Sir George Somers—dominates Ordnance Island. The dunking stool is a replica of the one used to dunk gossips, nagging wives, and suspected witches. Demonstrations are sometimes given, although volunteers report that getting dunked is no fun, even in jest.

Also on the island is the **Deliverance II,** a replica of one of the ships built by the survivors of the 1609 shipwreck. (Somers and his crew built two ships, the *Deliverance* and the *Patience,* to carry them to Jamestown, Virginia, after the incident.) *Ordnance Island, tel. 441/297–2750, www.bermudatourism.com. $3. Mar.–Nov., daily 9–5.*

⓴ ST. GEORGE'S HISTORICAL SOCIETY MUSEUM. Furnished to resemble its former incarnation as a private home, this typical Bermudian building from the early 1700s houses artifacts and documents pertaining to the island's earliest days. There's even a whale-blubber cutter. The cottage gardens behind the museum are beautiful, and there is no fee to view them. *Featherbed Alley,* *tel. 441/297–0423. $4 (includes admission to Featherbed Alley Printery). Apr.–Dec., weekdays 10–4; Jan.–Mar., weekdays 11–3.*

★ **23** **ST. PETER'S CHURCH.** Because parts of St. Peter's Church date back to its construction in 1620, it holds the distinction of being the oldest continuously operating Anglican church in the Western Hemisphere. It was not the first church to stand on this site, however. It replaced a 1612 structure of posts and palmetto leaves that was destroyed in a storm. The present church was extended in 1713, and the galleries on either side were added in 1833. The oldest part of the church is the area around the 17th-century triple-tier pulpit. The dark-red cedar altar is the oldest piece of woodwork in the colony, carved under the supervision of Richard Moore, a shipwright and Bermuda's first governor. The baptismal font, brought to the island by the early settlers, is about 500 years old, and the late-18th-century bishop's throne is believed to have been salvaged from a wreck. *Duke of York St., tel. 441/297–8359. Free (donations accepted). Daily 10–4:30.*

NEED A BREAK? Sitting almost cheek-by-jowl with St. Peter's Church, **TEMPTATIONS CAFE & BAKERY** (31 Duke of York St., tel. 441/297–1368) is a popular spot for heavenly pastries and sandwiches; it's open Monday–Saturday 8:30 AM–5 PM.

18 **SOMERS GARDEN.** After sailing to Jamestown and back in 1610, Sir George Somers fell ill and died. According to local lore, Somers told his nephew Matthew Somers to bury his heart in Bermuda, where it belonged. Matthew, who never seemed to pay much attention to his uncle's wishes, sailed for England soon afterward, sneaking Somers's body aboard in a cedar chest. (Somers's body is buried near his birthplace in Dorset.) When the tomb where Somers's heart was supposedly interred was opened many years later, only a few bones, a pebble, and some bottle fragments were found, so no one knows whether Matthew Somers ever carried out his uncle's wishes. Nonetheless, ceremonies were held at the

The Bermudian Roof

Typical Bermudian architecture is a limestone house, usually painted a pastel color, with a white tiered roof and most likely a white stone chimney. The style of this distinctive roof was chosen not for aesthetics but for the purpose of collecting rainwater, which is deposited in tanks underneath the house. Rainwater is the primary source of water on Bermuda, and it's used for drinking, bathing, cooking, you name it. The water is not purified, and yet no one has become ill as a result of drinking it. Nor has the island ever run out—supplies were taxed during World War II, however, when thousands of American soldiers were stationed on the island.

Bermuda's moon gates are another common architectural feature. You'll find these Chinese-inspired freestanding stone arches, which have been popular since the late 18th century, in gardens all over the island. These round (moonlike) gates are also favored as backdrops for wedding pictures.

empty grave upon the 1920 visit of the prince of Wales, during which the prince christened this pleasant, tree-shrouded park Somers Garden. Bordered by Shinbone Alley, Blockade Alley, and Duke of Kent and Duke of York Sts., no phone. Free. Daily 9–4.

15 TOWN HALL. St. George's administrative offices are housed in this two-story building that was constructed in 1808. The hall is paneled and furnished with cedar—go in and see the collection of mayoral photos or the "About St. George's" slide show. King's Sq., tel. 441/297–1425; 441/297–1532 information on "About St. George's." Free. Town Hall Mon.–Sat. 10–4; "About St. George's" Nov.–Mar., weekdays 10:05, 11:05, and 3:15 (call for hrs Apr.–Oct.).

24 TUCKER HOUSE. Antiques aficionados will find much of interest in this historic house, one of the showplaces of the Bermuda

National Trust, built of native limestone in 1711. Henry Tucker, president of the Governor's Council, lived here with his family from 1775 to 1807. His grandson donated most of the fine cedar and mahogany furnishings, which date from the mid-18th and early 19th centuries. *Water St., tel. 441/297–0545. $4; $5 combination ticket includes admission to Bermuda National Trust Museum and Verdmont Museum, in Smith's Parish. Mon.–Sat. 10–4.*

⑲ UNFINISHED CHURCH. Considering how much attention and affection are lavished on St. Peter's these days, it's hard to believe that residents in the 19th century wanted to replace the old church with a new one. Work began on this church in 1874, but construction was halted when a schism developed within the church. In 1992 the Bermuda National Trust obtained a 50-year lease on the church and is now repairing the structure. *Up Kent St. from King's Sq. (where Kent St. becomes Government Hill Rd. at intersection of Church Folly La.).*

WEST END

In contrast to Hamilton and St. George's, the West End is a rather bucolic part of Bermuda. With the notable exception of Dockyard, many of the attractions here are natural rather than man-made: nature reserves, wooded areas, and beautiful harbors and bays.

A Good Tour

Taking the ferry from Hamilton, disembark at the Dockyard landing to begin your walk through the **ROYAL NAVAL DOCKYARD** ㉕. Start at the former fortress that houses the **MARITIME MUSEUM** ㉖. The museum's collections are in several large stone buildings spread over 6 acres. Across the street is the Old Cooperage, a barre-maker's shop dating from 1831. It now houses the Neptune Cinema, as well as the Craft Market. For Bermudian art, stop next door at the **BERMUDA ARTS CENTRE AT DOCKYARD** ㉗. You can finish your tour here, or take the ferry to Somerset Island.

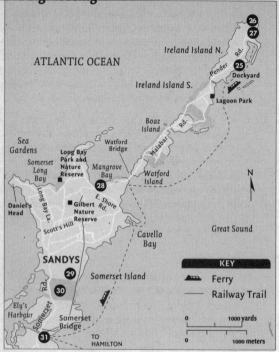

ATLANTIC OCEAN

Ireland Island N.

26
27

Pender Rd.

25
Dockyard

Ireland Island S.

Lagoon Park

Boaz
Island

Malabar Rd.

Sea
Gardens

Watford
Bridge

Long Bay Park and
Nature Reserve

Somerset
Long Bay

Mangrove
Bay

Watford
Island

N

Daniel's
Head

Long Bay La.

28

E. Shore Rd.

Gilbert
Nature
Reserve

Scott's Hill

Cavello
Bay

Great Sound

SANDYS

Somerset
Rd.

29

Somerset Island

30

KEY

Ely's
Harbour

Somerset
Bridge

31

TO
HAMILTON

Ferry

Railway Trail

0   1000 yards

0   1000 meters

Bermuda Arts
Centre at
Dockyard, 27

Fort Scaur, 30

Heydon Trust
Property, 29

Maritime
Museum, 26

Royal
Naval
Dockyard, 25

Somerset
Bridge, 31

Somerset
Village, 28

From here, you'll cross over Boaz and Watford islands to Somerset Island by ferry. The largest of all these islets, Somerset Island is fringed on both sides with beautiful secluded coves, inlets, and bays. Get off at Watford, for **SOMERSET VILLAGE** ㉘, which nestles sleepily beside pretty Mangrove Bay. If you're looking for some open space, some distance farther, opposite Willowbank guest house, is the entrance to the idyllic **HEYDON TRUST PROPERTY** ㉙. (The trek down Somerset Road past Gilbert Nature Reserve to Heydon may be too much for some, so consider a separate visit.) Just around the bend on your left is **FORT SCAUR** ㉚, which affords sweeping views of the Great Sound.

Linking Somerset Island with the rest of Bermuda is **SOMERSET BRIDGE** ㉛, said to have the world's smallest draw. Near the bridge is the Somerset ferry landing, where you can catch a ferry back to Hamilton. Across the bridge, Somerset Road becomes Middle Road, which leads into Southampton Parish.

TIMING

Allow the better part of a day for exploring this area. If you take the ferry to Somerset, look closely at the ferry schedule. The trip can take anywhere from a half hour to more than an hour, depending on which ferry you take. However, there are worse ways to while away an hour than churning across Bermuda's Great Sound. Take your bicycle or moped aboard the ferry, too, because after you stroll around Dockyard you'll need wheels to see other parts of the West End. Bus service is available twice an hour during the day along Somerset and Middle roads. But it's more sporadic during weekends, evenings, and holidays.

Sights to See

㉗ BERMUDA ARTS CENTRE AT DOCKYARD. Since it was opened by Princess Margaret in 1984, this spot has been a showcase for local artists and artisans and an excellent place to see Bermudians' work. Exhibits, which change often, include watercolors, oils, and photography. Beautifully crafted silver jewelry, hand-dyed scarves, and quilts are also sold. *Dockyard, tel. 441/234–2809. Free (donations accepted). Daily 10–5.*

30 **FORT SCAUR.** Perched on the highest hill in Somerset, the fort was completed in the 1870s. British troops were garrisoned here until World War I, and during World War II, American forces were stationed here. Little remains to be seen of that now, although the 22 acres of gardens are quite pretty, and the view of the Great Sound is fantastic. Almost worth the long climb is the Early Bermuda Weather Stone, the "perfect weather indicator." A handy plaque posted nearby explains all. *Somerset Rd., Ely's Harbour. Free. Apr.–Oct., daily 9–4:30; Nov.–Mar., daily 9–4.*

29 **HEYDON TRUST PROPERTY.** A reminder of what the island was like in its early days, this quiet, peaceful property of 41 acres has been maintained as undeveloped open space, disturbed only by citrus groves and flower gardens. If you persevere along the main path, you'll reach the tiny, rustic **Heydon Chapel,** which dates from before 1620. Services, which include Gregorian chant, are still held in the chapel at 3 PM Monday through Saturday. *Somerset Rd., tel. 441/234–1831. Free. Daily dawn–dusk.*

26 **MARITIME MUSEUM.** Opened by Queen Elizabeth II in 1975, the Maritime Museum is housed in Bermuda's largest fort, which was built to defend the Royal Naval Dockyard. You enter the museum over a moat. The exhibits are in six old munitions warehouses arranged around the parade grounds and the Keep Pond area. Bypass the tired displays pertaining to the *Sea Venture* and head for the artifacts and relics from some of the other approximately 300 ships wrecked on the island's reefs. Then seek out the restored ramparts with their commanding views of the Great Sound.

Across the street, the Neptune Cinema shows movies, and the Craft Market in the renovated **Cooperage Building** displays and sells the works of local craftspeople, including wood carvings and miniature cedar furniture. There's also a **Visitors Service Bureau** (tel. 441/234–3824) here that's open year-round, from

Monday through Friday 9:30 to 4, Sunday 11 to 3. *Dockyard, tel. 441/234–1418 Maritime Museum; 441/234–1333 Craft Market;. Maritime Museum $7.50, Craft Market free. Both daily 10–5.*

NEED A BREAK? Amid the shops in the Clocktower Building is **NANNINI'S HÄAGEN-DAZS** (tel. 441/234–2474), that staple of the sweet-tooth trade. Choose one of the 16 flavors of ice cream or nonfat soft yogurt or a cappuccino.

㉕ ROYAL NAVAL DOCKYARD. After the American Revolution, Britain found itself with neither an anchorage nor a major ship-repair yard in the western Atlantic. Around 1809, when Napoléon started to make threatening noises in Europe and British ships became increasingly vulnerable to pirate attack, Britain began construction of a major stronghold in Bermuda. The work was done by slaves and English convicts toiling under appalling conditions. Thousands of workers died before the project was completed. The shipyard functioned as such for nearly 150 years. It was closed in 1951, and the Royal Navy left Bermuda in 1995 after a 200-year presence.

Since then, the former shipyard has literally blossomed—vast stretches of concrete have been replaced with shrubs, trees, and grassy lawns. And every year seems to bring new Dockyard attractions. Besides serving as a cruise-ship terminal, there's a shopping arcade in the handsome, century-old Clocktower Building (now called the Clocktower Centre), plus a snorkel park, restaurants, and a marina with water-sports facilities.

You can reach the Dockyard in 40 minutes from Hamilton on an express bus that leaves the capital every 15 minutes or by ferry.

㉛ SOMERSET BRIDGE. Reputed to have the smallest draw in the world, this bridge on Somerset Road opens a mere 18 inches, just wide enough to accommodate a sailboat mast. When you cross over Somerset Bridge heading west, you are, as Bermudians say, "up the country."

28 SOMERSET VILLAGE. A quiet retreat, this village only has one road running through it. Somerset Village looks much as it did in 1962 when it was featured in *A Touch of Mink*, starring Doris Day and Cary Grant—a town of quiet streets and charming old buildings skirting lovely Mangrove Bay. Its few shops are mostly branches of Hamilton stores, along with two banks.

THE PARISHES

Bermuda's other points of interest—and there are many—are scattered throughout the island's parishes. This section covers the length and breadth of the colony, commenting on the major sights. Half the fun of exploring Bermuda, though, is wandering down forgotten lanes or discovering some little-known beach or cove. A moped or bicycle is ideal for this kind of travel, even though much of the island is served by buses and ferries.

TIMING

Pick a couple of close-by sights to visit rather than trying to hit them all. With roads as narrow and winding as Bermuda's it takes longer to traverse the island than you'd think. The parishes *are* less congested than the towns, but the area to the east of the capital—especially the traffic circle where Crow Lane intersects with the Lane and Trimingham Road—is very busy during morning and afternoon rush hours.

What to See

32 BERMUDA AQUARIUM, MUSEUM, AND ZOO. The aquarium has always been a pleasant diversion, but thanks to an ambitious expansion project it has become awesome. The state-of-the-art North Rock Exhibit, in the main gallery, is a 145,000-gallon tank that displays Bermuda's famed living coral reefs and colorful marine life. Other displays include a touch pool in the Local Tails Exhibit and a reptile walkway that gives you a close-up look at alligators and Galápagos tortoises. *Flatts Village, Smith's Parish, tel. 441/293–2727, www.bamz.org. $10. Daily 9–5 (last admission at 4:30), guided tours 1:10.*

34 **BERMUDA BIOLOGICAL STATION FOR RESEARCH.** In 1903—long before environmental issues were in fashion—scientists began researching marine life here. Research programs at the station deal with such issues as global change and the health of Bermuda's reefs and have focused extensively on acid rain. Guided tours of the grounds and laboratory are available to the public on Wednesday at 10 AM only, beginning in the main building. The Bermuda Biological Station for Research is also the leaving point for half-day eco-tours with David Wingate, every Thursday (weather permitting) to Non Such Island, a nature reserve with restricted access. The island is a living museum of what Bermuda was like, pre-human contact. Reservations are required for the Non Such Island tour, and lunch is included in the per-person rate. 17 *Biological La., Ferry Reach, St. George's Parish, tel. 441/297–1880. Free (donations accepted); Non Such tour $75.*

42 **BERMUDA NATIONAL TRUST.** The nonprofit organization that oversees the restoration and preservation of many of the island's gardens, open spaces, and historic buildings has its offices in Waterville, a rambling 18th-century house built by the Trimingham family. The drawing and dining rooms are open to the public during business hours. Waterville also houses the Trustworthy gift shop, which sells handmade crafts, novelties, and Trust logo items. 29 *The Lane, Paget Parish, tel. 441/236–6483, www.bnt.bm. Free (donations accepted). Bermuda National Trust weekdays 9–5, gift shop Mon.–Sat. 10–4.*

33 **BERMUDA PERFUMERY AND GARDENS.** In 1929 the Lili Perfume Factory began extracting natural fragrances from the island's flowers, and the enterprise eventually blossomed into the present perfumery and sightseeing attraction. You can take a guided tour of the factory, which is in a 200-year-old cottage with cedar beams, but the biggest draw is the aromatic nature trail teeming with oleander, frangipani, jasmine, orchids, and passionflowers that you can walk on your own. 212 *North Shore Rd., Hamilton Parish, tel. 441/293–0627 or 800/527–8213. Free. Apr.–Oct., Mon.–Sat. 9:15–5, Sun. 10–4; Nov.–Mar., Mon.–Sat. 9:15–4:30.*

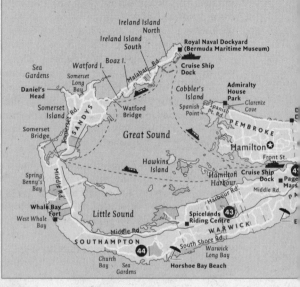

ATLANTIC OCEAN

Ireland Island North
Ireland Island South
Royal Naval Dockyard (Bermuda Maritime Museum)
Cruise Ship Dock
Sea Gardens
Watford I.
Boaz I.
Somerset Long Bay
Malabar Rd.
Daniel's Head
Cobbler's Island
Admiralty House Park
Clarence Cove
Spanish Pt. Rd.
Spanish Point
PEMBROKE
Somerset Island
Watford Bridge
SANDYS
Somerset Rd.
Somerset Bridge
Great Sound
Hamilton
Front St.
Spring Benny's Bay
Middle Rd.
Hawkins Island
Hamilton Harbour
Cruise Ship Dock
Page Mars
Whale Bay Fort
West Whale Bay
Little Sound
Harbour Rd.
Middle Rd.
Spicelands Riding Centre
43
WARWICK
SOUTHAMPTON
44
Middle Rd.
South Shore Rd.
Warwick Long Bay
Church Bay
Sea Gardens
Horshoe Bay Beach

Bermuda Aquarium, Museum, and Zoo, 32

Bermuda Biological Station for Research, 34

Bermuda National Trust, 42

Bermuda Perfumery and Gardens, 33

Botanical Gardens, 41

Christ Church, 43

Crystal Caves, 38

Fort St. Catherine, 35

Gates Fort, 36

Gibbs Hill Lighthouse, 44

St. David's Lighthouse, 37

Spittal Pond, 39

Verdmont, 40

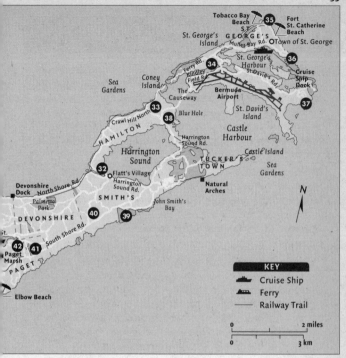

Tobacco Bay
Beach
St.
Fort
St. Catherine
Beach
St. George's GEORGE'S
Island
Muller Bay Rd. Town of St. George
St. George's
Harbour
Ferry Rd. St. David's Rd.
Kindley
Field Rd. Cruise
Ship
Dock
Sea
Gardens
Coney
Island
The
Causeway
Bermuda
Airport
St. David's
Island
HAMILTON
Crawl Hill North
Blue Hole
Harrington
Sound Rd.
Castle
Harbour
Castle Island
Harrington
Sound
TUCKER'S
TOWN
Sea
Gardens
Flatt's Village
Devonshire
Dock
North Shore Rd.
Palmetto
Park
Harrington
Sound Rd.
SMITH'S
Natural
Arches
DEVONSHIRE
John Smith's
Bay
South Shore Rd.
N
Paget
Marsh
PAGET
Elbow Beach

KEY	
Cruise Ship	
Ferry	
Railway Trail	

0   2 miles

0   3 km

The Bermuda Railway

The history of the Bermuda Railway is somewhat absurdly brief. Along with horse-drawn carriages, boats, and bicycles, it was the primary means of transportation on the island from 1931 to 1948. The Bermuda Public Works Department bandied about proposals for a railroad as early as 1899, and the Bermuda Parliament finally granted permission in 1922 for a line to run from Somerset to St. George's.

The laying of the tracks was a formidable undertaking, requiring the construction of long tunnels and swing bridges. By the time it was finished the railway had cost investors $1 million. Mile for mile, it was the most expensive railroad ever built, and the construction, which proceeded at a somnolent 2½ mi per year, was the slowest ever recorded.

Old Rattle and Shake, as it was nicknamed, began going downhill during World War II. Military personnel put the train to hard use, and it proved impossible to obtain the necessary maintenance equipment. At the end of the war the government acquired the distressed railway for $115,000. Automobiles came to Bermuda in 1946, and train service ended in 1948, when the government sold the railway in its entirety to British Guiana (now Guyana).

Today's secluded 18-mi Bermuda Railway Trail runs the length of the island along the route of the old Bermuda Railway. Restricted to pedestrians, horseback riders, and cyclists, the trail is a delightful way to see the island, away from the traffic and noise of main roads. Pick up "The Bermuda Railway Trail Guide," available at all Visitors Service Bureaus, which lists walking tours, ranging from about two to four hours, and an outline of sights to see along the way. Note that many of the trails are isolated—avoid setting out alone.

NEED A BREAK? **BAILEY'S ICE CREAM PARLOUR & FOOD D'LITES** (Blue Hole Hill, tel. 441/293–8605) has 40 varieties of freshly made natural ice cream, as well as shakes, sodas, yogurts, and sorbets. For something a bit stronger, cross the road for a rum swizzle and a "Swizzleburger" at the **SWIZZLE INN** (Blue Hole Hill, Hamilton Parish, tel. 441/293–1845).

---

41 BOTANICAL GARDENS. A fragrant haven for the island's exotic subtropical plants, flowers, and trees, the Botanical Gardens has within its 36 acres a miniature forest, an aviary, and a hibiscus garden with more than 150 species. Follow your nose to the garden filled with the scents of sweet geranium, lemon, lavender, and spices. Free 75-minute guided tours of the gardens are available several mornings a week. The pretty white house within the Gardens is **Camden** (tel. 441/236–5732), the official residence of Bermuda's premier. Camden is open for tours Tuesday and Friday noon–2 except when official functions are scheduled. *Point Finger Rd., Paget Parish, tel. 441/236–4201. Free. Daily dawn–dusk.*

43 CHRIST CHURCH. This one-story stone church with its soaring spire was built in 1719 and is reputedly the oldest Presbyterian house of worship in any British colony or dominion. It's open for Sunday services only. *Middle Rd., Warwick Parish, www.christchurch.bm.*

38 CRYSTAL CAVES. In 1907 while playing ball, two boys made a startling discovery. When the ball disappeared down a hole, the boys burrowed after it and found themselves in a vast cavern 120 ft underground, surrounded by fantastic stalagmite and stalactite formations. To visit the caves these days, you approach along a wet, sloping walkway and a wooden pontoon bridge across the underground lake—this is not for the white-glove club or the claustrophobic. After explaining the formation of stalactites and stalagmites, a tour guide uses a lighting system to make silhouettes. The caves are not open to children under 11. *8 Crystal Caves Rd., off*

Wilkinson Ave., Hamilton Parish, tel. 441/293–0640, fax 441/293–1656. $7.50. Apr.–Oct., daily 9:30–4:30; Nov.–Mar., call for hrs.

★ ☙ ❸❺ **FORT ST. CATHERINE.** Apart from Dockyard, this restored fortress is the most impressive on the island. It has enough cannons, tunnels, and ramparts to satisfy the most avid military historian— or scrambling child. The original fort was built around 1613, but it was remodeled and enlarged at least five times since then. In fact, work continued on it until late in the 19th century. As you travel through the tunnels, you'll come across some startlingly lifelike figures tucked into niches. Several dioramas depict the island's development, and an audiovisual presentation describes the building and significance of the fort. There is also a small but elaborate display of replicas of the Crown Jewels of England. 15 Coot Pond Rd., St. George's Parish, tel. 441/297–1920. $5. Daily 10–4:30.

❸❻ **GATES FORT.** St. George's has always had the greatest concentration of fortifications on Bermuda. Gates Fort is a reconstruction of a small militia fort dating from the 1620s. Don't expect turrets, towers, and tunnels, however. There is little to see here apart from the sea. The fort and Gates Bay, which it overlooks, were named for Sir Thomas Gates, the first survivor of the *Sea Venture* to reach dry land. Upon doing so, he is said to have shouted, "This is Gates, his bay!" Cut Rd., St. George's Parish, no phone. Free. Daily 10–4.

★ ☙ ❹❹ **GIBBS HILL LIGHTHOUSE.** The second cast-iron lighthouse ever built soars above Southampton Parish. Designed in London and opened in 1846, the tower stands 117 ft high and 362 ft above the sea. The light was originally produced by a concentrated burner of four large, circular wicks. Today the beam from the 1,000-watt bulb can be seen by ships 40 mi out to sea and by planes 120 mi away at 10,000 ft. The haul up the 185 spiral stairs is a long one, but you can stop to catch your breath at platforms along the way, where photographs and drawings of the lighthouse divert your attention. At the top you can stroll the balcony for a spectacular view of Bermuda. Lighthouse Rd., Southampton Parish, tel. 441/238–0524. $2.50. Daily 9–4:30.

NEED A
BREAK? A charming place to relax over breakfast, lunch, or tea and take in the island vistas is the **LIGHTHOUSE TEA ROOM,** (Lighthouse Rd., Southampton, tel. 441/238–8679) at Gibbs Hill in the lighthouse keeper's cottage.

37 ST. DAVID'S LIGHTHOUSE. Built in 1879 of Bermuda stone and occupying the highest point on Bermuda's eastern end, the lighthouse rises 208 ft above the sea. Although only about half the height of Gibbs Hill Lighthouse in Southampton Parish, it nevertheless has spectacular views. From the balcony you can see St. David's and St. George's, Castle Harbour, and the reef-fringed south shore. The lighthouse is not always open. Check with the Park Ranger's Office (tel. 441/236–5902) for hours. *St. George's Parish.*

NEED A
BREAK? Right on the water near St. David's Lighthouse, the casual **BLACK HORSE TAVERN** (Clarkes Hill, tel. 441/297–1991) serves delicious, sandwiches, shark hash, and curried conch stew. It's closed Monday.

★ **39 SPITTAL POND.** A showcase of the Bermuda National Trust, this nature park has 60 acres for carefree roaming, although you're asked to keep to the walkways. More than 25 species of waterfowl winter here between November and May. On a high bluff overlooking the ocean, Spanish Rock stands out as an oddity. Early settlers found this rock crudely carved with the date 1543 and other markings that were unclear. It's now believed that a Portuguese ship was wrecked on the island in 1543 and that her sailors built a new ship on which they departed. The carvings are thought to be the initials RP (for *Rex Portugaline,* King of Portugal) and the cross to be a badge of the Portuguese Order of Christ. The rock was removed to prevent further damage by erosion, and the site is marked by a bronze casting of the original carving. A plaster-of-paris cast of the Spanish Rock is also on display at the Bermuda

Smart Sightseeings

Savvy travelers and others who take their sightseeing seriously have skills worth knowing about.

DON'T PLAN YOUR VISIT IN YOUR HOTEL ROOM Don't wait until your plane lands to decide how to spend your days. It's inevitable that there will be much more to see and do than you'll have time for: choose sights in advance.

ORGANIZE YOUR TOURING Note the places that most interest you on a map, and visit places that are near each other during the same morning or afternoon.

START THE DAY WELL EQUIPPED Leave your hotel in the morning with everything you need for the day—maps, medicines, extra film, your guidebook, bathing suit, and a change of clothing.

TOUR MUSEUMS EARLY If you're there when the doors open you'll have an intimate experience of the collection.

EASY DOES IT See museums in the mornings, when you're fresh, and visit sit-down attractions later on. Take breaks before you need them.

STRIKE UP A CONVERSATION Only curmudgeons don't respond to a smile and a polite request for information. Most people appreciate your interest in their home town. And your conversations may end up being your most vivid memories.

GET LOST When you do, you never know what you'll find—but you can count on it being memorable. Use your guidebook to help you get back on track. Build wandering-around time into every day.

QUIT BEFORE YOU'RE TIRED There's no point in seeing that one extra sight if you're too exhausted to enjoy it.

TAKE YOUR MOTHER'S ADVICE Go to the bathroom when you have the chance. You never know what lies ahead.

Historical Society Museum, in Hamilton. *South Shore Rd., Smith's Parish, no phone. Free. Daily dawn–dusk.*

★ ⓐ **VERDMONT.** Now owned by the Bermuda National Trust, Verdmont was opened as a museum in 1956. It's not definitively known, but the house may have been built by prominent shipowner John Dickinson around 1710. It resembles a small English manor house and has an unusual double roof and four large chimneys: each of the eight rooms has its own fireplace. Elegant cornice moldings and paneled shutters grace the two large reception rooms downstairs, originally the drawing room and formal dining room. Some of the furniture is imported from England—there is an exquisite early 19th-century piano—but most of it is fine 18th-century cedar, crafted by Bermudian cabinetmakers. A china coffee service, said to have been a gift from Napoléon to President Madison, is also on display. The president never received it. The ship bearing it across the Atlantic was seized by a Bermudian privateer and brought to Bermuda. *Collector's Hill, Smith's Parish, tel. 441/236–7369. $3; $5 combination ticket with Bermuda National Trust Museum and Tucker House in St. George's. Tues.–Sat. 10–4.*

The night air is warm and humid, and a group of friends are among the many hopping from bar to bar in and around the quaint Front Street area. As they wander, different sounds of pop, dance, and Soca music come and ago from open doorways, drowning out the sounds of laughter and muzzled talking from inside. Diners sit and watch the world go by from open-fronted eateries, as do guests on board the giant cruise ships that line Hamilton Harbour as they stand on deck catching some of the heavy air. In the distance, somewhere out in the darkness of the harbor, the lights of boats can be seen and the drums of Soca music heard as locals and tourists take their socializing out on the ocean waves. There's a lot to do, but will they manage to do it all during their stay? They will certainly have fun trying.

In This Chapter

How and Where 167 • Sources 167 • Bars and Lounges 168 • After Hours 171 • Music Clubs 172

Revised by Karen Smith

nightlife

BECAUSE BERMUDA HAS NO CASINOS and only a few nightclubs, you'll find most of the action in pubs (many of which serve light fare), lounges, and hotel bars; on evening boat excursions; and at beach parties and local hangouts. But don't overlook the work of local musicians: Bermuda has a long tradition of producing superb jazz artists and hosts an annual jazz festival in the fall. One of the best places to catch a jam session is at Hubie's Bar on Friday night; it's a typical smoky jazz bar, with an obscure entrance in a somewhat dicey area of town. However, everyone knows where Hubie's is—and it's the kind of club where you'll see the common man rubbing shoulders with members of Parliament.

HOW AND WHERE

As a general rule, men tend to dress smart casual for clubs. This means you may not want to wear your T-shirts, jeans, or running shoes. For women the dress code is casual chic, or just plain casual. Pubs and clubs begin to fill up around 9:30 or 10.

SOURCES

Most venues are open year-round. Check *This Week in Bermuda* and *Preview of Bermuda,* free publications available in all hotels and tourist-information centers, for the latest information on who's playing or what's going on.

BARS AND LOUNGES

Most of these bars serve light pub fare, in addition to a mean rum swizzle or a Dark and Stormy, two local rum-based drinks.

Hamilton

THE BEACH (Front St., tel. 441/292–0219). If what you're looking for is a reasonably priced drink without the pretensions of upscale bars, then the Beach is your place. For the locals, it's the spot to hang out either straight from work or when everywhere else has closed. It attracts a mixed crowd, has seating outside, and is open until 3 AM daily.

BLUE JUICE (Bermuda House La., off Front St., Hamilton, tel. 441/292–4507). One of the newest bars in Bermuda and certainly the trendiest, Blue Juice (next to Tuscany, an Italian restaurant) attracts the younger set and has an open-air courtyard area with a video screen, as well as an indoor bar. If the rain does come down, as is common in Bermuda, a canvas roof is pulled out in seconds. Appetizers are served at lunch and dinner, and the bar stays open until 3 AM daily. Its popularity means you should be prepared to wait.

CASEY'S (Queen St., across from the Little Theatre, tel. 441/292–9994). If you like to toss a few back in a hard-core bar, consider Casey's, a narrow room with a jukebox and a few tables. It's by no means fancy or touristy, and it really packs them in, especially on Friday night. Casey's is open 10–10 every day except Sunday.

COCONUT ROCK (20 Reid St., tel. 441/292–1043). With a trendy Bermudian restaurant on one level and an even trendier sushi bar called Yashi in the back, this place is filled with music and Hamilton's young and beautiful. Yet it's interesting and fun, and open daily for lunch and dinner (Sunday dinner only). Don't confuse this place with Coconuts, the upscale restaurant at the Reefs resort in Southampton.

DOCKSIDER (Front St., tel. 441/296–3333). This pub attracts a mixed crowd of visitors and locals with a new sports-and-entertainment big-screen TV. If the activity at the long cedar bar is too noisy, opt for the wine bar, which is quieter and more intimate, or the poolroom. A nightclub ($10 cover) in the back room plays dance, pop, and Soca music (a fast, steel pan–based music whose name is derived from "the soul of calypso"). Docksider is open until 1 AM Sunday through Thursday and 2 AM on Friday and Saturday.

FLANAGAN'S IRISH PUB & RESTAURANT (69 Front St., tel. 441/295–8299). On the second floor of the Emporium Building, this pub is a favorite for folks who like to dance and talk over drinks. Lots of exotic, fun drinks, like frozen mudslides, are on offer. Local music groups entertain Wednesday through Saturday nights during high season—they go on after 10. Otherwise a giant TV screen flickers with sporting events. It's open daily year-round, 11 AM to 1 AM.

FRESCO'S WINE BAR & RESTAURANT (2 Chancery La., tel. 441/295–5058). A great place for a bottle or glass of wine or dessert, Fresco's (formerly the Chancery Wine Bar) has enclosed the European-style patio for year-round use. It's open daily for lunch, dinner, or drinks at the upstairs bar.

HOG PENNY (Burnaby St., tel. 441/292–2534). Small and cozy, the Hog Penny is decked out in dark wood and resembles a down-to-earth English country pub. Lunch and dinner are reasonably priced, and it's particularly popular on the weekend. During the summer a live band plays most nights—in winter, just Friday and Saturday—and the floor is cleared for dancing, sometimes even on the tables. It's open to 1 AM daily, but be warned—it can be very busy.

M. R. ONIONS (Par-la-Ville Rd.,, tel. 441/292–5012). Off the beaten track, friendly M. R.'s likes to market itself as a sports bar—you can watch any number of sports on several wide-screen TVs and also access the Internet ($10 for the first hour and

$5 thereafter)—but it's also a restaurant in its own right. At press time, a major face-lift was planned.

THE PICKLED ONION (53 Front St., tel. 441/295–2263). This restaurant and bar caters to a well-heeled crowd of locals and visitors. Live music—usually jazz and pop—plays nightly from about 10:30 PM to 1 AM in the high season and irregularly off-season.

ROBIN HOOD (Richmond Rd., tel. 441/295–3314). The casual and friendly Robin Hood is popular at night for pub fare, pizza, and patio dining under the stars. Sports can be watched almost anytime it seems on the TV screens.

Outside Hamilton

FROG AND ONION (Cooperage Building, Dockyard, Sandys, tel. 441/234–2900). A very popular eating place, the Frog and Onion serves a splendid variety of down-to-earth pub fare in a dark wood, barnlike setting. If you're spending the day at Dockyard, it's a great place to recharge your batteries. Plus it's open every day until late.

HENRY VIII (South Shore Rd., Southampton, tel. 441/238–1977). There's always local or visiting entertainment at this ever-popular watering hole. The dark pub is decorated with rich oak paneling and polished brass. A competent menu of English and Bermudian fare is also offered for lunch and dinner. However, those looking for a quiet chat in the late evening may find the volume of music off-putting.

THE LOYALTY INN (Somerset Rd., Somerset, tel. 441/234–4502). Reopened in 2001 after several years of inactivity, Loyalty aims to please the whole family, kids and all, and has a relaxed atmosphere, a small restaurant area, and live music. Kids have the run of a children's play area on site.

SWIZZLE INN (3 Blue Hole Hill, Hamilton Parish, tel. 441/293–1854). "Swizzle Inn, swagger out" is the motto at this watering hole catering to a young crowd. Decor elements include a dartboard, a jukebox that plays soft and hard rock, and business cards from all over the world tacked on the walls, ceilings, and doors. The food is actually quite good, and because Swizzle Inn is in the Bailey's Bay area, between Hamilton and St. George's, it makes an ideal stop-off when going to or from the nearby airport.

WHARF TAVERN (Somers Wharf, St. George's, tel. 441/297–1515). The yachting crowd gathers here for rum swizzles and nautical talk. There's also a moderately priced pub-style menu.

Dance Clubs

CLUB AZURE (511 South Side St., St. David's, tel. 441/297–3070). This is a trendy club where the hip people go on a night out in the island's east end. It's busiest on weekends, of course, and is open until the early hours—sometimes with thematic dance nights and performers. Be prepared to boogie.

ESCAPE VENUE (Par-la-Ville Rd., below M. R. Onions, Hamilton, tel. 441/292–7978). Reopened in 2000, Escape attracts young trendy things who seriously like to dance. It tends to be open Thursday, Friday, and Saturday nights until about 3 AM, but you should call beforehand to check.

THE OASIS (Emporium Bldg., Front St., Hamilton, tel. 441/292–4978 or 441/292–3379). A hot dance spot for rock and disco, the Oasis draws a somewhat younger crowd who gladly pay the $10 cover charge. In high season, there's dancing nightly from 9 PM to 3 AM. One of Bermuda's top bands, the Kennel Boys, plays Wednesday–Saturday, beginning at midnight.

AFTER HOURS

Around 3 AM, when bars and clubs close, head for the **ICE QUEEN** (Middle Rd., Paget, tel. 441/236–3136). It's like a drive-in movie without the movie: The parking lot is just jammed with cars and mopeds. The main attraction are the $3.25 burgers, or the fish

The Local Music Scene

A tiny music scene has emerged from Bermuda's population of 60,000. The island's longtime superstar **GENE STEEDE**—a guitarist, singer, and comedian who has been described as Tony Bennett, Harry Belafonte, and Johnny Carson rolled into one—can usually be found, with his band, at the airport arrivals hall greeting visitors with bouncy island music. He plays other venues, too. Other popular acts to seek out are the **COCA-COLA STEEL BAND** and the calypso-playing **BERMUDA STROLLERS**. **SHARX** is a rock band, heard at many conventions and private parties. A band that has been around a few years but is just now getting the recognition it deserves is the **KENNEL BOYS**, who perform at the Oasis. **TROPICAL HEAT**, with a reggae-calypso-Soca-Latin sound, is a regular at Hawkins Island's "Don't Stop the Carnival" party, which runs from May to October. Some of the Bermuda bands list their performance dates and venues at www.bermuda.com.

on a bun for $5.50, which taste terrific after a night on the town. The Ice Queen opens at 10 AM, which also makes it a good stop for an afternoon ice cream break.

As the name indicates, **AFTER HOURS** (117 South Rd., past intersection with Middle Rd., Paget, tel. 441/236-8563) is another late-night spot. It opens at midnight and serves good curries, hamburgers, and sandwiches until 4 AM.

MUSIC CLUBS

Given that the island is 500 mi from the United States, and much farther from anywhere else, it makes sense that in Bermuda the music scene is pretty much dominated by local bands, playing the hotel-and-pub circuit. Outside performers are billed occasionally, particularly during the Bermuda Festival (☞ Cultural Activities). Music is generally Afro-Caribbean–inspired, with reggae, calypso, and steel-drum bands at the forefront. Jazz is a big deal on Bermuda, too, which culminates in the annual Bermuda Jazz Festival.

Calypso

CLAYHOUSE INN (North Shore Rd., Devonshire, tel. 441/292–3193). Clayhouse is the place to be. Expect a rowdy show starring limbo dancers, the Bermuda Strollers, the Coca-Cola Steel Band, and an occasional big name. Shows are at 10:15 Monday through Thursday. About $23 covers the entry fee plus two drinks. A range of entertainment is laid on for the weekend.

Folk

BERMUDA FOLK CLUB (Old Colony Club, Trott Rd., Hamilton, tel. 441/296–6362). Monthly get-togethers, which usually take place at 8:30 on the first Saturday of the month, constitute Bermuda's only folk music venue, although the musicians might cover any number of musical styles besides folk. Drinks are often served at happy-hour prices, and the cover is $6 but can rise to more than $20 for off-island acts. It's worth calling for nights other than first Saturdays, too, as unpublicized gigs and events sometimes pop up.

Jazz

BERMUDA JAZZ FESTIVAL (441/292–0023 for information; 441/295–4839 for tickets). Tickets are available through **TicketWeb** (tel. 800/965–4827 in the U.S., www.ticketweb.com). The often sold-out Bermuda Jazz Festival, which celebrates its seventh year in 2002, kicks off each fall at Dockyard, usually during a long weekend in September. Local and internationally known jazz artists pump out the tunes, and tickets go fast. Shop around for hotel-and-festival combination packages.

Hotel Bars and Lounges

Too lazy to call a cab and too prettied up to ride your moped? Some of the island's nightlife takes place at hotel bars—maybe even yours. Non-guests are welcome, too.

Ariel Sands: Caliban's beachside Brownies Bar in Devonshire is the bar du jour. While in here, don't neglect to browse actor-and-owner Michael Douglas's personal photographs, which adorn the walls.

Cambridge Beaches: The serious dark-wood British pub and lovely outdoor terrace have music nightly (in season). Because it's a West End resort, you'll mostly mingle with hotel guests or those benefiting from a dine-around program.

Elbow Beach: Near Hamilton, yet not Hamilton, Café Lido and the Veranda Bar are both open until midnight (or 1 [am] in season). Café Lido has indoor and outdoor seating, and the Veranda Bar is more of a piano bar (live music nightly), with an adjacent cigar room.

Fairmont Southampton Princess: The spacious Neptune Lounge and dance floor has nightly live music starting around 9:30 until midnight.

The Reefs: Nightly piano or Calypso music brings lots of folks to the clubhouse cocktail lounge strewn with sofas, tiny tables, a long bar. It's an especially good spot to stop if you're staying east of Warwick.

HUBIE'S BAR (Angle St., Hamilton, tel. 441/293–9287). Hubie's, located off Court Street, attracts jovial locals and visitors who appreciate good live jazz at a weekly session on Friday from 7 to 10 PM. It's best to take a cab, as the area can be dangerous at night. There is a cover charge of $5.

THE LOFT (Somerset Rd., next to Thel's Cafe, Somerset). Strictly for jazz and blues lovers, the Loft opened at the end of 2000 and hosts live performers on a Friday and Saturday night between 8 PM and midnight.

A poet sitting in one of the overstuffed chairs of a local coffeehouse sips a double café latte while chatting with his friend, a well-known painter. "Bermuda," the poet declares solemnly, "is in the midst of an artistic renaissance." The painter shakes his head affably while nibbling on biscotti, pulls out his work to discuss a show at the Bermuda National Gallery. For such a small island, Bermuda has a surprisingly diverse cultural scene. Like so much else here, some of the island's best cultural events are slightly tucked away. But it's always worth the extra effort it takes to discover them.

In This Chapter

Sources 177 • Venues and Societies 178 • Dance 179 • Film 180 • Kids' Stuff 181 • Music 182 • Readings and Talks 183 • Theater 183 • Tours 185

By Kim Dismont Robinson

cultural activities and events

EXCEPT WHAT HAMILTON'S NUMEROUS ART GALLERIES and the in-the-know Reid Street coffeehouse, Rock Island Coffee Cafe, provide, Bermuda doesn't have a cultural center per se. In fact, if you are arts-inclined, consider a stop at Rock Island, where you can kill two birds with one stone—it's become the unofficial watering hole for Bermuda's eclectic group of artists and doubles as an informal art space. Bermudian poet Andra Simons often works behind the counter and he introduced open-mike poetry to the island with Flow Sunday, an event at which you can also meet a number of other local artists who can give you the lowdown on weekly events.

If you're looking for a more formal show, Bermuda's best bet is the Bermuda National Gallery. For dramatic and musical performances, the City Hall Theatre and the Ruth Seaton James Auditorium host the country's best, including the annual Bermuda Festival. For music, *see* Nightlife.

SOURCES

The Bermuda Department of Tourism and all of its Visitors Service Bureaus give away the "Bermuda Calendar of Events" brochure. The informative *Preview of Bermuda* also describes upcoming island events. The glossy monthly magazine *The Bermudian* ($4) has a calendar of events, as does *RG Magazine*, another glossy monthly magazine that is included free in the

Bermuda Festival

In January and February, the **BERMUDA FESTIVAL** brings internationally renowned artists to the island. The two-month program includes theater and classical and jazz concerts. In 2001 the Bermuda Festival featured an impressive list of performers that included a capella vocal ensemble I Fagiolini, bass singer Willard White's tribute to Paul Robeson, the Philadelphia Virtuosi Chamber Orchestra, and the Ballethnic Dance Company. Most shows take place in City Hall, with additional lunchtime and cocktail-hour concerts at various venues. Ticket prices range from $15 to $35. For information and reservations, contact Bermuda Festivals Ltd. (Suite 480, 48 Par-la-Ville Rd., Hamilton HM 11, tel. 441/292–8572 Dec.–Feb.; 441/295–1291 Mar.–Nov.; fax 441/295–7403 Dec.–Feb.; 441/295–7403 Mar.–Nov.;, www.bermudafestival.com) or the Bermuda Department of Tourism.

Royal Gazette newspaper on or around the first of the month. Some hotels carry a **TV STATION** that broadcasts information about cultural events and nightlife on the island. **RADIO VSB**, FM 1450, gives a lineup of events daily at 11:15 AM. Or you can **DIAL 974** for recorded information on nature walks, tours, cultural events, afternoon teas, and seasonal events. **ROCK ISLAND COFFEE CAFE** (48 Reid St., Hamilton, tel. 441/296–5241) is also a good place to stop and ask what's going on.

VENUES AND SOCIETIES

Because the arts scene in Bermuda is so casual, many of the events and performing groups listed below operate on a seasonal or part-time basis. If you see a bulletin board, inspect it for posters advertising upcoming events.

Meet local painters and see some of their work at the **BERMUDA SOCIETY OF ARTS** (Front St., Hamilton, tel. 441/292–3824, fax 441/296–0699, www.bermuda.bm/bsoa), on the top floor of City Hall.

CITY HALL THEATRE (City Hall, Church St., Hamilton) is the major venue for a number of top-quality cultural events each year. Contact the **BOX OFFICE** (Visitors Service Bureau, tel. 441/295–1727) for reservations and for information about all cultural events on the island.

DANCE

The **BERMUDA CIVIC BALLET** (Box HM 661, Hamilton HMCX, tel. 441/293–4147) performs classical ballet at various venues during the academic year. Internationally known artists sometimes appear as guests. The group is affiliated with the Bermuda School of Russian Ballet.

The **BERMUDA SCHOOL OF RUSSIAN BALLET** (Box HM 661, Hamilton HM CX, tel. 441/293–4147 or 441/295–8621) has been around for half a century and presents unique ballet and modern dance performances. Show times and venues vary, so call for details.

The **JACKSON SCHOOL OF PERFORMING ARTS** (Arcade Bldg., Burnaby St., Hamilton, tel. 441/292–5815 or 441/292–2927) is comparable to U.S. schools which train talented young artists. Seek out their innovative gymnastics and dance program performances.

The **NATIONAL DANCE THEATRE OF BERMUDA** (Box 1759, Hamilton HM HX, tel. 441/239–4091) began in 1980 and has enjoyed much success in Bermuda and abroad. The company presents classical, modern, and jazz performances throughout the academic year.

UNITED DANCE PRODUCTIONS (UDP; Alexandrina Hall, 75 Court St., Hamilton, tel. 441/295–9933 or 441/295–0397), under

Gombey Dancers

The Gombey dancer is one of the island's most enduring and uniquely Bermudian cultural icons. The Gombey (pronounced gum-bay) tradition here dates from at least the mid-18th century when enslaved Africans and Native Americans covertly practiced a unique form of dance, also incorporating West Indian, British, and biblical influences. Nowadays, Gombeys mainly perform on major holidays, during which time Bermudians will go to "dance with the Gombeys".

The Gombey name originates from a West African word which means, literally, "rustic drum." The masked, exclusively male dancers move to the accompaniment of Congolese-style drums and the shrill, whistle-blown commands of the troupe's captain. The whistle commands, the staccato drum accompaniment, and the ritualistic, often frenetic movements of the dancers are passed from generation to generation.

The dancers' colorful costumes include tall headdresses decorated with peacock feathers and capes covered with intricate embroidery, ribbons, and tiny mirrors. It's traditional to toss money at the dancers' feet. Performance times and locations vary, but check out the No. 1 Shed on Front Street on Tuesday afternoons around 3 or consult the Bermuda Department of Tourism.

the artistic direction of Suzette Harvey, has been around for more than a decade. UDP has a reputation for producing some of the island's most funky, creative dance shows featuring modern, African, hip-hop, ballet, jazz, and tap dance. Show times and venues vary, so call for details.

FILM

Bermuda has four cinemas showing first-run movies: two in Hamilton, one in St. George's, and another in the West End. Check the listings in the *Royal Gazette* for movies and show times.

The **BERMUDA INTERNATIONAL FILM FESTIVAL** (Box HM 2963, Hamilton HM MX, tel. 441/293–3456, fax 441/293–7769, www.bermudafilmfest.com) is a relatively new festival celebrating an international array of independent films. Screening lasts a full week during late April or early May at the cinemas in Hamilton. Directors and stars mingle with a congenial audience of visitors and locals. Tickets are sold for individual films as well as for workshops and seminars on topics that include screenwriting, camera techniques, and the marketing of independent films. Festival parties are also popular as Hamilton mimics—for a few days at least—the Hollywood-style glamour of Sundance, minus stretch limos.

LIBERTY THEATRE (Union and Victoria Sts., Hamilton, tel. 441/291–2035) is a 270-seat cinema with four daily show times, including a daily matinee. The area immediately outside the theater is safe during the day, but you should not linger in this neighborhood after dark.

The **LITTLE THEATRE** (Queen St., Hamilton, tel. 441/292–2135) is a 173-seat theater across the street from Casey's Bar. There are usually three show times per night.

NEPTUNE CINEMA (The Cooperage, Dockyard, tel. 441/291–2035) is a 118-seat cinema that typically shows feature films twice nightly, with matinees Friday, Saturday, and Sunday.

SOUTHSIDE CINEMA (1 Kindley Field Rd., St. David's, tel. 441/297–2821) is the island's largest theater. It's a fairly new facility, located on the former U.S. military base near the airport. Show times are usually 7:30 nightly. Advanced tickets are available at **UNLIMITED SUPPLIES** (2 Woodlands Rd., Hamilton, tel. 441/295–9229).

KIDS' STUFF

The whole family can play a few games of mini-golf at the **BERMUDA GOLF ACADEMY AND DRIVING RANGE** (Industrial

Park Rd. off Middle Rd., Southampton, tel. 441/238–8800). It's open daily from 9 AM to 10 PM. Admission is $7.50.

The Youth Branch of the **BERMUDA NATIONAL LIBRARY** (74 Church St., Hamilton, tel. 441/295–0487) has a number of programs including a weekly Movie Day and Story Time.

Several island **PLAYGROUNDS,** especially near the beaches, can add extra fun to family day by the sea. Some of the best ones are those at Shelly Bay, St. George's, Clearwater, Warwick, and Dockyard.

ROCK RAMBLERS (tel. 441/238–3438), a local eco-heritage group, leads walks on the Tribe Roads, beaches, and fort grounds. The tours are about $10–$15 per person and usually last for about an hour and a half. Children under 12 are free but must be accompanied by an adult. The tours can be customized for children's interests with advance notice.

The Town Crier of St. George (E. Michael Jones, who acts as a kind of cultural ambassador) hosts **TOASTED MARSHMALLOW & FIRESIDE CHATS** (tel. 441/297–8000) most weekends January through April. The guided tour includes a visit to the St. George's Historical Society Museum. A fire is lit in the museum garden, and toasted marshmallows are shared along with Bermuda folklore. Tickets are $20 for adults, and children under 16 are free.

MUSIC

The **BERMUDA CONSERVATORY OF MUSIC** (BCM; Colony Club, Trott Rd., Hamilton, tel. 441/296–5100) was formed in 1997 by merging the country's two leading music schools. Concerts are presented periodically during the academic year at various venues.

The **BERMUDA PHILHARMONIC SOCIETY** (Box HM 552, Hamilton HM CX, tel. 441/291–6690, fax 441/295–3770), now in its 40th season, presents several programs throughout the year featuring both the full orchestra and various soloists. Students of the Menuhin Foundation, established in Bermuda by the late violin virtuoso Yehudi Menuhin, sometimes perform with the orchestra. Visiting musicians often participate in these events.

The **GILBERT & SULLIVAN SOCIETY OF BERMUDA** (Box HM 3098, Hamilton HM NX, tel. 441/295–3218, fax 441/295–6812), devoted to performing the works of the famous libretto- and playwriting duo, began in 1972 under the name Warwick Players. The society puts on a musical each year, usually in October. In addition to Gilbert and Sullivan operettas, the group occasionally stages Broadway shows.

READINGS AND TALKS

There are two major open-mike poetry hot spots in Bermuda. Both start with hip-hop and jazz music played on turntables by DJ Beatnik.

FLOW SUNDAY (Andra Simons, tel. 441/296–6457), founded in 1997 by poet Andra Simons, was the first island event in which poets and musicians were allowed a no-holds-barred forum for artistic expression. Flow is held on alternate Sunday nights, sometimes at Rock Island Coffee Cafe. Contact Simons for the venue.

The mission statement of open-mike poetry session **NENO LETU** is "Bring the Word." Founded in 1999, the group meets alternate Wednesdays at **Hubie's Bar** (Angle St., Hamilton, tel. 441/293–9287).

The **BERMUDA NATIONAL GALLERY** (City Hall, Church St., Hamilton, tel. 441/295–9428) often hosts a series of lunchtime lectures on art and film. You can stop by or call the gallery for a schedule.

THEATER

The **BERMUDA MUSICAL & DRAMATIC SOCIETY** (Box DV 631, Devonshire DV BX, tel. 441/292–0848 or 441/295–5584) has

Bermuda Books

Bermuda has a small literary legacy involving Eugene O'Neill, Noel Coward, and James Thurber, who used the island as a writing retreat, and lots of locals whose books you may want to acquaint yourself with during your visit.

For a history of the island from the Sea Venture wreck to the present, check out historian W. S. Zuill's The Story of Bermuda and Her People. Cyril Outerbridge Packwood's Chained on the Rock is an extensive historical account of slavery in Bermuda. Two popular books of childhood recollections include Nothin' but a Pond Dog and the sequel, The Fires of Pembroke, by Llewellyn Emery.

Your Bermuda, by George Rushe, is an excellent, alphabetical pocket encyclopedia covering a multitude of Bermudian subjects. Another World: Bermuda and the Rise of Modern Tourism is an extensive and sometimes humorous analysis written by Duncan McDowall.

For fiction buffs, Palmetto Wine and An Isle So Long Unknown are two good short story collections. If you're interested in social commentary, check out collected essays by local journalists such as Vernon Jackson's Paradise Found, Almost! and Larry Burchall's The Other Side: Looking Behind the Shield. Younger readers might like Elizabeth Musson Kawaley's The Island That Disappeared, historical fiction about Bermuda during the 1920s, and Bermudian artist Elizabeth Mulderig's three Tiny the Tree Frog books.

Eric Amos's Birds of Bermuda and Bermuda's Botanical Wonderland by Christine Watlington are two good picks for the nature lover.

For these and other titles, check with the Bermuda Book Store (tel. 441/ 295–3698) or True Reflections (tel. 441/295–9424) in Hamilton—most are hard to find off island.

some good amateur actors on its roster. Formed in 1944, this active theater society stages performances year-round in the society's Daylesford headquarters, one block north of City Hall. The Christmas pantomime is always a sellout, as are most other performances. Visit or call the box office at Daylesford, on Dundonald Street, for reservations and information. Tickets are about $10.

Debuting in 2000, the **FESTIVAL FRINGE,** held at the same time as the annual Bermuda Festival, was designed to complement the more formal Bermuda Festival performances with smaller, avant-garde ones by local and visiting artists. Schedules and ticket information are available from the Bermuda Department of Tourism (tel. 441/292–0023 in Bermuda; tel. 800/223–6106 in the U.S.) or from the Bermuda Department of Cultural Affairs (tel. 441/292–9447).

Bermuda is the only place outside the United States where Harvard University's **HASTY PUDDING THEATRICALS** performs. For almost 30 years this satirical troupe has entertained the island during Bermuda College Weeks (March–April). Produced by the Bermuda Musical and Dramatic Society, each of these Bermuda-based shows incorporates political and social issues of the past year. They're all staged at the City Hall Theatre (☞ *above*). Tickets are about $20.

TOURS
Garden and Wildlife Tours

Free 75-minute guided tours of the **BOTANICAL GARDENS** (tel. 441/236–5291 or 441/236–4201) leave at 10:30 AM from the car park by the Berry Hill Road entrance year-round: Tuesday, Wednesday, and Friday from April to October, and Tuesday and Friday from November to March. You can also take a tour by special arrangement with the curator of the gardens, in exchange for a donation to the Botanical Society.

DAVID WINGATE (Bermuda Biological Institute, 17 Biological La., Ferry Reach, St. George's Parish, tel. 441/297–1880) is a local celebrity for his passionate commitment to Bermuda's wildlife and environment. Almost single-handedly, Wingate has revivified the cahow bird population and cedar trees on Bermuda. His significant role on the island dates at least as far back as 1962, when Wingate's project began on Non Such Island, an uninhabited island in northeast Bermuda that acts as an environmental microcosm of Bermuda. Because of its somewhat quarantined state, Non Such became an ideal setting for birds, plants, and other near-extinct species to be safely reintroduced. On a tour here, you can see the natural world restoring itself to its precolonial state and learn about the ecological relationships of Bermuda's various indigenous wildlife. Nature tours with Wingate ($75; 3–4 hours) include a 15-minute boat ride to the island and lunch and can be arranged through the Bermuda Biological Institute.

In spring, the **GARDEN CLUB OF BERMUDA** (Visitors Service Bureau, tel. 441/295–1480) arranges tours to three different houses each Wednesday between 1 and 4. Admission is $12.

The enjoyable walking tours organized by **NATIVE ADVENTURES** (tel. 441/295–2957) allow you to experience Bermuda's natural beauty and remote corners through the eyes of a professional photographer. Tamell Simons leads 3-hour tours at $95 per person. The cost includes film and developing, and groups of six receive a 15% discount. Advance bookings are recommended.

Historical Tours

The **BERMUDA DEPARTMENT OF TOURISM** (BDT; tel. 441/292–0023) publishes brochures with self-guided tours of Hamilton, St. George's, the West End, and the Railway Trail. Available free at all Visitor Service Bureaus and at hotels and guest houses, the brochures also contain detailed directions for walkers and cyclists as well as historical notes and anecdotes.

From November through March, the BDT coordinates walking tours of Hamilton, St. George's, Spittal Pond Nature Reserve, the Royal Naval Dockyard, and Somerset. The tours of Hamilton and St. George's, as well as most of the Royal Naval Dockyard tours, take in historic buildings, while the Spittal Pond and Somerset tours focus on the island's flora.

OUT & ABOUT BERMUDA (tel. 441/295–2595, www.bermudashorts. bm/outandabout) leads walking tours through some of Bermuda's most scenic nature reserves, parks, residential neighborhoods, and historic areas. The cost is $20–$30 per person, and tours are limited to about six.

TIM ROGERS (tel. 441/234–4082, fax 441/238–2773), a witty British transplant who has lived on Bermuda for more than a decade, leads exceptional walks (and seated talks) about various Bermuda topics that other historians or guides sticking to their textbooks may be hesitant to relay. Rogers's humorous and conversational tours yield intriguing historical material on piracy, local ghosts and lore, and the island's more interesting architectural motifs. Rogers operates out of several hotels, like the Southampton Princess and Daniel's Head Village Resort near Somerset on the West End. Nonguests are welcome to join the tour. A 90-minute walking tour costs $15. Rogers also offers private tours at $35 per hour.

The **WALKING CLUB OF BERMUDA** (Laura Gorham, tel. 441/ 295–9428, www.walk.free.bm) is an exercise club that provides visitors with a social opportunity to meet Bermudians while seeing the island. Walks are of varied length and refreshments included in the fee are served afterward. A $20 yearly membership fee is required. Donations are welcome for non-members at the beginning of the walk.

Horse-drawn Carriage Tours

You can hire carriages on Front Street in Hamilton—a Bermuda tradition among the just-married. Rates for a one- or two-horse

Winter Festivals and Events

Planning a snow-free Christmas? With these seasonal activities, you won't miss shoveling the walk one little bit. Contact the Bermuda Department of Tourism (800/Bermuda or www.bermudatourism.com) for more information.

DECEMBER

Christmas Boat Parade: A parade of lighted yachts and boats of many sizes in Hamilton Harbour, culminating in a fireworks extravaganza.

Hamilton Jaycees Santa Claus Parade: Just before Christmas, Father Christmas visits Front Street, along with bands and floats.

Christmas Eve: Midnight candlelight services are held in churches of all denominations.

Christmas: A public holiday—with dramatic hotel brunches.

Boxing Day: (Dec. 26) A public holiday, traditionally for visiting friends and family. Look for a variety of sports events, and the Bermuda Gombey Dancers around town.

St. George's New Year's Eve Celebration: King's Square and Ordnance Island have food stalls, rides for children, and continuous entertainment by local musicians. A midnight countdown and dropping of the "onion" are followed by fireworks.

JANUARY

New Year's Day: A public holiday, yet all sightseeing attractions and restaurants remain open.

Bermuda International Race Weekend: (Early Jan.) Top international runners participate in marathon and other races. Most races and a 10-km walk are open to all.

Bermuda Festival: This two-month program attracts internationally known artists for concerts, dance and theater.

carriage for up to four passengers are approximately $20 for 30 minutes. Each adult is charged an additional $5 per half hour when more than five people ride in one carriage.

Taxi and Minibus Tours

For an independent tour of Bermuda, a taxi is a good but more expensive alternative to a group tour. A blue flag on the hood of a cab indicates that the driver is a qualified tour guide. These cabs can be difficult to find, but most of their drivers are friendly, entertaining—they sometimes bend the truth for a good yarn— and well informed about the island and its history. Ask your hotel to arrange a tour with a knowledgeable driver.

Cabs seat four or six, and the legal rate for island tours (minimum three hours) is $30 per hour for one to four passengers and $42 per hour for five or six passengers. Two children under 12 equal an adult.

➤ TAXI & MINIBUS TOUR OPERATORS: **Bee-Line Transport Ltd.** (Box HM 2270, Hamilton HM, tel. 441/293–0303, fax 441/293–8015). **Bermuda Hosts Ltd.** (Box CR 46, Crawl, Hamilton CR, tel. 441/ 293–1334, fax 441/293–1335). **Destination Bermuda Ltd.** (Box HM 1822, Hamilton HM HX, tel. 441/292–2325, fax 441/292–2252).

As the visiting English couple eat breakfast on the sunny hotel veranda, a man dressed in a blazer, Bermuda shorts, and kneesocks slowly passes by, then returns to their table. "I couldn't help overhearing . . ." the man begins, launching into a spirited discussion with the couple about the island's latest cricket match. It is not until a waiter taps the man on the shoulder to alert him to a phone call that the couple realize this man is the hotel's proprietor. Whether in small lodgings like this one or larger affairs, the warmth and friendliness of Bermuda's hotel staff—from housekeepers to owners—are legendary. . . .

In This Chapter

Prices 192 • Resort Hotels 193 • Small Hotels 198 • Cottage Colonies 206 • Housekeeping Cottages and Apartments 212 • Guest Houses and Breakfasts 223

Revised and updated by Rachel Christmas Derrick

where to stay

THE MOST FAMOUS BERMUDIAN LODGING is the beachfront cottage colony—freestanding cottages painted pastels (usually pink), with white trim and gleaming white tiered roofs. While there are a few large, multistory hotels, most of the island's other accommodations are guest houses, housekeeping apartments or individual cottages, and small (often family-run) hotels. Bermuda is noted for its lovely gardens and manicured lawns, and the grounds of almost every accommodation are filled with subtropical trees, flowers, and shrubs.

The greatest concentration of lodgings is along the south shore, in Paget, Warwick, and Southampton parishes, which have the best beaches. Hotels near Front Street in Hamilton, or one of the many Hamilton Harbour properties (which are a 5- to 10-minute ferry ride from the capital), put you close to a slew of shops and restaurants. Fortunately, Bermuda is so small that, no matter where you stay, you won't travel far to see and do everything you want.

CATEGORY	COST*
$$$$	over $300
$$$	$200–$300
$$	$100–$200
$	under $100

*All prices are for a standard double room in peak season, excluding 7.25% tax and 10% service charge).

PRICES

Rates at Bermuda's luxury resorts are comparable to those at posh hotels in New York, London, and Paris. Thus, some travelers are surprised to discover that high-end perks such as 24-hour room service and same-day laundry service are rare. Fortunately, however, personalized attention, exceptionally comfortable rooms, and trim, scenic surroundings are not.

A 7.25% government occupancy tax is tacked on to all hotel bills, and a service charge is levied. Some hotels calculate a service charge as 10% of the bill, whereas others charge a per diem amount. All guests must make a two-night deposit two to three weeks before their arrival.

Fortunately, virtually every hotel on the island offers at least one vacation package—frequently some kind of honeymoon special—and many of these are extraordinarily good deals. Of course, Guest Houses/Bed & Breakfasts are typically under $150.

You can also shave about 40% off your hotel bill by visiting Bermuda in low or shoulder seasons. The trick is trying to pin down the dates. Low season runs roughly from November through March. However, each property sets its own schedule, which may even change from year to year. Some hotels begin high-season rates on April 1, others April 15, and a few kick in as late as May 1. So it's best to call and ask about low- and shoulder-season rates.

Most lodgings offer a choice of meal plans, several with "dine-around" privileges at other island restaurants. Some room rates, however, include a mandatory meal plan that covers either breakfast or both breakfast and dinner. Unless otherwise noted, the rates quoted below are based on the European Plan (EP), which includes no meals.

We also assume that all properties are air-conditioned; exceptions are noted.

RESORT HOTELS

$$$$ ELBOW BEACH HOTEL. You would never guess from its pristine appearance that this is Bermuda's oldest seaside resort: it opened in 1908. After traversing the long driveway, you approach the huge entryway pillars, and once you're inside, the marble floors and wood-paneled lobby confirm that this is definitely a luxe resort. All rooms and suites have a balcony or patio, ocean or garden view, Internet access, and 24-hour room service. Rooms are comfortably sized with marble bathrooms. The jewel of the resort is the two-floor Penthouse with filled bookshelves, a small kitchen, butler-maid quarters across the hall, master and junior bedrooms, two balconies (one with a whirlpool) with perfect ocean views. The resort's beachside Cafe Lido offers one of the island's very best inside and outside dining venues. *60 South Shore Rd., Paget PG 04 (Box HM 455, Hamilton HM BX); tel. 441/236–3535; 800/223–7434 in the U.S. and Canada; fax 441/236–8043; www.elbowbeach.com. 169 rooms, 75 suites. 3 restaurants, 4 bars, in-room safes, minibars, room service, pool, hair salon, hot tub, putting green, 5 tennis courts, croquet, gym, beach, motorbikes, shops, children's programs, concierge, business services. AE, DC, MC, V. EP.*

$$$$ ★ THE FAIRMONT HAMILTON PRINCESS. This big pink landmark opened in 1885 and is credited with launching Bermuda's tourist industry. It's named in honor of Princess Louise, Queen Victoria's daughter, who visited the island in 1883. The atmosphere today is still slightly formal, and the staff provides swift, courteous service. The walls at the entrance to the Tiara Room restaurant are covered with pictures of the politicians and royals who have stopped by through the years. Ideally located on Hamilton Harbour, the hotel caters to businesspeople (voice mail and Internet access available), convention groups, and others who want to be near downtown Hamilton. A ferry makes regular runs across the harbor to the Fairmont Southampton Princess, which has a golf course and other sports facilities (at extra cost). The Hamilton Princess has no beach, but you may use the one at the Southampton

Princess. The dine-around plan between the two Princess hotels offers a choice of nine restaurants—from casual to formal. *76 Pitts Bay Rd., Hamilton HM 08 (Box HM 837, Hamilton HM CS); tel. 441/295–3000 or 800/441–1414, fax 441/295–1914, www.fairmont.com. 413 rooms, 60 suites. 3 restaurants, 2 bars, in-room data ports, in-room safes, minibars, 2 pools, hair salon, spa, putting green, tennis court, gym, motorbikes, shops, laundry service, concierge, business services. AE, DC, MC, V. BP, EP, MAP.*

$$$$ **THE FAIRMONT SOUTHAMPTON PRINCESS.** This modern, six-
★ story hotel crowning a hilltop near Gibbs Hill Lighthouse is the island's most complete full-service resort. It's not the place for a quiet retreat, but its extensive activities, the island's top children's program, and several of its best restaurants make it very appealing. The 300-year-old Waterlot Inn occupies a dockside spot on the north side, and the Whaler Inn beach club is perched above the surf on the south-shore side. A jitney churns over hill and dale to connect them all. The oceanfront deluxe rooms are the nicest. Avoid rooms on the first three floors of the west and north wings, as they overlook rooftops. Two beautiful penthouses and two magnificent wood-paneled duplex suites with enormous windows overlooking the ocean are also available. Use of the health club, par-3 golf course, and tennis courts all cost extra. A first-class spa is planned for winter 2002. The excellent Dolphin Quest program, in a 3-acre, open-to-the-sea lagoon, allows you to interact with friendly bottlenose dolphins for $105. Admission is often by lottery during the busy summer season. *101 South Shore Rd., Southampton SN02 (Box HM 1379, Hamilton HM FX); tel. 441/238–8000 or 800/441–1414, fax 441/238–8968, www.fairmont.com. 594 rooms, 24 suites. 5 restaurants, 4 bars, minibars, no-smoking room, pool, hair salon, spa, 18-hole golf course, 11 tennis courts, croquet, health club, beach, motorbikes, shops, nightclub, theater, children's programs, concierge. AE, DC, MC, V. MAP.*

$$$$ **SONESTA BEACH RESORT.** Set on a low promontory fringed by coral reefs, this six-story modern building has a stunning ocean

view and direct access to three superb beaches. The rooms are rather generic, but the hotel caters to those who want an outdoor, action-packed vacation. An activities director coordinates bingo games, theme parties, movies, water sports, an excellent children's program, teen activities, and other diversions. South Side Scuba Watersports has a rental outlet here, and dive and snorkel boats leave the resort daily from April through November and on request the rest of the year. A shuttle takes you to the hotel's beach at Cross Bay, but beach lovers should insist on a Bay Wing Beachfront Junior Suite that opens onto a private sandy beach. All rooms on the 25-acre property have balconies, but island-view rooms in the main building have just that—land views only. The Sonesta also has a popular health and beauty spa, and special spa packages are available. A shuttle bus transports guests between the hotel and South Road, where buses to Hamilton are available. *6 Sonesta Dr., off South Shore Rd., Southampton SN 02 (Box HM 1070, Hamilton HM EX); tel. 441/238–8122; 800/766–3782 in the U.S.; fax 441/238–8463; www.sonesta.com. 365 rooms, 34 suites. 3 restaurants, 2 bars, in-room safes, minibars, 2 pools, hot tub, massage, spa, steam room, 6 tennis courts, gym, beach, motorbikes, shops, children's programs, playground, concierge. AE, DC, MC, V. EP (BP and MAP on request).*

$$$ GROTTO BAY BEACH RESORT. Grotto Bay, a mile from the airport, is set among 21 acres of gardens and has an enclosed bay with a fish-feeding aquarium and two illuminated underground attractions: the Cathedral Cave and Prospero's Cave. Traditional Bermudiana character bathes the reception, lounge, and dining areas, with wooden floors, potted palms, a pastel palette, and natural lighting. The 11 three-story lodges each contain between 15 and 30 sunny rooms. All have private balconies or patios and water views. The hotel has its own excursion boat for sightseeing, and scuba diving and snorkeling trips leave from a private deepwater dock. Grotto Bay offers an all-inclusive package in addition to its regular rates, which are among Bermuda's most affordable for a beach resort. *11 Blue Hole Hill, Hamilton Parish CR 04, tel. 441/293–8333 or 800/582–3190, fax 441/293–2306,*

bermuda lodging

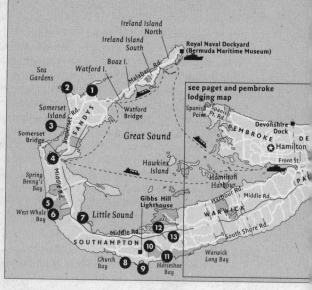

ATLANTIC OCEAN

Ireland Island
North

Ireland Island
South

Royal Naval Dockyard
(Bermuda Maritime Museum)

Boaz I.

Watford I.

Sea
Gardens

Watford
Bridge

Somerset
Island

Great Sound

Somerset
Bridge

Hawkins
Island

Spring
Benny's
Bay

West Whale
Bay

Little Sound

Gibbs Hill
Lighthouse

SOUTHAMPTON

Middle Rd.

Church
Bay

Horseshoe
Bay

see paget and pembroke
lodging map

Spanish
Point

Spanish
Pt. Rd.

Devonshire
Dock

PEMBROKE

DE

Hamilton

Front St.

Hamilton
Harbour

Harbour Rd.

Middle Rd.

WARWICK

South Shore Rd.

Warwick
Long Bay

Angel's Grotto, 18
Ariel Sands, 14
Aunt Nea's Inn at
Hillcrest, 21
Brightside Guest
Apartments, 16
Burch's Guest
Apartments, 15
Cambridge
Beaches, 1

Clear View Suites
and Villas, 17
Daniel's Head
Village, 2
The Fairmont
Southampton
Princess, 11
Garden House, 4
Greene's
Guest House, 7

Grotto Bay
Beach Resort, 20
Munro Beach
Cottages, 6
Ocean Terrace, 12
Pink Beach Club
& Cottages, 19
Pompano Beach
Club, 5
The Reefs, 8

Royal Heights
Guest House, 10
St. George's Club, 22
Sonesta Beach
Resort, 9
Sound View
Cottage, 13
Willowbank, 3

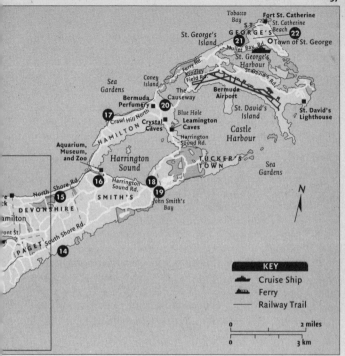

Tobacco Bay

Fort St. Catherine

St. George's Island

St. Catherine Beach

ST. GEORGE'S

21

Town of St. George

St. George's Harbour

Mullet Bay Rd.

St. David's Rd.

22

Ferry Rd.

Kindley Field Rd.

Coney Island

Sea Gardens

Bermuda Perfumery

The Causeway

20

Bermuda Airport

St. David's Island

St. David's Lighthouse

17

Crawl Hill North Shore Rd.

Crystal Caves

Blue Hole

Leamington Caves

Harrington Sound Rd.

Castle Harbour

HAMILTON

Aquarium, Museum, and Zoo

Harrington Sound

TUCKER'S TOWN

Sea Gardens

16

Harrington Sound Rd.

18

19

N

North Shore Rd.

15

SMITH'S

John Smith's Bay

DEVONSHIRE

Hamilton

Front St.

PAGET

South Shore Rd.

14

KEY	
🚢	Cruise Ship
⛴	Ferry
—	Railway Trail

0   2 miles

0   3 km

www.netlinkbermuda.com/grottobay. 198 rooms, 3 suites. Restaurant, 2 bars, pool, 4 tennis courts, gym, shuffleboard, beach, dive shop, boating, motorbikes, video games, children's programs, playground, concierge, business services, meeting room. AE, MC, V. BP, EP, FAP, MAP.

SMALL HOTELS

$$$$ HARMONY CLUB. Nestled in lovely gardens, this two-story pink-and-white all-inclusive hotel was built in the 1930s as a private home. The base rate covers everything, including airport transfers, meals, alcohol, and even two-seat scooters. The hotel is adult-oriented and has a couples-only policy, but a couple can be two friends, two cousins, or any other combination. A spacious reception area has Bermuda cedar paneling and a club lounge with a large-screen TV and an assortment of games. All guest rooms are spacious and luxuriously decorated. Most have a patio or balcony. The hotel is not on the water, but has a heated pool, and the south-shore beaches are about five minutes away by moped. In high season a host of activities from informal barbecues to formal dances keep things lively. 109 South Shore Rd., Paget PG 03 (Box PG 299, Paget PG BX); tel. 441/236–3500; 888/427–6664 in the U.S.; fax 441/236–2624; www.harmonyclub.com. 68 rooms. Restaurant, bar, pool, hot tub, sauna, putting green, 2 tennis courts, motorbikes. AE, DC, MC, V. AP.

$$$$ NEWSTEAD. A stone's throw from the Hamilton ferry at Hodson's Landing, this charming renovated manor house and its guest cottages are in classic Bermudian colonial style but have also happily kept up with the times. Among the latest additions are business suites, two conference centers, a gym, outside dining area and bar, and high-speed Internet connections in each room. The large guest rooms have polished mahogany campaign chests and sliding glass doors opening onto balconies. Brick steps and walkways lead to poolside suites and cottages. The hotel has no beach, but it does have three private docks for deepwater swimming and boating. There is also access to the Coral Beach

Specialty Sleeps

While each of Bermuda's varied accommodations has something special to offer, some are unique in a big way. Far off the beaten path at Bermuda's eastern end in historic St. George's, **AUNT NEA'S INN AT HILLCREST** is a one of-a-kind guest house. Here in this stately Georgian-style family home, the queen-size beds—from sleigh beds to fantastical canopy beds—are all works of art, and instead of being hidden in bathrooms, whirlpool tubs are right in bedrooms. Clear across the island in Sandys at **DANIEL'S HEAD VILLAGE,** you can pretend you're camping out: upscale cottages made from tentlike fabric sit on stilts above the water, and windows on the floor offer views of marine life.

Looking for pampering? Then head to the spa at **CAMBRIDGE BEACHES** in Sandys, **SONESTA BEACH RESORT** in Southampton, or **ARIEL SANDS** in Devonshire—these resorts draw lots of honeymooners detoxing after the big day. Newlyweds also flock to **ELBOW BEACH HOTEL** in Paget, **GROTTO BAY BEACH RESORT** (one of the island's most affordable beach hotels) in Hamilton Parish, and **POMPANO BEACH** in Southampton, which is also a great choice for families with children.

Bermuda is not traditionally a family destination, but that has started to change. Most hotels, cottage colonies, guest houses, and housekeeping apartments welcome families with children, and most will make baby-sitting arrangements. Some offer supervised children's programs (usually just during summer months) that include crafts-making, sports, and island excursions. Some are free to guests while others charge a daily fee. Among those with the best "kids camps" are the **FAIRMONT SOUTHAMPTON PRINCESS** in Southampton, **ELBOW BEACH, GROTTO BAY,** and **WILLOWBANK,** a Christian retreat in Sandys.

& Tennis Club facilities on the south shore, about 10 minutes away by taxi. The Rockfish Grill restaurant overlooking the water serves Asian-inspired dishes. (27 Harbour Rd., Paget PG BX (Box PG 196, Paget PG BX); tel. 441/236–6060; 800/468–4111 in the U.S.; fax 441/236–7454. www.newsteadhotel.com. 38 rooms, 6 suites. Restaurant, bar, pool, barbershop, hair salon, massage, putting green, 2 tennis courts, gym, dock, boating, concierge, business services, meeting room. AE, MC, V. BP.

$$$$ ★ **POMPANO BEACH CLUB.** Expect a friendly, personal welcome at this family-run hotel, which was a fishing club (the island's first) until 1956. Pompano is tucked away between the Port Royal Golf Course and attractive woodland and the south shore, the views of which are spectacular from here, especially at sunset. The pink-and-white crescent-shape main building houses the dining room (with alfresco tables), a small pub, a cozy lounge, and a fitness center, all with sea views. Terraced up a hillside are the rooms and one-bedroom suites, all with balconies or patios and ocean views. The best value is the "superior" rooms, which are larger than the suites and have ocean views from the bedroom (suites have an ocean view through the living-room windows). More spacious (and only a few dollars extra) are the "deluxe" rooms. A heated swimming pool and a children's wading pool sit on a spacious cliff-side patio high above the ocean. The beach has been enlarged over the years to almost four times its original size, but the real boon is the low-tide stroll 250 yards into waist-high crystal-clear waters. 36 Pompano Beach Rd., Southampton SB 03, tel. 441/234–0222; 800/343–4155 in the U.S.; fax 441/234–1694; www.pompano.bm. 36 rooms, 20 suites. Restaurant, bar, in-room safes, refrigerators, pool, wading pool, 2 outdoor hot tubs, tennis court, gym, beach, windsurfing, boating. AE, MC, V. BP, MAP.

$$$$ ★ **THE REEFS.** This small, elegant, and relaxed resort hugs the cliffs that wind into the sea around Christian Bay, giving it unparalleled south-shore ocean and coastline views. A popular wedding and honeymoon getaway, the Reefs also welcomes families among its many repeat guests. A traditional pink Bermuda cottage clubhouse houses the dining room and comfortable lounge bar where local entertainers play nightly. But be sure to try the less formal Coconuts: it has the island's best waterfront dining setting, perfect for casual lunches or candlelight dinners. The guest rooms near the beach are the most expensive, but for seclusion and tranquillity the cliff-side "deluxe" and "superior" rooms perched above wave-washed boulders at the far end of the resort are best. Tiled floors, vibrant fabrics, and rattan predominate in the modestly sized but airy rooms (TVs and VCRs available on request). All have ocean views and balconies. There are also eight cottage accommodations, some with garden whirlpools. 56 South Rd., Southampton SN 02, tel. 441/238–0222; 800/742–2008 in the U.S. and Canada; fax 441/238–8372; www.thereefs.com. 58 rooms, 1 suite, 8 cottage suites. 3 restaurants, 2 bars, lounge, fans, in-room data ports, in-room safes, refrigerators, pool, 2 tennis courts, gym, beach, motorbikes, piano, baby-sitting, laundry service. AE, MC, V. BP, MAP.

$$$$ STONINGTON BEACH HOTEL. This training ground for students of the Hospitality and Culinary Institute of Bermuda has one of the friendliest and hardest-working staffs on the island. Situated 10 minutes from Hamilton on the south shore Bermuda College grounds, Stonington has access to the largest multimedia meeting space on the island, the college gym and sports field, and even lectures. The spa and sports facilities at the Elbow Beach Hotel are also open to guests. The guest rooms, set in two-story terraced lodges, face one of the island's best beaches, which gives the hotel its name. The identical rooms have tile floors, handsome wood furniture, balconies or patios, and ocean views. Rooms nearest the ocean are in a beachfront cottage housing a one-bedroom and a three-bedroom apartment, both with kitchens. The spacious lobby looks out to the ocean. Regency furnishings, well-stocked bookshelves, a fireplace, and a large-screen TV in the adjoining library make it a comfortable place to relax. Creative dishes can be savored in the Norwood Room restaurant. 8 College Dr., Paget PG 04.(Box HM 523, Hamilton HM CX); tel. 441/236–5416; 800/447–7462 in the U.S. and Canada; fax 441/236–0371; www.

stoningtonbeach.com. *64 rooms, 2 cottages. Restaurant, bar, in-room safes, refrigerators, pool, 2 tennis courts, beach, snorkeling, motorbikes, library. AE, DC, MC, V. BP, MAP.*

$$$$ WATERLOO HOUSE. ★ This quiet Relais & Châteaux retreat has a long history. An archway and steps leading to the flower-filled patio from Pitts Bay Road were later additions to a house that predates 1815, when it was renamed in honor of the defeat of Napoléon. Facing the harbor, its spacious terrace is used for outdoor dining and entertainment—piano, jazz, and calypso. Flower arrangements fill the stately lounge, which has a large fireplace. Most antiques-filled rooms are in the main house; some are in the two-story stone buildings beside the pool and patio. The luxurious bathrooms have whirlpools. All rooms have water views. Picnic cruises on the property's launch provide views of Bermuda's outer islands. The hotel's Wellington Room won a *Wine Spectator* magazine award (2000) for the second year in a row for having one of the world's outstanding restaurant wine lists. Waterloo's dining plan allows dine-around privileges at the sister properties of Horizons & Cottages and the Coral Beach & Tennis Club. You can also use the short golf course at Horizons and all facilities at the Coral Beach. Transportation is provided. *100 Pitts Bay Rd., Hamilton HM 11 (Box HM 333, Hamilton HM BX); tel. 441/295–4480; 800/468–4100 in the U.S.; fax 441/295–2585; www.waterloohouse.com. 28 rooms, 6 suites. Restaurant, bar, pool. AE, MC, V. BP, MAP.*

$$$$ WHITE SANDS HOTEL & COTTAGES. Perched high above the south shore, this small hotel is a three-minute walk from the white sands of Grape Bay Beach. The dining room, with bentwood chairs upholstered in plush fabrics, commands a dazzling view of the sea. The cozy lounge has a fireplace and a terrace with yet more stunning views. You can have lunch in the lounge or on the pool terrace, which has its own snack bar and barbecue grill. Guest rooms are in the three-story main house and in cottages, each of which has two or three bedrooms with bath, living room, and kitchen. The best rooms have both a balcony and an ocean view. The standard rooms in the main house are smaller and have no balcony but do have a sea view. "Moderate" balconied rooms have sea glimpses, and standard rooms in the terrace wing have a balcony overlooking the gardens. The modern, tiled bathrooms have tubs and showers. Tea is served each afternoon, and a full breakfast is included in the rate. *55 White Sands Rd., Paget PG BX (Box PG 174, Paget PG BX, tel. 441/236–2023; 800/548–0547 in the U.S.; 800/228–3196 in Canada; fax 441/236–2486; www.white-sands-bermuda.com. 37 rooms, 3 housekeeping cottages. Restaurant, bar, in-room data ports, in-room safes, refrigerators, pool. AE, MC, V. BP, MAP.*

$$$ ROSEDON. Notable for its spacious veranda and majestic garden approach, this stately Bermuda manor house has the attentive service and decor details to match the formal exterior. The spacious guest rooms in the main house are the most traditional, with antiques and reproductions, but the other rooms, situated in two-story buildings around a large heated pool, enjoy an exotic garden setting. The four newest, built in 2001, are luxury bungalows with colonial-style four-poster beds, love seats, VCRs, and whirlpool bathtubs. All the cheerfully decorated rooms at Rosedon have balconies or patios. Rosedon has no restaurant, but breakfast, sandwiches, and light meals are served either in your room or under umbrellas by the pool. Afternoon tea is offered in the large lounges in the main house, where films are shown nightly. The hotel has no beach, but guests have access to the Stonington Beach Hotel facilities with complimentary transportation. *61 Pitts Bay Rd., Pembroke HM 06 (Box HM 290, Hamilton HM AX); tel. 441/295–1640; 800/742–5008 in the U.S. and Canada; fax 441/295–5904; www.rosedonbermuda.com. 47 rooms. Bar, 2 lounges, in-room safes, refrigerators, pool, laundry service. AE, MC, V. BP, EP.*

$$$ SURF SIDE BEACH CLUB. Those seeking privacy may find it here, on the south shore. The homey cottages housing the spacious apartments are tucked into cliffs and are built on terraced levels, so that each has a view of the ocean and long stretch of beach below. Each has cable TV, phone, and porch, and most have a fully

paget and pembroke lodging

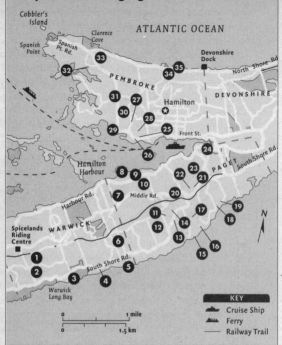

Astwood Cove, 3
Barnsdale Guest Apartments, 20
Clairfont Apts., 2
Dawkins Manor, 17
Edgehill Manor, 30
Elbow Beach Hotel, 15
The Fairmont Hamilton Princess, 29
Fourways Inn, 7
Grape Bay Cottages, 19
Greenbank Cottages, 8

Hamiltonian Hotel & Island Club, 34
Harmony Club, 22
Horizons & Cottages, 12
Little Pomander Guest House, 24
Loughlands Guest House & Cottage, 14
Marula Apts., 32
Marley Beach Cottages, 4
Mazarine by the Sea, 35

Newstead, 10
Oxford House, 27
Paraquet Guest Apts., 13
Robin's Nest, 33
Rosedon, 28
Rosemont, 25
Royal Palms Hotel, 31
Salt Kettle House, 9
Sandpiper Apartments, 6
Serendipity, 21
Skytop Cottages, 11

Stonington Beach Hotel, 16
Surf Side Beach Club, 5
Syl-Den, 1
Valley Cottages and Apts., 23
Waterloo House, 26
White Sands Hotel & Cottages, 18

equipped kitchen. All are decorated with light-wood furnishings, bright island fabrics, and wall-to-wall carpeting or tile floors. The poolside Palms restaurant has a thoughtful set menu from one of the island's most talented chefs (special diets, including vegetarian, are particularly well catered). *90 South Shore Rd., Warwick, WK 7 (Box WK 101, Warwick WK BX); tel. 441/236–7100 or 800/553–9990, fax 441/236–9765, www.surfside.bm. 10 apartments, 23 studios, 3 suites, 2 penthouse units. Restaurant, bar, room service, pool, hair salon, massage, sauna, spa, beach, coin laundry. AE, MC, V. BP. MAP.*

$$$ WILLOWBANK. This former estate, located on 6 acres of landscaped gardens overlooking Ely's Harbour, was converted to a family-style hotel by a Christian trust. Morning devotions are held in a lounge and grace is said before meals, which are announced by an ancient ship's bell and served family style. But there is no proselytizing. Willowbank is simply a serene and restful alternative to the glitzy resorts, with wonderful views and marvelous beaches nonetheless. The two large lounges are the focal point for quiet conversations and afternoon tea. Guests also meet for fellowship in the library and the Loaves and Fishes dining room. You may have liquor in your room, but there is no bar. The guest rooms, many with an ocean or harbor view, are in one-story white cottages. They are large and simply furnished but have neither phones nor TVs. There is a free summer children's program including crafts and trips around the island. No service charge is added to the bill, but most guests tip on their own. *126 Somerset Rd., Sandys MA 06 (Box MA 296, Sandys MA BX); tel. 441/234–1616 or 800/752–8493, fax 441/234–3373, www.willowbank.bm. 64 rooms. Restaurant, 2 lounges, pool, 2 tennis courts, 2 beaches, dock, snorkeling, children's programs. MC, V. MAP.*

$$–$$$ ROYAL PALMS HOTEL. The brother-and-sister team of Richard ★ Smith and Susan Weare have transformed this grand home into a hotel with standards that are second to none. The main house, a former mansion built around 1903, and three other buildings are set in lush gardens of tall palms and trees bearing avocado, grapefruit, oranges, peaches, guava, and bananas. Canopied swinging chairs here are excellent spots for contemplating the greenery. The hotel's proximity to Hamilton (it's a five-minute walk) and reasonable rate make Royal Palms a good choice, despite its distance from beaches. You can choose from individually decorated rooms, cottages, and minisuites with kitchenettes. Many guests like to relax and read around the outdoor kidney-bean-shape pool. Ascots restaurant, popular among locals, has one of the island's most imaginative menus. During the summer lunch and dinner are served out back on the main-house terrace. *24 Rosemont Ave., Pembroke HM o6 (Box HM 499, Hamilton HM CX); tel. 441/292–1854; 800/678–0783 in the U.S.; 800/799–0824 in Canada; fax 441/292–1946; www.royalpalms.bm. 25 rooms. Restaurant, bar, lounge, in-room data ports, pool, laundry service. AE, MC, V. CP.*

$$ HAMILTONIAN HOTEL & ISLAND CLUB. High on Langton Hill overlooking Pembroke Parish and the city of Hamilton, this generic hotel also offers stunning ocean views from all of its 32 suites. The rooms are decorated in summery pastel shades and have tiled hallways and living rooms and carpeted bedrooms. All have sofa beds, a balcony, and TV (no cable). Suites have a refrigerator, a microwave, a toaster, and a coffeemaker. Centrally located in a tropical garden setting on the outskirts of Hamilton, the hotel is a two-minute walk to a bus stop that will take you to the city center in about five minutes. A large outdoor pool and sun deck have great sea views. There's a golf course nearby. *Langton Hill, Pembroke (Box HM 1738, Hamilton HM GX); tel. 441/295–5608; 401/848–7870 in the U.S.; fax 441/295–7481. 32 suites. Pool, 3 tennis courts. AE, MC, V. EP.*

COTTAGE COLONIES

$$$$ ARIEL SANDS. Spreading out behind a sandy Cox's Bay beach in ★ Devonshire Parish is a statue of Ariel, the sprite in Shakespeare's *The Tempest*. She is the namesake of this informal cottage colony owned by the family of actor Michael Douglas. The snorkeling is

Pretty in Pink: Bermuda's Cottage Colonies

Long before Bermuda's tourism heyday, in the golden age of cruise-ship travel, the beautiful people began transforming Bermuda into a chic getaway. Would-be hoteliers could see that this exclusive clientele would want seclusion, British colonial sophistication, and traditional Bermudian hospitality. And so the cottage colony was born—a plush home-away-from-home that left no comfort unexplored, no luxury ignored.

Since Cambridge Beaches, the first cottage colony, was built at the turn of the 20th century, six more official colonies have sprung up, many still frequented by a glamorous set: Ariel Sands, Fourways Inn, Horizons & Cottages, Pink Beach Club & Cottages, the St. George's Club, and Willowbank. However, despite this demarcation, visitors are often baffled by the island's numerous lodgings that have the word "cottage" in their name.

The definitive line over what does and does not qualify as a cottage colony continues to blur, but generally speaking it describes a beachfront collection of traditional cottages, separated from a main building that often houses the front desk, restaurants, bars, and lounge areas. Distinctive island architecture and interior design styles are common features, such as gleaming white limestone stair-step roofs, spacious living and dining areas, open fireplaces, terraces or balconies, often cedar-beamed ceilings and furniture, and British country-style fabrics and ornaments. Most have either stunning water views or colorful garden settings.

Originally the guest rooms were in small detached cottages with kitchens where maids prepared breakfast. Newer complexes, however, can include much larger guest houses, some of more modern design. Rooms may be offered individually, or adjoining. Breakfast prepared en suite may or may not be part of the deal.

Whatever a cottage colony is, it certainly isn't basic or budget. And while many offer a unique holiday experience, they won't suit everyone. The emphasis is on peace and quiet, and they're just the ticket for vacationers seeking gracious living than merely a hotel room.

superb here, and there are two ocean-fed pools and a heated freshwater pool. The Bermudian cottage–style clubhouse has a comfortable lounge and dining room with ocean view. Many locals enjoy the quiet atmosphere and come to sip cocktails in the bar after a game of tennis or before having dinner at Caliban's. (A dine-around program is available.) On the sloping, tree-shaded grounds are 12 cottages with two to eight guest rooms in each. All rooms have unobstructed ocean views. The playful New-Age decor includes transparent inflatable throw pillows and geometric canopies over beds. The spa offers a variety of relaxing and customized treatments. *34 South Shore Rd., Devonshire DV 07 (Box HM 334, Hamilton HM BX); tel. 441/236–1010; 800/468–6610 in the U.S.; fax 441/236–0087; www.arielsands.com. 47 rooms, 3 suites, 2 cottages. Restaurant, 2 bars, in-room data ports, 2 saltwater pools, pool, spa, putting green, 3 tennis courts, gym, volleyball, beach, concierge, business services, meeting room. AE, MC, V. BP, MAP.*

$$$$ **CAMBRIDGE BEACHES.** This top resort occupies a beautiful
★ peninsula edged with private coves and five pink-sand beaches, and is Bermuda's original cottage colony. It remains a favorite among royals and celebrities. The range of accommodations allows for many budgets: Pegem, on the high end, is a 300-year-old, two-bedroom Bermuda cottage with a cedar-beam ceiling, den, sunporch, and English antiques. Built in 2001, yet capturing the resort's historic flavor, are rooms and suites on the Hill, the highest point on the grounds. Less expensive rooms have land views. (But you'll have splendid views of Mangrove Bay from the Tamarisk restaurant and terrace.) Many rooms have whirlpools and fireplaces. The resort's health and beauty spa is staffed by European-trained professionals. A complimentary shopping launch to Hamilton leaves three times a week during high season, and the marina has Windsurfers, Boston Whalers, three types of sailboats, snorkel equipment, canoes, and kayaks. Children must be supervised at all times, and those under five are allowed in the dining room only by special arrangement. *30 King's Point Rd., Sandys MA 02, tel. 441/234–0331; 800/468–7300 in the U.S.; fax 441/*

234–3352; www.cambridgebeaches.com. 66 rooms, 25 suites, 2 two-bedroom cottages. 2 restaurants, 2 bars, in-room data ports, pool, saltwater pool, spa, putting green, 3 tennis courts, croquet, gym, beach, dock, boating, marina. MC, V. MAP.

$$$$ **HORIZONS & COTTAGES.** Oriental rugs, polished wood floors,
★ cathedral ceilings, and open fireplaces are elegant reminders of the 18th century, when the main house in this resort was a private home. A Relais & Châteaux property, this resort works continually to maintain its high standards. Horizons, the outstanding restaurant, is both a chic and intimate dining spot. In nice weather, tables are set on the terrace. Menus are created under the guidance of chef Jonathan Roberts, and the hotel has dine-around arrangements with sister properties Waterloo House and Coral Beach & Tennis Club. Guest cottages are spread out across the terraced lawns. Most have a large common room with a fireplace, library, and board games, and all have terraces. Each has a distinct personality and decor. Some have white wicker furnishings, while others have a traditional European flavor. Most cottages also have a kitchen, where a maid prepares breakfast before bringing it to your room. The hotel has no beach of its own, but guests may use the facilities at Coral Beach, a private club, including the spa. *33 South Shore Rd., Paget PG 04 (Box PG 198, Paget PG BX); tel. 441/236–0048; 800/468–0022 in the U.S.; fax 441/236–1981; www.horizonscottages.com. 45 rooms, 3 suites. Restaurant, in-room safes, pool, golf, 3 tennis courts, croquet. No credit cards. BP, MAP.*

$$$$ **PINK BEACH CLUB & COTTAGES.** With its two pretty pink beaches,
★ this secluded colony is Bermuda's largest and a favorite with celebrities. The location is ideal: 10 minutes from the airport, 15 minutes by moped from Hamilton's Front Street, and moments from nearby golfing. Opened as a cottage colony in 1947, the main house has a clubby ambience reflected in its dark-wood paneling, large fireplace, and beam ceilings. Paved paths wend their way through 16½ acres of gardens, leading to the beaches and 25 pink cottages. Single or multiple cottage units range from junior

suites to two-bedroom executive suites with two bathrooms and twin terraces. All are spacious, with sliding glass doors that open onto a balcony or terrace. Most have ocean views. A full breakfast is served in your room. Evenings can begin or end with drinks in the bar or lounge while international dishes are available in the formal dining room. Casual poolside dining with nightly entertainment is an alternative. *1016 South Shore Rd., Tucker's Town, Smith's HS 01 (Box HM 1017, Hamilton HM DX); tel. 441/293–1666; 800/355–6161 in the U.S. and Canada; fax 441/293–8935; www.pinkbeach.com. 91 suites. Restaurant, bar, pool, massage, 2 tennis courts, gym, beach. AE, MC, V. BP, MAP.*

$$$ ST. GEORGE'S CLUB. Within walking distance of King's Square in St. George's, this resort and hotel in a residential neighborhood adjoins a golf course designed by Robert Trent Jones. The sleek, three-story main building contains the lobby, business center, cottages, Tillie's Restaurant and pub, and a convenience store where you can buy everything from champagne to suntan lotion. The individually decorated cottage units, set on more than 18 acres of grounds, are huge and sunny. Each has a fully equipped kitchen. Bathrooms are large; some have oversize tubs. *6 Rose Hill, St. George's Parish GE 05 (Box GE 92, St. George's GE BX); tel. 441/297–1200, fax 441/297–8003, www.stgeorgeclub.com. 71 cottages. Restaurant, bar, 3 pools, 18-hole golf course, putting green, 3 tennis courts. AE, MC, V. EP.*

$$–$$$ DANIEL'S HEAD VILLAGE. Bermuda's first new resort in more than two decades, Daniel's Head is like nothing the island has ever seen before: This environmentally sensitive vacation playground has unique tent cottages (framed with weatherproof fabric instead of walls), scattered across 19 acres studded with casuarina pines and flowering bushes. To minimize any adverse effects on the natural surroundings, these cottages stand on stilts. In fact, the over-the-water units have windows in their floors for viewing the vibrant marine life below. Balconies and wraparound windows in all take in views of the ocean. Although they're built from recycled materials, and use some solar power, accommodations come with hotel-room-style features such as queen-size beds, housekeeping service, telephones, coffeemakers, and in-room baths with showers (and some with colorful Mexican ceramic sinks). One- or two-bedroom hillside ocean-view suites are more secluded. Various beaches are tucked between the boulders along the dramatic coastline—a designated protected region—of the Daniel's Head Peninsula. Only water sports powered by people or Mother Nature are permitted here, such as sea-kayaking, sailing, snorkeling, and diving. Hotel staff can make arrangements for dive trips to nearby wrecks, fishing excursions, catamaran cruises, and eco-tours. *4 Daniel's Head La., Sandys MA BX (Box MA341, Sandys MA BX); tel. 441/234–4272 or 877/418–1723, fax 441/234–4270, www.danielsheadvillage.com. 96 cottages, 19 one- and two-bedroom suites. Restaurant, bar, fans, in-room safes, pool, beach, snorkeling, windsurfing. MC, V. CP, MAP.*

$$–$$$ **FOURWAYS INN.** This small luxury inn and cottage colony has a formal, sedate ambience. Centrally located, Fourways is about a five-minute walk from the ferry landing and a five-minute bus ride to south-shore beaches. The architecture is typically Bermudian: the main building is a former family home that dates from 1727, and each of the five cottages, set in a profusion of greenery and flowers, has a poolside suite and a deluxe upper-floor room. Marble floors and marble bathrooms are common throughout, as are plenty of fresh flowers; each room also has a balcony or terrace and large closets paneled with full-length mirrors. Perks include bathrobes and slippers. You receive a complimentary fruit basket on arrival, and homemade pastries and the morning paper are delivered daily to your door. Fourways' award-winning restaurant has around 8,000 bottles in its wine cellar and 650 selections. *1 Middle Rd., Paget PG 01 (Box PG 294, Paget PG BX); tel. 441/236–6517; 800/962–7654 in the U.S.; fax 441/236–5528. www.fourwaysinn.com. 6 rooms, 4 suites. Restaurant, bar, minibars, kitchenettes, pool, business services. AE, MC, V. CP.*

HOUSEKEEPING COTTAGES AND APARTMENTS

$$$$ **GRAPE BAY COTTAGES.** These two almost-identical cottages sit within a whistle of the soft sands of Grape Bay Beach. Beach Crest and Beach Home are two-bedroom cottages with open fireplaces, hardwood floors, phones, and full-size kitchens. The comfortable furnishings include king-size beds. You can't step directly from door to beach, but the stroll down takes little more than two minutes. This is a very quiet, secluded location, ideal for beach lovers who like to cook for themselves, and do serious sand-and-surf time. The cottages are a bit costly for one couple, but for two couples sharing expenses this is an eminently affordable choice. The beach house of the American consulate is right next door to Beach Home. A grocery store and cycle shop are nearby. *Box HM 1851, Hamilton HM HX, tel. 441/296–0563; 800/637–4116 in the U.S.; fax 441/296–0563. 2 cottages. Kitchenettes. AE, MC, V. EP.*

$$$ **MARLEY BEACH COTTAGES.** Scenes from the films *Chapter Two* and *The Deep* were filmed here, and it's easy to see why: the setting is breathtaking. Near Astwood Park, on the south shore, the resort sits high on a cliff overlooking a private beach, stunning coastline, and dramatic reefs. A long path leads down to the sand and the sea. (If you plan to stay here, pack light. There are a lot of steep steps.) Each cottage contains a suite and a studio apartment, which can be rented separately or together. Some furnishings could benefit from modernization, but all accommodations have large sunny rooms, superb ocean views, private porches or patios, phones, and fully equipped kitchens with microwave and coffeemaker. The Heaven's Above and Seasong deluxe suites are spacious, and each has a fireplace. You can have groceries delivered, and there is daily maid service. If you're a pet lover, the resort's namesake—Marley, a pretty tabby cat—might keep you company. *South Shore Rd., Warwick (Box PG 278, Paget PG BX); tel. 441/236–1143 ext. 42; 800/637–4116 in the U.S.; fax 441/236–1984. 6 studios, 4 suites, 3 executive suites. Pool, hot tub, beach, snorkeling, fishing, baby-sitting. AE, MC, V. EP.*

$$$ MUNRO BEACH COTTAGES. Seclusion and privacy are the key words at this small group of cottages spread over 5 acres at Whitney Bay on the western end of the south shore. A beautiful palm-fringed beach is the view from the duplex cottages hidden away behind one of Bermuda's (and maybe the world's) most picturesque golf courses, Port Royal. What these cottages lack in facilities (there is no club room, restaurant, or activities provided) they make up for in tranquillity and views of stunning sunsets. All standard units have a king-size bed or two twin beds and a double sofa bed and can accommodate up to four people. All have fully equipped kitchens, telephones, TVs, and radios, although some of the furnishings are a little dated. Barbecues are available and daily maid service is included. The resort is a 20-minute walk across the golf course to the nearest South Shore Road bus stop, so a moped is recommended . *2 Port Royal Golf Course Rd., Southampton SN BX (Box SN 99, Southampton SN BX); tel. 441/234–1175, fax 441/234–3528, www.munrobeach.com. 9 cottages. In-room safes, kitchenettes, beach, fishing. AE, DC, MC, V. EP.*

$$$ ROSEMONT. This modern family-owned hilltop complex of nearly 50 poolside or garden suites was the first to corner Bermuda's self-catering niche, and it's not hard to see why. Ideally located in a quiet residential area with excellent views of Hamilton Harbour and the Great Sound, Rosemont is also just a stone's throw from the capital, ferries, shops, and restaurants. Accommodations comprise bedroom, sitting area, kitchen, full bathroom, and private entrance and are simply but attractively decorated. Each has its own private patio or balcony. The penthouse suite—a two-bedroom unit that can be converted into three deluxe rooms—has panoramic views, balconies, and whirlpools. *Box HM 37, Hamilton HM AX, tel. 441/292–1055, fax 441/295–3913, www.rosemont.bm. 47 apartments. Kitchenettes, in-room data ports, pool. No credit cards. EP.*

$$–$$$ CLEAR VIEW SUITES & VILLAS. These spacious north-shore waterfront suites and villas offer breathtaking ocean views and quiet seclusion. One- to four-bedroom units are available, and all have kitchenettes and living and dining areas. The decor is modern, with carefully chosen fabrics and tasteful wooden furniture. If you don't want to cook, Clear View's delightful cliff-top Landfall Restaurant, designed with a mix of British colonial and Bermudian architecture, offers hearty breakfast, lunch, dinner, and Sunday brunch. The property is ideally located for walkers, who can take advantage of one of the most attractive coastal stretches of the Bermuda Railway Trail. Special packages such as the Learn and Leisure and the Educational Focus programs incorporate field trips, museum visits, and local history and art. A conference room is available and maid service is included. *Sandy La., Hamilton Parish CR 02, tel. 441/293–0484; 800/468–9600 in the U.S.; fax 441/293–0267; www.bermuda-online.org/clearview.htm. 12 apartments. Restaurant, pool, tennis, snorkeling, coin laundry, business services. AE, DC, MC, V. EP.*

$$ ANGEL'S GROTTO. Some 30 years ago, this was a swinging nightclub and one of the hottest spots on Bermuda. It's now a quiet residential apartment house on the south shore of Harrington Sound. Proprietor Helene Hart and her hardworking staff have won top Department of Tourism honors four years running for these charmingly decorated, immaculately maintained flats. Rooms have cable TVs, radios, phones, and fully equipped kitchens. There is no beach, but the pink sands of John Smith's Bay, on the south shore, are a five-minute walk away. Most guests are couples. The secluded Honeymoon Cottage is particularly appealing if you want privacy. The two-bedroom, two-bath apartment in the main house is a good buy for two couples traveling together. The large patio is ideal for cocktails, and there is also a barbecue. Deepwater swimming is available in Harrington Sound. *83 Harrington Sound Road, Smith's Box HS 81, Smith's HSG BX, tel. 441/293–1986; 800/550–6288 in the U.S.; fax 441/236–1984; www.angelsgrotto.com. 7 apartments. Kitchenettes. AE, MC, V. EP.*

$$ ASTWOOD COVE. With access to the nearby south-shore beaches and a good smattering of restaurants within a 2-mi radius, these gleaming white apartments are a boon for beach-loving budget travelers. As a guest you can help yourself to the fruits of the terraced orchards around which the apartments are set. Standard and superior studios and suites have either a full kitchen or a microwave and refrigerator. The poolside rooms are a favorite with families, and the upstairs suites offer excellent value with views over Astwood Park and glimpses of the sea. Rooms are spanking clean, with wicker, rattan, and hardwood furnishings. There are no TVs apart from the communal one in the barbecue pavilion. Bathrooms have showers only. There are barbecue grills as well as a coin-operated laundry room and sauna (at extra charge). *49 South Rd., Warwick WK 07, tel. 441/236–0984, fax 441/236–1164, www.astwoodcove.com. 20 apartments. Pool. MC, V. EP.*

$$ BARNSDALE GUEST APARTMENTS. Budget travelers who want to be near south-shore beaches and the Hamilton ferry should consider the small apartments in this two-story, terra-cotta house. On the bus route in a residential neighborhood and close to a grocery store, the apartments are set in a garden with an orchard of loquat, banana, and peach trees—all of whose fruits you are encouraged to sample. Stay a week and you'll benefit: Barnsdale treats guests to every seventh night free. All apartments are neat and clean efficiencies, each with a private entrance. Rooms are simply decorated and annually spruced up and sleep up to four guests—although the kitchen area can seem awfully close to the sleeping area. An outdoor barbecue gives you a chance to enjoy those balmy Bermuda nights, and diving trips and tours can be arranged. *2 Barnes Valley, Box DV 628, Devonshire DV BX, tel. 441/236–0164 or 800/637–4116, fax 441/236–4709, www.bermuda.com/barnsdale. 7 apartments. Fans, kitchenettes, pool. AE, MC, V. EP.*

$$ BRIGHTSIDE GUEST APARTMENTS. This attractive property with verandas overlooking picture-postcard Flatts Inlet combines great views with access to the village. Ideal for an informal and relaxing vacation, these nine fully equipped housekeeping apartments are minutes from the Bermuda Aquarium, Museum & Zoo. The two-floor cottage is the most spacious, and all rooms are clean and modern. There is no beach, but a patio and huge pool stand in as substitutes. Brightside is 15 minutes by bus from Hamilton and also well located for a visit to historic St. George's about 25 minutes away by bus. *38 North Shore Rd., Flatts Village, FL BX (Box FL 319, Flatts FL 07); tel. 441/292–8410, fax 441/295–6968, www.bermuda.com/brightside. 9 apartments. Pool. No credit cards. EP.*

$$ CLAIRFONT APARTMENTS. These clean and quiet apartments perched on a hill close to the south-shore beaches offer excellent value for money. The six spacious one-bedroom apartments and two studios are simply decorated, and all have fully equipped kitchens, phones, radios, and TVs (cable is an extra $2 per day). Daily maid service is included. The four sunny upstairs units have balconies and lovely views across the valley toward the south shore. Downstairs apartments have patios leading onto a communal lawn. Children are welcome and can take advantage of a good playground that's a five-minute walk away and the use of the pool area. Cheap monthly off-season rates start from $1,000. Early booking is advised. *6 Warwickshire Rd., Warwick WK 02 (Box WK 85, Warwick WK 02); tel. 441/238–0149 or 800/637–4116, fax 441/238–3503, www.bermudareservation.net. 8 apartments. Kitchenettes, pool. AE, MC, V. EP.*

$$ DAWKINS MANOR. These homey but modern housekeeping apartments tucked away in the rural lanes of Paget enjoy an idyllic garden setting. The friendly and informal atmosphere ensures you will get a taste of real Bermuda life here. Apartments have private patios, modern bathrooms, cable TVs, clock radios, and phones—the furnishings are simple, Caribbean style. Units without kitchens have king-size beds, refrigerator, a hot pot for drinks, and some dishes. The apartments are well located for south-shore beaches, shops and restaurants, and cycle rentals. Hamilton is 10 minutes away by bus. *29 St. Michaels's Rd., Box PG*

34, Paget PG BX, tel. 441/236–7419 or 800/637–4116, fax 441/236–7088, www.bermuda-charm.com. 6 apartments. In-room data ports, in-room VCRs, pool, coin laundry, business services. AE, MC, V. EP.

$$ GARDEN HOUSE. Hospitable owner and manager Rosanne Galloway will make sure you feel at home at her beautiful harborside Bermudian property near the Somerset Bridge. Here you can choose from a studio, a one-bedroom cottage with separate living room and kitchen, or a two-bedroom cottage with a huge living room that leads to a separate kitchen. Beds are either kings or two twins, except for the larger cottage, which has an antique four-poster. Living rooms are furnished in British country-house style with some Bermudian cedar furniture pieces. All rooms have phones, kitchens, and patios approaching the lovely gardens. A stroll to the end of the lawn will lead you onto Elys Harbour, where you can swim as long as you don't mind diving into deep water right off the shore. Children under 12 stay free. Maid service is included daily. *4 Middle Rd., Sandys SB 01, tel. 441/234–1435, fax 441/234–3006. 5 apartments. Kitchenettes, no-smoking room, pool. AE, MC, V. Closed Dec.–Feb. EP.*

$$ GREENBANK COTTAGES. On a quiet lane less than a minute's walk from the Salt Kettle ferry landing, these single-story cottages nestle among tall trees next to Hamilton Harbour. They're small and family-oriented rather than grand, but they come with plenty of personal attention from the Ashton family. The lounge in the 200-year-old main house has hardwood floors, a TV, and a grand piano. There are four apartments with kitchens in the main house. All others are self-contained, with kitchens, private entrances, and shaded verandas. (Only two include breakfast in the rate.) The waterside cottages, especially Salt Winds, have particularly lovely harbor views. Rooms themselves are simply furnished, without seeming too generic. There is a private dock for deepwater swimming, and the beaches are less than 10 minutes away by taxi or moped. One of the island's best water-sports operators—Salt Kettle Yacht Charters—is on the property. *17 Salt Kettle Rd., Paget*

PG 01 (Box PG 201, Paget PG BX); tel. 441/236–3615; 800/637–4116 in the U.S.; fax 441/236–2427; www.bermudamall.com/greenbank. *3 rooms, 8 apartments. Kitchenettes, dock. AE, MC, V. CP, EP.*

$$ MARULA APARTMENTS. Spacious grounds on the water's edge of Mills Creek in Pembroke Parish make an idyllic setting for these apartments. The hustle and bustle of Hamilton may seem miles away while you're lounging by the pool overlooking the ocean, but in fact it's just a five-minute bus ride into town. There are five housekeeping units and a two-bedroom self-contained cottage. All accommodations are comfortable and roomy, with full kitchens (microwaves are available on request), separate bedrooms, phones, and cable TV. Marula is also good for walks in nearby Admiralty House Park and only a stone's throw from Clarence Cove where you can sunbathe or swim. *17 Mariners La., Pembroke HM 02 (Box HM 576, Hamilton HM CX); tel. 441/295–2893, fax 441/292–3985. 6 apartments. Fans, kitchenettes, pool, laundry service. AE, MC, V. EP.*

$$ MAZARINE BY THE SEA. These cozy efficiencies perched on the water's edge a mile from Hamilton are ideal for those on a budget. Five of the seven units have ocean views. Each has a bedroom, bathroom, kitchenette, and small patio or balcony overlooking gardens or sea. All have microwaves, phones, and TVs. The whitewashed rooms are clean and well maintained. There is no beach, but there is deepwater swimming and good reef snorkeling at the doorstep. Those who are not strong swimmers can use the pool overlooking the sea. A grocery store and bus stops are a short walk away. *91 North Shore Rd., Pembroke (Box HM 91, Hamilton HM AX); tel. 441/292–1659, fax 441/292–6891, www.mazarinebythesea.com. 7 apartments. Kitchenettes, pool, snorkeling, fishing. AE, MC, V. EP.*

$$ OCEAN TERRACE. Perched on Southampton's Scenic Heights, these self-contained studios enjoy spectacular all-round panoramic views of the island and ocean. The three spacious and modern apartments each have a queen bed, sofa, full kitchen, private entrance and veranda, and cable TV. A roll-out bed can also be arranged. Although it's in a residential area, Ocean Terrace is well located for beaches. A five-minute walk to the bottom of the hill will bring you to Horseshoe Bay, and the South Shore Road bus goes into Hamilton (a 30-minute ride) or toward Dockyard. This traditional Bermudian coral-color property, with a whitewashed roof and white shutters, has been owner-occupied for more than 20 years. A small pool and terrace are dotted with tables, chairs, and sun loungers. *2 Scenic Heights La., Southampton, SN03 (Box SN 501, Southampton SN BX); tel. 441/238–0019; 800/637–4116 in the U.S.; fax 441/238–4673. 4 apartments. Pool, coin laundry. AE, MC, V. EP.*

$$ PARAQUET GUEST APARTMENTS. Good for cost-conscious travelers who plan to eat in, these apartments (pronounced "parakeet") have an ideal location—a five-minute walk from Elbow Beach, five minutes to Hamilton by moped, and a short walk to the grocery store. Rooms are spartan but spacious and sunny. Nine have kitchenettes, the rest refrigerators and coffeemakers. Ask for a room with inland views and a private patio. While most apartments have showers only, some efficiency units have full baths. Use of in-room telephones costs $2.50 per day extra. When sunning yourself all day makes cooking a chore, try the casual home-style meals at the restaurant, which are enjoyed by locals. For special evenings out, the fine restaurants at Horizons & Cottages and the Stonington Beach Hotel are within walking distance. *72 South Rd., Paget PG 04 (Box PG 173, Paget PG BX); tel. 441/236–5842, fax 441/236–1665. 12 rooms. Restaurant, kitchenettes. No credit cards. EP.*

$$ ROBIN'S NEST. Tucked away in its own valley in a residential area off the North Shore Road, this is a real find for those who like to cook for themselves and enjoy true garden tranquility. All apartments are spacious and modern and have kitchens. Three of the four open onto lush, intimate gardens. All have cable TVs and phones. The small number of rooms means you are more than likely to enjoy the good-size pool and patio all to yourself. There is only one elevated apartment, which has sea views from its small rooftop patio. Repeat guests and business travelers alike enjoy the proximity to Hamilton, Admiralty Park, and snorkeling on the north shore. *10 Vale Close, Pembroke West HM 04, tel. 441/ 292–4347, www.bermudareservation.net. 4 apartments. In-room safes, kitchenettes, pool. No credit cards. EP.*

$$ SANDPIPER APARTMENTS. These spacious, simple, cheerfully decorated apartments in Warwick Parish are ideally located for south-shore beaches and bus routes. The 14 whitewashed units include five one-bedroom apartments and nine studios. Most can accommodate up to four people, and all have full kitchen with microwave and dining area and full bath, plus balconies or patios, radios and cable TVs. Tiled floors and bold floral-print curtains and bedspreads predominate, and daily maid service is included. Sandpiper is set in lush gardens with a pool and whirlpool, just off the main South Road and Hamilton bus route (a 15- to 20-minute bus ride into town). Paw-Paws restaurant is also within walking distance, and you can use the nearby beach and bar at Surf Side Beach Club. *Box HM 685, Hamilton HM CX, tel. 441/236– 7093, fax 441/236–3898, www.bermudareservation.net. 14 apartments. Kitchenettes, pool, hot tub, coin laundry. AE, MC, V. EP.*

$$ SKY TOP COTTAGES. This aptly named hilltop property has spectacular views of the island's southern coastline and the azure ocean beyond. Runners and walkers will appreciate their proximity to Elbow Beach, one of Bermuda's best stretches of sand for a workout. Neat, sloping lawns and carefully tended gardens with sun loungers and paved walks provide a pleasant setting for studios and one-bedroom apartments. Owners John and Andrea Flood refurbish the properties annually. The individually decorated units have attractive prints and carefully coordinated colors. Studios have shower baths, and one-bedrooms have full baths. The very private one-bedroom Frangipani apartment has an eat-in kitchen, a king-size bed, and a sofa bed. All units have good kitchenette facilities, phones, and cable TVs. Barbecue grills are available. *65 South Rd., Paget PG 03 (Box PG 227, Paget PG BX); tel.*

441/236–7984, fax 441/232–0446, www.bermuda.com/skytop. 11 apartments. Kitchenettes, volleyball. MC, V. EP.

$$ SYL-DEN. These well-located guest apartments are an affordable option for the budget-minded beach lover who wants a place near the south shore. Set back on a hill from the South Shore Road, Syl-Den is a 5- to 10-minute walk to Warwick Long Bay and minutes by bus to Horseshoe Bay and the other beaches. It takes about 25 minutes to reach Hamilton by bus. Most of the spacious rooms have tiled floors and are clean but simply decorated. Each unit has cable TV, phone, bath and shower, and full kitchen. Three have a private patio or garden. Guests can also take advantage of a large pool and small sun terrace. 8 Warwickshire Estate, Warwick WK 02, tel. 441/238–1834, fax 441/238–3205, www.bermudareservation.net. 12 apartments. In-room safes, kitchenettes, pool, coin laundry. AE, MC, V. EP.

$$ VALLEY COTTAGES & APARTMENTS. These pretty, informal Bermuda cottages and apartments are perfect for beach lovers, with one of the island's top stretches of sand—Elbow Beach—a short walk away. Choose from modern self-contained studio apartments or a larger one-bedroom cottage suite that can house up to four guests. Room are set in three attractive and traditional pink buildings. Palm trees and lush greenery surround the property. Most apartments have an accompanying patio or garden area, and all have kitchens or kitchenettes, phones, and cable TVs. A peaceful terrace and secluded spa pool are perfect for tanning and relaxing. You'll also have the use of the tennis courts at the Harmony Club. Valley Rd., Paget PG BX (Box PG 173, Paget PG BX); tel. 441/236–0628; 800/637–4116 in the U.S.; fax 441/236–3895. 9 apartments. Pool. AE, MC, V. EP.

$ BURCH'S GUEST APARTMENTS. This smart-looking whitewashed house with red shutters and panoramic views is situated right in the middle of the island, in a residential area. Hamilton is a five-minute bus ride away, and there is a small grocery store within walking distance. Apartments are simply furnished, but all have kitchenettes, phones, and cable TV. The most spacious of the five is at the front of the building and has the best views of the ocean. Three beds make it ideal for families with small children. The four smaller units have twin beds. Studios 6 and 7 have sea glimpses. There is a small garden at the back of the building with a pool. *110 North Shore Rd., Devonshire FL 03, tel. 441/292–5746 or 800/637–4116, fax 441/295–3794. 5 apartments. Kitchenettes, pool. No credit cards. EP.*

$ SERENDIPITY. These two studio guest apartments tucked away in a residential area in Paget are part of the family residence of Albert and Judy Corday, and those staying here have use of the owners' large family pool and benefit from a flat rate with no tax (an exemption applies to properties accommodating up to 5 people). Both ground-floor apartments are clean and pleasantly decorated. They have fully equipped kitchenettes, bathrooms with showers only, TVs (no cable), phones, and small private patios. One apartment has a queen-size bed with a love-seat sofa bed; the other has two single beds. There is no view, but a 15-minute walk will take you to Elbow Beach. It's a stone's throw from two grocery stores, a take-out restaurant, and other services. A bus stop is located just outside the front gate. Maid service can be arranged. *6 Rural Dr., Paget PG 06, tel. 441/236–1192, fax 441/232–0010. 2 studio apartments. Kitchenettes, no-smoking room, pool, laundry service. No credit cards. EP.*

$ SOUND VIEW COTTAGE. This Bermudian cottage with three housekeeping apartments is set in an elevated residential area overlooking the Great Sound. All rooms are tastefully decorated and have full kitchen facilities. The cottage also has a pool, patio, and barbecue and is very convenient to the south-shore beaches. The cottage has enviable views of both the south shore and Great Sound. Furthermore, the personal attention bestowed upon you by hosts Barbara and Eldon Raynor has brought them many repeat guests (most of whom request the same room year after year) and local hospitality awards. *9 Bowe La., Southampton SN 04, tel. 441/238–0064. 3 apartments. Kitchenettes, pool. No credit cards. EP.*

GUEST HOUSES/BED AND BREAKFASTS

$$–$$$$ **AUNT NEA'S INN AT HILLCREST.** Fine furniture and attention to
★ detail have transformed this charming 18th-century house into
an enchanting inn. The crowning glory of each of the 18 individually
decorated accommodations are the first-class beds. From
handsome oak canopy four-posters to wicker sleigh beds, each
one is a work of art. One cozy suite, for example, has a fantastic
wrought-iron Corsican-designed bed, a living room with open
fireplace, heavy Chinese rosewood chairs inlaid with mother-of-
pearl, and access to the public balcony that overlooks a lawn and
St. George. A Continental breakfast buffet, featuring freshly baked
muffins, is enjoyed family style at a large communal table. Your
enthusiastic hosts, Delaey Robinson and Andrea Dismont, will give
new guests a tour of the property. The self-catering suites and
cottages across from the main house are ideal for families. Aunt
Nea's, nestled in the historic town of St. George's, is about 45
minutes from Hamilton by bus. Nearby Tobacco Bay Beach and
the adjoining secluded coves have good snorkeling. The St.
George golf course is almost within putting distance. 1 Nea's Alley,
St. George, GE 05 (Box GE 96, St. George's GE BX); tel. 441/297–1630,
fax 441/297–1908, www.auntneas.com. 12 rooms, 4 one-bedroom suites,
2 two-bedroom suites. Breakfast room, lounge, refrigerators. AE, MC, V.
CP.

$$ **EDGEHILL MANOR.** Atop a high hill surrounded by gardens and
shrubs, this large colonial house is easy walking distance from
Hamilton and less than 15 minutes by moped from the best south-
shore beaches. The welcoming staff are attentive and add to the
cozy feel. In the morning you can feast on home-baked muffins
and scones in the cheery breakfast room. The guest rooms, which
are individually decorated with French provincial furniture and
colorful quilted bedspreads, have large windows and terraces
and benefit from recent bathroom upgrades. There's a large
poolside room with a kitchen that's suitable for families. All rooms
have cable TV. If you're traveling alone on a tight budget, ask for

the small ground-level room with a kitchen and private terrace. *36 Rosemont Ave., Hamilton HM EX (Box HM 1048, Hamilton HM EX); tel. 441/295–7124, fax 441/295–3850. 9 rooms. Breakfast room, in-room safes, refrigerators, pool. No credit cards. CP.*

$$ GREENE'S GUEST HOUSE. Set in the quiet western end of Southampton Parish on part of the Bermuda Railway Trail, this family-run guest house is a tranquil retreat with beautiful views of the Great Sound. All rooms are clean and modern, and each has a refrigerator, coffeemaker, cable TV, VCR, radio, and phone. A large swimming pool at the back of the house has lovely views over Jennings Bay and the ocean. Greene's is a two-minute walk to bus stops on the main Middle Road for south-shore beaches (it's a five-minute ride). Hamilton is 30 minutes away. Port Royal Golf Course and moped rentals can be reached in minutes by bus, and it is just a short walk to the Golf Academy, where you can practice your technique. A full breakfast is included. *Jennings Bay, Southampton SN BX (Box SN 395, Southampton SN BX); tel. 441/238–0834; 800/637–4116 in the U.S.; fax 441/238–8980. 6 rooms. Breakfast room, lounge, in-room VCRs, refrigerators, pool. No credit cards. BP.*

$$ LITTLE POMANDER GUEST HOUSE. In a quiet residential area on
★ Hamilton Harbour, the Little Pomander is a find if you're seeking affordable accommodation near the capital. The rooms, in a charming waterside cottage, are decorated with plump, pastel comforters, and coordinated fabrics. All rooms have microwaves, phones, refrigerators, and cable TV. Often guests congregate at sunset on the waterside lawn to enjoy views of Hamilton Harbour and stay to cook dinner on the barbecue grill. For a $10 fee you can play tennis across the road at the Pomander Tennis Club. Continental breakfast is served in a sunny room. *16 Pomander Rd., Paget PG 02 (Box HM 384, Hamilton HM BX); tel. 441/236–7635, fax 441/236–8332. 5 rooms. Refrigerators, breakfast room. AE, MC, V. CP.*

$$ LOUGHLANDS GUEST HOUSE & COTTAGE. This stately white mansion has seen grander days, but it still retains a charm and character accessible to the budget traveler. Set in spacious grounds above the South Shore Road, this 1920 house is loaded with fine antiques and European china. Lladro figurines grace the mantelpiece in the formal parlor, antique grandfather clocks stand in corners, and handsome breakfronts display Wedgwood china and Baccarat and Waterford crystal. Less than a five-minute walk from Elbow Beach, this guest house offers a Continental breakfast of cereals, fruit juice, prunes, croissants, Danishes, and coffee. The economical guest rooms tend to be somewhat worn, but most have large, comfortable chairs and cotton bedspreads. Singles, doubles, triples, and quads are available, and a large cottage near the main house has additional rooms. *79 South Rd., Paget PG 03, tel. 441/236–1253. 18 rooms with bath, 6 with shared bath. Pool, tennis court. No credit cards. CP.*

$$ ★ OXFORD HOUSE. This elegant Bermuda-style town house is a five-minute walk from the capital's shops, ferries, and buses. The family-owned and -operated two-story establishment, recipient of the Department of Tourism's highest award in its category for several years running, is popular with business travelers as well as tourists. Polished cedar-wood floors, a fireplace, and handsome Chippendale chairs lend warmth and class to the breakfast room, where you can sample scones, English muffins, fresh fruit, boiled eggs, and cereal each morning. The bright, airy rooms (doubles, triples, and quads) are individually decorated with bold fabrics, whitewashed walls, and some with antique furniture. A small bookcase in the upstairs hall is crammed with paperbacks that you're welcome to borrow. *20 Woodbourne Ave., Pembroke (Box HM 374, Hamilton HM BX); tel. 441/295–0503; 800/548–7758 in the U.S.; 800/272–2306 in Canada; fax 441/295–0250; www.oxfordhouse.com. Breakfast room, laundry service. AE, MC, V. CP.*

$$ ★ ROYAL HEIGHTS GUEST HOUSE. At the top of a nearly vertical driveway, this modern bed-and-breakfast has views of Gibbs Hill Lighthouse and a fantastic panorama of the Great Sound. Breathtaking sunsets can be viewed from the spacious, carpeted living room or by the pool. The rooms are large, each with private

Where to Stay with Kids

Families with children find Bermuda's larger hotels, housekeeping cottages, or holiday apartments the most comfortable and convenient. Along with pools, beaches, and family-friendly restaurants, most of the island's beach hotels offer summer children's programs: You can drop the kids off to participate in sand castle competitions, treasure hunts, face painting, and arts and crafts, or send them on trips to the aquarium or botanical gardens, or on a ferry ride. Activities on the premises are generally complimentary, while there is an additional charge for off-property excursions. Most children's programs are divided into two groups, one for preteens and teenagers, the other for younger children. The age ranges vary from hotel to hotel.

Although Pompano Beach Club does not have a children's program, the facilities seem designed for families with younger editions. The very shallow beach and the "kiddies" pool beside the larger pool put parents at ease when their children hit the water. Paddleboats and rafts are available at the boat house. A clay tennis court is on the premises and there is a miniature golf course nearby. The spacious two-room suites are popular among families.

Two smaller properties (with smaller price tags) are also excellent choices for families with children. Whale Bay Inn offers one-bedroom apartments and is within strolling distance of the beach. Salt Kettle House has homelike cottages (with fully equipped kitchens) and a hearty breakfast is included in the rates.

Most hotels in Bermuda allow children under a certain age to stay in their parents' room at no extra charge, but others charge for them as extra adults. Be sure to find out the cutoff age for children's discounts.

entrance, big windows, and a terrace. While all rooms benefit from great views, Nos. 3 and 6 are popular for their overlooks of the Great Sound. The matching drapes and quilted spreads in good-quality fabrics give rooms a cozy domestic feel, and there is ample closet space. Room No. 5, with its double bed and daybed, is good for families. All rooms have cable TVs and some have microwaves. Breakfast includes pastries, muffins, fruit, and sometimes egg dishes. Special honeymoon packages are available. The Fairmont Southampton Princess's golf course and some of the island's finest dining are within walking distance. *4 Crown Hill, Southampton SN 03 (Box SN 144, Southampton SN BX); tel. 441/238–0043, fax 441/238–8445. 7 rooms. Refrigerators, saltwater pool. AE, MC, V. CP.*

$ SALT KETTLE HOUSE. Set behind a screen of palm trees on a bay adjoining Hamilton Harbour, only a quick walk from the Hamilton ferry, this small, secluded guest house is a gem for the budget traveler looking for the best of British hospitality. Just left of the entrance is a cozy lounge with a fireplace where guests gather for cocktails and conversation. A hearty English breakfast is served family style in the dining room, which has water views. The main house has two guest rooms, and an adjoining apartment has a bedroom, bathroom, living room, and kitchen. Four waterside cottages have shaded patios and lounge chairs, bedrooms, sitting rooms, and kitchens. Guest rooms are small but well kept, and the decor is charming. The owner, Hazel Lowe, loves to chat with guests and make sightseeing and dining recommendations. She can refer you to a nearby cove for swimming. *10 Salt Kettle Rd., Paget PG 01, tel. 441/236–0407, fax 441/236–8639. 3 rooms in main house, 4 cottages. Lounge. No credit cards. BP.*

Imagine entering a world where a staff, which outnumbers the guests by three to one, remembers your name and is eager to take care of your every need. That is the essence of luxury pampering. You are immersed in a fantasy of care, attention, and detail to relax, inspire, and rejuvenate you. You can indulge in nearly every treatment you've ever heard of: aromatherapy, dulse scrubs, haysack wraps, and more.

In This Chapter

Cambridge Beaches 229 • Sonesta Beach Resort • 231

spas

IF THE CONCEPT OF LUXURY PAMPERING seems mysterious to you, try a little guided imagery:

Picture your day beginning with an early morning walk along lush garden paths teeming with bougainvillea, a light breakfast brought to your room, an invigorating game of tennis or an ocean kayak trip, and a sumptuous lunch, which in no way involves cottage cheese or a pineapple ring.

Next, imagine yourself relaxing under a beach umbrella with a book or taking a casual stroll on the beach or a dip in the ocean. Cap off the day with a series of indulgent treatments—perhaps a seaweed wrap or a salt-glow skin polish followed by a massage— then a good night's sleep under luxurious linens. As you close your eyes, your mind feels calm and your worries distant, knowing tomorrow will bring with it the same kindnesses. You drift off to sleep hearing not the sounds of your faraway responsibilities calling you, but the faint chirpings of the Bermudian birds and frogs and the sounds of the lapping ocean waves.

CAMBRIDGE BEACHES

Set on a 25-acre peninsula with five private coves on the ocean and a marina on the bay, Cambridge Beaches draws a mix of international travelers, many of whom return year after year. This is the type of place where guests gather for high tea in the afternoon, then dress for a formal dinner in the elegant main house. Evenings often end with dancing to live music on a terrace that overlooks the resort's private marina.

Sunlight dapples the indoor swimming pools at the Ocean Spa, a traditional Bermudian cottage with pink-stucco walls and a ridged roof. Guests here relax on a terrace where refreshments are served. The glass dome that covers the pools is open during warm months.

The spa offers treatments hard to find outside Europe. Cathiodermie facials by Guinot of Paris incorporate gentle stimulation of skin tissue with rollers that cause a tingling sensation. Using a clay mask, the therapist dissolves impurities and toxins, leaving the tissue feeling rejuvenated. Ionithermie treatments using electrical stimuli firm and tone skin and help rid the body of cellulite. These treatments can be combined with body wraps using seaweed, plant extracts, and other natural ingredients.

The Classic Spa Day package might start with a consultation with a therapist who conducts a computerized body-fat analysis, followed by exercise, sauna, and massage. A half-day program for men includes massage, facial, and hair treatment. Both full-day and half-day packages include lunch on a bayside terrace.

Accommodations are in cottage rooms and suites with traditional furnishings. Most have a whirlpool bath. Only a handful of the rooms have televisions, but there are others that can be rented.

Cambridge Beaches is in Somerset, a tiny parish of shady lanes and old homes. A short hike from Cambridge Beaches brings you to Scaur Hill Fort, built in the 1870s to protect the Royal Naval Dockyard. Now it's a 22-acre park with breathtaking views of the Great Sound and its armada of sailboats. You can charter a sailboat here or go snorkeling at an underwater trail for novice snorkelers. *30 Kings Point Rd., Sandys MA 02, Bermuda, tel. 441/234-0331 or 800/468-7300, fax 441/234-3352. www.privilege-spa.com. 69 rooms, 19 suites. Nightly rate $295–$420 per room. 5-night spa package $2,049 per person, includes meals and spa treatments. MC, V.*

EQUIPMENT
Free weights, stair climbers, stationary bikes, treadmills, weight-training circuit.

SERVICES
Aromatherapy, massage, paraffin body wraps, reflexology, reiki, salt glow, seaweed wrap.

SWIMMING
Indoor and outdoor pools, beaches.

CLASSES AND PROGRAMS
Computerized body-fat analysis, fitness consultation, nutrition consultation.

RECREATION
Bikes, boating, canoeing, croquet, kayaking, mopeds, snorkeling, tennis, windsurfing.

MEALS
Meals are included. Breakfast buffet. Lunch in the Mangrove Bay Terrace or the Café. Dinner in the Tamarisk Room.

➤ **SAMPLE MEALS:** Pesto pasta with shrimp and lemon, fish chowder, chicken–macadamia nut salad (lunch); seafood jambalaya, chicken breast with couscous, linguini with shrimp (dinner).

SONESTA BEACH RESORT
You'll find the pinkest beaches you've ever seen at the Sonesta Resort, located right in the middle of Bermuda's South Shore, a privileged area close to island attractions yet secluded and peaceful.

Boasting an impressive array of treatments and exercise equipment in a compact space, the Bersalon Spa is a great place to drop by between business meetings or rounds of golf. The facility has 11 treatment rooms, an aerobics studio, a strength-training and cardiovascular room, and well-equipped lounges for men and women.

If you simply want to be pampered, there are four-day spa sampler packages that allow you to try treatments not available in the United states, such as the Oriental Wisdom, which combines Chinese- and Japanese-style massage with aromatherapy.

Set on a 25-acre peninsula, the resort has three beaches with gentle surf, tennis courts, and water sports. For swimmers, the freshwater swimming pool has an all-weather glass-dome enclosure.

The guest rooms and suites are in a six-story structure with ocean and bay views. Rooms have a balcony or patio. Spacious split-level units have a sitting area and dressing room, modern rattan furniture, and floor-to-ceiling windows. Bring the kids to this big resort. While youngsters enjoy summer camp, you can be pampered at the spa. *Box HM 1070, Shore Rd., Southampton, Bermuda SN02, tel. 441/238-8122 or 800/766-3782, fax 441/238-8463. www.senesta.com. 403 rooms. Nightly rate $115–$440 per room. 3-night spa sampler package $895–$2,085, single or double occupancy. AE, DC, MC, V.*

EQUIPMENT
Free weights, stair climbers, stationary bikes, treadmills, weight-training circuit.

SERVICES
Aromatherapy, herbal wrap, loofah body scrub, paraffin body treatment, reflexology, salt-glow skin polish.

SWIMMING
Indoor and outdoor pools, beaches.

CLASSES AND PROGRAMS
Personal training, snorkeling instruction, tennis lessons.

RECREATION
Badminton, croquet, scuba diving, shuffleboard, Ping-Pong, tennis, volleyball, windsurfing.

CHILDREN'S PROGRAMS
Activities for ages 5–12.

MEALS
Meals à la carte. Lunch served at the SeaGrape and Boat Bay Club.

➤ **SAMPLE MEALS:** Vegetarian quesadillas, avocado sandwich with tomato and cheese (lunch); grilled swordfish, vegetarian lasagna, vegetable skewers with sea scallops (dinner).

portraits of bermuda

AMERICA'S REBEL COLONIES AND BERMUDA: GETTING A BANG FOR THEIR BUCKWHEAT

When the American War of Independence began, Bermudians at first felt little personal concern. There was some sympathy for the colonists; quarrels between arbitrary executive power and people, which in America had now led to real trouble, had also been part of Bermuda's history, and besides this there were ties of blood and friendship to make for a common understanding. But for all that, Bermudians, while expressing discreet sympathy, were chiefly concerned for their ships and carrying trade, and, realizing their helpless position, they believed their wisest course lay in continued loyalty to the Crown. The wisdom of this policy was suddenly brought into question when the Continental Congress placed an embargo on all trade with Britain and the loyal colonies, for as nearly all essential food supplies came from the Continent, the island faced starvation unless the decree was relaxed. Thus there was a swift realization that Bermuda's fate was deeply involved in the war.

The drama now began to unfold and soon developed into a struggle between the governor, George Bruere, and the dominant Bermuda clique led by the Tuckers of the West End. Bruere's chief characteristic was unswerving, unquestioning loyalty, and the fact that two of his sons were fighting with the royalist forces in America—one of them was killed at Bunker Hill—made the ambiguous behavior of Bermudians intolerable to him, both as a father and as an Englishman.

Of the Tuckers, the most prominent member of the family at this time was Colonel Henry, of the Grove, Southampton. His eldest son, Henry, colonial treasurer and councillor, had married the governor's daughter, Frances Bruere, and lived at St. George's. There were also two sons in America, Thomas Tudor, a doctor settled in Charleston, and St. George, the youngest, a lawyer in Virginia. The two boys in America, caught up in the events around them and far removed from the delicacies of the Bermuda situation, openly took the side of the Colonists.

Up to the time of the outbreak of the war there had been warm friendship between the Tuckers and the Brueres, a relationship made closer by the marriage of Henry Tucker to Frances Bruere. But when it became known in Bermuda that the Tuckers abroad were backing the Americans, Bruere publicly denounced them as rebels and broke off relations with every member of the family except his son-in-law. But Colonel Henry was more concerned with the situation in Bermuda than he was with the rights and wrongs of the conflict itself, and he believed that unless someone acted, the island faced serious disaster. So, privately, through his sons in America, he began to sound out some of the delegates to the Continental Congress as to whether the embargo would be relaxed in exchange for salt. This move, never in any way official, had the backing of a powerful group, and before long it was decided to send the colonel with two or three others to Philadelphia to see what could be arranged. Meanwhile, another less powerful faction took form and likewise held meetings, the object of which was to oppose in every way these potential rebellions.

Colonel Henry and his colleagues reached Philadelphia in July 1775, and on the 11th delivered their appeal to Congress. Though larded with unctuous flattery, the address met a stony reception, but a hint was thrown out that although salt was not wanted, any vessel bringing arms or powder would find herself free from the embargo. The fact that there was a useful store of powder at St. George's was by now common knowledge in America, for the Tucker boys had told their friends about it and the information had reached General Washington. Thus, before long, the question of seizing this powder for the Americans was in the forefront of the discussions.

Colonel Henry was in a tight corner. Never for an instant feeling that his own loyalty was in question, he had believed himself fully justified in coming to Philadelphia to offer salt in exchange for food. But these new suggestions that were now being put to him went far beyond anything he had contemplated, and he was dismayed at the ugly situation that confronted him. It is evident that the forces at work were too strong for him. The desperate situation in Bermuda, verging on starvation, could only be relieved by supplies from America, and an adamant Congress held the whip hand. After some agonizing heart-searching, Colonel Henry gave in and agreed with Benjamin Franklin to trade the powder at St. George's for an exemption of Bermuda ships from the embargo.

Henry returned home at once, arriving on July 25. His son St. George, coming from Virginia, arrived about the same time, while two other ships from America, sent especially to fetch the powder, were already on their way.

On August 14, 1775, there was secret but feverish activity among the conspirators as whaleboats from various parts of the island assembled at Somerset. As soon as it was dark, the party, under the command, it is believed, of son-in-law Henry and a Captain Morgan, set off for St. George's. St. George, lately from Virginia and sure to be suspect, spent the night at St. George's, possibly at the home of his brother Henry, and at midnight was seen ostentatiously walking up and down the Parade with Chief Justice Burch, thus establishing a watertight alibi. Meanwhile, the landing party, leaving the boats at Tobacco Bay on the north side of St. George's, reached the unguarded magazine. The door was quickly forced, and before long, kegs of powder were rolling over the grass of the Governor's Park toward the bay, where they were speedily stowed in the boats. The work went on steadily until the first streaks of dawn drove the party from the scene. By that time 100 barrels of powder were on the way to guns that would discharge the powder against the king's men.

When Bruere heard the news he was frantic. A vessel that he rightly believed had the stolen powder on board was still in sight from Retreat Hill, and he determined to give chase. Rushing into town, the distraught man issued a hysterical proclamation:

POWDER STEAL
Advt
Save your Country from Ruin, which
may hereafter happen. The Powder
stole out of the Magazine late last
night cannot be carried far as the
wind is so light.

A GREAT REWARD
will be given to any person that can
make a proper discovery before the
Magistrates.

News of the outrage and copies of the proclamation were hurried through the colony as fast as riders could travel. The legislature was summoned to meet the following day. Many members of the Assembly doubtless knew a good deal, but officially all was dark and the legislature did its duty by voting a reward and sending a wordy message expressing its abhorrence of the crime.

But no practical help was forthcoming, and after several days of helpless frustration Bruere determined to send a vessel to Boston to inform Admiral Howe what had happened. At first no vessels were to be had anywhere in the island; then, when one was found, the owner was threatened with sabotage, so he withdrew his offer. Another vessel was found, but there was no crew, and for three whole weeks, in an island teeming with mariners, no one could be found to go to sea. At last, on September 3, the governor's ship put to sea, but not without a final incident, for she was boarded offshore by a group of men who searched the captain and crew for letters. These had been prudently hidden away in the ballast with the governor's slave, who remained undiscovered. The captain hotly denied having any confidential papers, so the disappointed boarders beat him up and left.

In due course the ship reached Boston, and Admiral Howe at once sent the *Scorpion* to Bermuda to help Bruere keep order. Thereafter, for several years, His Majesty's ships kept a watchful eye on the activities of Bermudians, and in 1778 these were replaced by a garrison. It has always seemed extraordinary that no rumor of this bargain with the Americans reached Bruere before the actual robbery took place. It is even more amazing that within a stone's throw of Government House such a desperate undertaking could have continued steadily throughout the night without discovery.

The loss of the powder coincided with the disappearance of a French officer, a prisoner on parole. At the time it was thought that he had been in league with the Americans and had made his escape with them; but 100 years later, when the foundation for the Unfinished Church was being excavated, the skeleton of a man dressed in French uniform was disclosed. It is now believed that he must have come on the scene while the robbery was in progress and, in the dark, been mistaken for a British officer. Before he could utter a sound, he must have been killed outright by these desperate men and quickly buried on the governor's doorstep.

–*William Zuill*

A native Bermudian and former member of the Bermuda House of Assembly, William Zuill wrote several historical works about the island. This excerpt about the role of Bermuda in the American War of Independence is taken from his book *Bermuda Journey*. William Zuill died in 1989.

PRACTICAL INFORMATION

Addresses

Until recently, many houses in Bermuda didn't have street numbers. Some establishments are still mentioned only by their street, so **call for directions** if you're getting somewhere on your own.

The 180 islands that compose Bermuda are divided into nine parishes: Sandys (pronounced Sands), Southampton, Warwick, Paget, Pembroke, Devonshire, Smith's, Hamilton, and St. George's. Their import is pretty much historical these days, although they often appear on addresses following or in lieu of the street. It can get confusing, however, since Hamilton is both a city and a parish. The City of Hamilton is actually in Pembroke Parish. St. George is a city within the parish of the same name. We indicate Hamilton Parish and St. George's Parish when we refer to a property that falls outside the respective city proper.

Air Travel

CARRIERS

American has several nonstop flights, with two daily flights from New York and one from Boston in high season, April through October. Frequency drops November–March. **Continental** flies daily from Newark, New Jersey. **Delta** has one daily flight from Atlanta and one from Boston. **Trans World Airlines** flies daily to Bermuda from St. Louis, connecting through Atlanta. **US Airways** has daily service from New York, Baltimore, and Philadelphia. Service from New York is nonstop from April through September but connects through Philadelphia during low season. **Air Canada** has one daily flight from Toronto. **British Airways** flies every day except Wednesday during high season and three times a week during low season from London's Gatwick Airport.

➤ **MAJOR AIRLINES: Air Canada** (tel. 888/247–2262). **American** (tel. 800/433–7300). **Continental** (tel. 800/231–0856). **Delta Airlines** (tel. 800/241–4141). **Trans World Airlines** (tel. 800/221–2000). **US Airways** (tel. 800/428–4322).

➤ **FROM THE U.K.: British Airways** (tel. 0845/77–333–77).

CHECK-IN & BOARDING

Bermuda has occasional delays or cancellations due to high winds or crosswinds, particularly in the late summer and fall. Before you leave home for the airport, you should always **call to confirm whether or not there are Bermuda-bound delays.**

Bermuda-bound travelers are rarely bumped, even during the island's busiest summer season. Instead, when overbooking occurs, some airlines switch to a larger aircraft. In the event that passengers are bumped, however, the first to go are typically those who checked in late and those flying on discounted tickets, so **check in and get to the gate as early as possible.**

At many airports outside Bermuda, travelers with only carry-on luggage can bypass the airline's front desk and check in at the gate. But in Bermuda, everyone checks in at the airline's front desk. U.S. customs has a desk here, too, so you won't have to clear customs at home when you land.

Have your passport handy. Bermuda is rather scrupulous about ID, and you'll be asked to show your passport when checking in and again when boarding.

FLYING TIMES

Flying time to Bermuda from New York, Newark, Boston, Philadelphia, and Baltimore is about 2 hours; from Atlanta, 2¾ hours; and from Toronto, 3 hours.

Airports & Transfers

Bermuda's gateway is Bermuda International Airport, on the east end of the island, approximately 9 mi from Hamilton and 17 mi from Somerset.

➤ **AIRPORT INFORMATION: Bermuda International Airport** (2 Kindley Field Rd., St. George's, tel. 441/293–2470 ext. 4814).

TRANSFERS

Taxis are readily available at the airport. The approximate fare (not including tip) to Hamilton is $21; to St. George's, $12; to south-shore hotels, $28; and to Sandys (Somerset), $35. A surcharge of 25¢ is added for each piece of luggage stored in the trunk or on the roof. Fares are 25% higher between midnight and 6 AM and all day on Sunday and public holidays. Depending on traffic, the driving time to Hamilton is about 30 minutes; to Sandys, about one hour.

Bermuda Hosts Ltd. has round-trip transportation to hotels and guest houses aboard air-conditioned 6- to 25-seat vans and buses. Reservations are recommended. One-way fares, based on zones, are as follows: Zone 1 (to Grotto Bay Beach Hotel), $5; Zone 2 (to the Flatts Village area), $7; Zone 3 (to Cobb's Hill Road), $10; Zone 4 (to Church Road), $12; and Zone 5 (westward to Dockyard), $15.

➤ **BUS TRANSFERS: Bermuda Hosts Ltd.** (tel. 441/293–1334, fax 441/293–1335).

Boat & Ferry Travel

FARES & SCHEDULES

Ferries sail every day from Hamilton's ferry terminal, with routes to Paget, Warwick, and across the Great Sound to Somerset, in the West End. On weekdays, the Paget and Warwick ferries run until 9 PM; the last ferry from Hamilton to Somerset leaves at 5:30 PM. Sunday service is limited and ends around 7 PM. A one-way fare to Paget or Warwick is $2.50; to Somerset, $4. You can bring a bicycle on board free of charge, but you'll pay $4 extra to take a motor scooter to Somerset, and scooters are not allowed on the smaller Paget and Warwick ferries. Discounted one-, three-, and seven-day passes are available for use on both ferries and buses. The helpful ferry operators will answer questions about routes and schedules and will even help get your bike on board. Schedules are available at the ferry terminal, central bus terminal, and most hotels and are posted at each landing.

➤ BOAT & FERRY INFORMATION: Hamilton Ferry Terminal (8 Front St., near Queen St., tel. 441/295–4506).

Bus Travel

Bermuda's pink-and-blue buses travel the island from east to west. To find a bus stop outside Hamilton, look for either a stone shelter or a pink-and-blue striped pole. For buses heading to Hamilton, the top of the pole is pink; for those traveling away from Hamilton, the top is blue. Remember to **wait on the proper side of the road.** Driving in Bermuda is on the left. Bus drivers will not make change, so **purchase tickets or discounted tokens** or carry plenty of coins.

In addition to public buses, private minibuses serve St. George's. The minibus fare depends upon the destination, but you won't pay more than $5. Minibuses, which you can flag down, drop you wherever you want to go in this parish. They operate daily from about 7:30 to midnight, April through October, and 8–8 the rest of the year.

FARES & SCHEDULES

Bermuda is divided into 14 bus zones, each about 2 mi long. Within the first three zones, the rate is $2.50 (coins only). For longer distances, the fare is $4. If you plan to travel by public transportation often, buy a booklet of tickets (15 fourteen-zone tickets for $24, or 15 three-zone tickets for $15). You can also buy a few tokens, which, unlike tickets, are sold individually. Ticket booklets (and discounted but cumbersome "bags" of tokens) are available at the Hamilton bus terminal and at post offices. One-, three-, and seven-day adult passes ($10, $21, and $34, respectively) are available at the bus terminal, the Bermuda Department of Tourism in Hamilton, and at the airport. Passes for children (ages 5–15) are $5, $10, or $15. Passes are accepted on both buses and ferries.

Hamilton buses arrive and depart from the Central Bus Terminal. A small kiosk here is open weekdays 7:15–5:30, Saturday 8–3, and Sunday 9–5; it's the only place to buy money-saving tokens.

Buses run about every 15 minutes, except on Sunday, when they usually come every half hour or every hour, depending on the route. Bus schedules, which also contain ferry timetables, are available at the bus terminal in Hamilton and at many hotels. Upon request, the driver will be happy to tell you when you've reached your stop. **Be sure to greet the bus driver when boarding**—it's considered rude in Bermuda to ask a bus driver a question, such as the fare or details on your destination, without first greeting him or her.

➤ **BUS INFORMATION: Central Bus Terminal** (Washington and Church Sts., Hamilton, tel. 441/292–3854 or 441/295–4311). **St. George's Minibus Service** (tel. 441/297–8199).

Business Hours

BANKS & OFFICES

Branches of the Bank of Bermuda and the Bank of Butterfield are open Monday–Thursday 9:30–3, Friday 9:30–4:30. Bermuda Commercial Bank (opposite the Anglican Cathedral on Church Street in Hamilton) operates Monday–Thursday 9:30–3, Friday 9:30–4:30.

SHOPS

Most stores are open Monday through Saturday from around 9 until 5 or 6. Some of the larger department stores, like Trimingham's, are open until 9 PM on Friday. Some Hamilton stores keep evening hours when cruise ships are in port. Dockyard shops are generally open Monday through Saturday 10–5, Sunday 11–5. Otherwise, most shops are closed on

Sunday. Those that are open—mainly gas stations, grocery stores, and pharmacies—have abbreviated hours.

Car Travel

You cannot rent a car in Bermuda. Bermuda has strict laws governing against overcrowded roads, so even Bermudians are only allowed one car per household. A popular (albeit somewhat dangerous) alternative is to rent mopeds or scooters (☞ Moped & Scooter Rental, *below*), which are better for negotiating the island's narrow roads.

Cruise Travel

Concerned about overcrowding, the government of Bermuda limits the number of cruise ships that can visit the island on a weekly basis. At press time, five cruise lines were making regular sailings—Celebrity Cruises, Norwegian Cruise Line, Princess Cruises, and Royal Caribbean International.

To get the best deal on a cruise, **consult a cruise-only travel agency.** Weeklong cruises to Bermuda leave from New York, Boston, and other east-coast U.S. ports.

SHORE EXCURSIONS

Since you may just have one day to explore, **check where your ship docks.** The traditional port is Hamilton, the capital and the island's most commercial area, the best choice for shoppers. Many ships tie up at St. George's, where you walk off the vessel into Bermuda's equivalent of Colonial Williamsburg, a charming town of 17th-century buildings, narrow lanes, and a smattering of small boutiques. The West End, Bermuda's third port of call, is fast becoming the preferred one. Its Royal Naval Dockyard, an erstwhile shipyard that was the British Royal Navy's headquarters until 1995, has been beautifully restored as a minivillage with shops, restaurants, a maritime museum, an art gallery, and a crafts market. There are also occasional special events and a marina, with rental boats, submarine cruises, parasailing excursions, and a snorkeling area.

Bermuda tours are also organized by the cruise line and sold aboard the ship. You'll pay a bit more for these tours than if you book them independently, but some passengers find that the convenience is worth the price. Tours typically last between two and three hours and cost between $30 and $40 per person, although snorkeling and helmet diving cost a bit more.

Of course, you are always free to explore on your own. With its excellent taxi service, Bermuda is also a good island for hiring a car and driver.

➤ **CRUISE LINES INFORMATION: Celebrity Cruise Line** (Ship: *Horizon*. Built: 1990. Size: 46,811 tons. Capacity: 1,354 passengers. Cruise style: Semiformal. Ship: *Zenith* Built: 1992. Size: 47,255 tons. Capacity: 1,374 passengers. Cruise style: Semiformal. 1050 Caribbean Way, Miami, FL 33132, tel. 800/437–3111). **Norwegian Cruise Line** (Ship: *Norwegian Majesty*. Built: 1992, stretched 1999. Size: 40,876 tons. Capacity: 1,462 passengers. Cruise style: Casual. 7665 Corporate Center Dr., Miami, FL 33126, tel. 305/436–0866 or 800/327–7030). **Princess Cruises** (Ship: *Pacific Princess*. Built: 1972. Size: 20,000 tons. Capacity: 620 passengers. Cruise style: Semiformal. 10100 Santa Monica Blvd., Los Angeles, CA 90067, tel. 800/774–6237). **Royal Caribbean International** (Ship: *Nordic Empress*. Built: 1990. Size: 48,563 tons. Capacity: 1,600 passengers. Cruise style: Casual. 1050 Caribbean Way, Miami, FL 33132, tel. 800/327–6700 reservations; 800/255–4373 brochures only).

Customs & Duties

When shopping, **keep receipts** for all purchases. Upon reentering the country, **be ready to show customs officials what you've bought.** If you feel a duty is incorrect or object to the way your clearance was handled, note the inspector's badge number and ask to see a supervisor. If the problem isn't resolved, write to the appropriate authorities, beginning with the port director at your point of entry.

IN BERMUDA

On entering Bermuda, you can bring in duty-free up to 50 cigars, 200 cigarettes, and 1 pound of tobacco; 1.137 liters of wine and 1.137 liters of spirits; and other goods with a total maximum value of $30. To import plants, fruits, vegetables, or pets, you must get an import permit in advance from the Department of Agriculture and Fisheries. Merchandise and sales materials for use at conventions must be cleared with the hotel concerned before you arrive.

➤ **INFORMATION: Department of Agriculture and Fisheries** (HM 834, Hamilton HM CX, tel. 441/236–4201, fax 441/236–7582, www.agfish£bdagovt.bm).

IN AUSTRALIA

Australian residents who are 18 or older may bring home $A400 worth of souvenirs and gifts (including jewelry), 250 cigarettes or 250 grams of tobacco, and 1,125 ml of alcohol (including wine, beer, and spirits). Residents under 18 may bring back $A200 worth of goods. Prohibited items include meat products. Seeds, plants, and fruits need to be declared upon arrival.

➤ **INFORMATION: Australian Customs Service** (Regional Director, Box 8, Sydney, NSW 2001, tel. 02/9213–2000, fax 02/9213–4000).

IN CANADA

Canadian residents who have been out of Canada for at least seven days may bring home C$750 worth of goods duty-free. If you've been away less than seven days but more than 48 hours, the duty-free allowance drops to C$200. If your trip lasts 24–48 hours, the allowance is C$50. You may not pool allowances with family members. Goods claimed under the C$750 exemption may follow you by mail. Those claimed under the lesser exemptions must accompany you. Alcohol and tobacco products may be included in the seven-day and 48-hour exemptions but not in the 24-hour exemption. If you meet the age requirements of the province or territory through which you reenter Canada, you may bring in, duty-free, 1.14 liters (40 imperial ounces) of liquor or 1.5 liters of wine or 24 12-ounce cans or bottles of beer or ale. If you are 16 or older you may bring in, duty-free, 200 cigarettes and 50 cigars. Check ahead of time with Revenue Canada or the Department of Agriculture for policies regarding meat products, seeds, plants, and fruits.

You may send an unlimited number of gifts worth up to C$60 each duty-free to Canada. Label the package UNSOLICITED GIFT—VALUE UNDER $60. Alcohol and tobacco are excluded.

➤ **INFORMATION: Revenue Canada** (2265 St. Laurent Blvd. S, Ottawa, Ontario K1G 4K3, tel. 613/993–0534; 800/461–9999 in Canada; fax 613/957–8911, www.ccra-adrc.gc.ca).

IN NEW ZEALAND

Homeward-bound residents 17 or older may bring back $700 worth of souvenirs and gifts. Your duty-free allowance also includes 4.5 liters of wine or beer; one 1,125-ml bottle of spirits; and either 200 cigarettes, 250 grams of tobacco, 50 cigars, or a combination of the three up to 250 grams. Prohibited items include meat products, seeds, plants, and fruits.

➤ **INFORMATION: New Zealand Customs** (Custom House, 50 Anzac Ave., Box 29, Auckland, New Zealand, tel. 09/359–6655, fax 09/359–6732, www.customs.govt.nz).

IN THE U.K.

From countries outside the EU, including Bermuda, you may bring home, duty-free, 200 cigarettes or 50 cigars; 1 liter of spirits or 2 liters of fortified or sparkling wine or liqueurs; 2 liters of still table wine; 60 ml of perfume; 250 ml of toilet water; plus £145 worth of other goods, including gifts and souvenirs. If you are returning from outside the EU, prohibited items include meat products, seeds, plants, and fruits.

➤ **INFORMATION: HM Customs and Excise** (Dorset House, Stamford St., Bromley, Kent BR1 1XX, tel. 020/7202–4227, www.hmce.gov.uk).

IN THE U.S.

U.S. residents who have been out of the country for at least 48 hours (and who have not used the $400 allowance or any part of it in the past 30 days) may bring home $400 worth of foreign goods duty-free.

U.S. residents 21 and older may bring back 1 liter of alcohol duty-free. In addition, regardless of your age, you are allowed 200 cigarettes and 100 non-Cuban cigars. Antiques, which the U.S. Customs Service defines as objects more than 100 years old, enter duty-free, as do original works of art done entirely by hand, including paintings, drawings, and sculptures.

You may also send packages home duty-free: up to $200 worth of goods for personal use, with a limit of one parcel per addressee per day (except alcohol or tobacco products or perfume worth more than $5); label the package PERSONAL USE and attach a list of its contents and their retail value. Do not label the package UNSOLICITED GIFT or your duty-free exemption will drop to $100. Mailed items do not affect your duty-free allowance on your return.

➤ **INFORMATION: U.S. Customs Service** (1300 Pennsylvania Ave. NW, Washington, DC 20229, tel. 202/354–1000 inquiries, www.customs.gov; complaints c/o Office of Regulations and Rulings; registration of equipment c/o Resource Management, tel. 202/927–0540).

Electricity

Local electrical current is the same as in the United States and Canada: 110 volt, 60 cycle AC. All appliances that can be used in North America can be used in Bermuda without adapters.

Emergencies

➤ **DOCTORS & DENTISTS REFERRAL: Government Health Clinic** (67 Victoria St., Hamilton, tel. 441/236–0224, fax 441/292–7627).

➤ **EMERGENCIES: Police, fire, ambulance** (tel. 911). **Air/Sea Rescue** (tel. 441/297–1010, fax 441/297–1530, www. rccbermuda.bm).

➤ **HOSPITALS: King Edward VII Memorial Hospital** (7 Point Finger Rd., outside Hamilton near the Botanical Gardens, tel. 441/236–2345, fax 441/236–3691) is open 24 hours.

➤ **PHARMACIES: Clarendon Pharmacy** (Clarendon Bldg., Bermudiana Rd., Hamilton, tel. 441/295–6144), open Monday–Saturday 8–6. **Collector's Hill Apothecary** (South Shore Rd. and Collector's Hill, Smith's, tel. 441/236–8664 or 441/236–9878), open Monday–Saturday 8–8, Sunday 11–7. **Hamilton Pharmacy** (Parliament St., Hamilton, tel. 441/295–7004 or 441/292–7986), open Monday–Saturday 8–9. **Paget Pharmacy** (Rural Hill Plaza, Middle Rd., Paget, tel. 441/236–2681 or 441/236–7275), open Monday–Saturday 8–8, Sunday 10–6. **Phoenix Centre** (3 Reid St., Hamilton, tel. 441/295–3838 or 441/295–0698), open Monday–Saturday 8–6, Sunday noon–6. **Robertson's Drug Store** (York St. and Customs House Sq., tel. 441/297–1736 or 441/297–1828), open Monday–Saturday 8–7:30, Sunday 4–6. **Woodbourne Chemist** (Gorham Rd., Pembroke, on outskirts of Hamilton, tel. 441/295–1073 or 441/295–2663), open Monday–Saturday 8–6.

Etiquette & Behavior

Bermudians tend to be quite formal in attire as well as in personal interactions. Casual dress, including bathing suits, are acceptable at hotels and resorts, but locals never venture into Hamilton in anything less than slacks and sports shirts for men, and dresses for women. Most restaurants and clubs request that men wear jackets, and more formal establishments require ties during dinner.

In downtown Hamilton, the classic Bermuda shorts are often worn by banking and insurance executives, but the outfit always includes high black socks, dress shoes, and jacket and tie. **When it comes to dress, err on the formal side.** It is an offense in

Bermuda to appear in public without a shirt, even for joggers. This rule may seem arcane, but most Bermudians appreciate this decorum. This also holds true for the beach—thong bathing suits and topless sunbathing are not acceptable.

Courtesy is the rule when locals interact among themselves. In business and social gatherings use the more formal Mr. and Ms. instead of first names, at least until a friendship has been established, which sometimes takes just a few minutes. Always greet bus drivers with a friendly "Good morning" or "Good afternoon" when you board public buses. This is an island custom, and it's nice to see each passenger offer a smile and sincere greeting when boarding and exiting the bus.

Food & Drink

The major cultural influences that have shaped modern-day Bermuda—British, Caribbean, and American—have inspired its food as well. Truly local specialties are few and far between, but do search out mussel pie, fish sandwiches, cassava pie, shark hash, and the succulent Bermuda spiny lobster (available September–March).

Eating out, like most everything else on the island, is quite expensive, but the quality tends to be high and the range of options—from extremely casual pubs and local beach shacks to top-rated hotel dining rooms and elegant colonial-style restaurants—is typical of an area that caters to visitors. One thing you won't find on the island are fast-food chains, with the exception of a solitary Kentucky Fried Chicken in Hamilton.

Many hotels offer a choice of meal plans. Those willing to give up a little culinary independence in exchange for convenience, and often substantial savings, should investigate these options when booking. Some resorts have a dine-around program, which allows you to trade a meal at your resort for a meal at another. Numerous "self-catering" lodgings involve doing some shopping and cooking for yourself but you'll certainly eat for less.

For more information on eating out in Bermuda, and reviews of the island's best dining spots, *see* Eating Out. The restaurants we list are the cream of the crop in their price categories. Unless otherwise noted, the restaurants listed in this guide are open daily for lunch and dinner.

PAYING

Most restaurants on Bermuda, even smaller ones, accept all major credit cards, but always check first if you are relying on this. **Check your bill before you tip.** A 15% service charge is almost always automatically added.

RESERVATIONS & DRESS

Reservations are always a good idea. We mention them only when they're essential or are not accepted. Book as far ahead as you can, and reconfirm as soon as you arrive, especially in high season. Also be aware that many restaurants close—or curtail hours or days of service—in the off-season, so **call ahead before setting out for lunch or dinner.**

Bermudians on the whole are a dressy lot, and dinner attire is no exception. Even when not required, a jacket for men is never out of place in upscale restaurants. In our restaurant reviews, we mention dress only when men are required to wear a jacket or a jacket and tie.

WINE, BEER, & SPIRITS

Bermuda is known for its fine rum and spirits, and in addition many restaurants now have extraordinary wine cellars as well. There are numerous wine and spirit merchants along Front Street that do a good business catering to cruise passengers, and many towns on the island have shops that provide excellent bottled rum varieties at reasonable prices.

To take liquor back duty-free, visit one of the larger shops and **arrange for your purchases to be delivered to the airport or your cruise ship** at no extra charge. There are good savings, with liters of rum costing approximately $10 duty-free (it's about $20 for regular purchases). Make sure you leave enough time for the shop to make the delivery (one to two days is ideal).

Gay & Lesbian Travel

Bermuda remains socially conservative in many respects, so same-sex couples may encounter some stares and whispers. However, discriminating against anyone based on sexual orientation is against the law.

➤ **GAY- & LESBIAN-FRIENDLY TRAVEL AGENCIES: Different Roads Travel** (8383 Wilshire Blvd., Suite 902, Beverly Hills, CA 90211, tel. 323/651–5557 or 800/429–8747, fax 323/651–3678). **Kennedy Travel** (314 Jericho Turnpike, Floral Park, NY 11001, tel. 516/352–4888 or 800/237–7433, fax 516/354–8849, www. kennedytravel.com). **Now Voyager** (4406 18th St., San Francisco, CA 94114, tel. 415/626–1169 or 800/255–6951, fax 415/626–8626, www.nowvoyager.com). **Skylink Travel and Tour** (1006 Mendocino Ave., Santa Rosa, CA 95401, tel. 707/546–9888 or 800/225–5759, fax 707/546–9891, www.skylinktravel.com), serving lesbian travelers.

Health

Sunburn and sunstroke are legitimate concerns if you're traveling to Bermuda in the summer. On hot, sunny days, **wear a hat, a beach cover-up, and lots of sunblock.** These are essential for a day on a boat but are also advisable for midday at the beach. Be sure to take the same kind of precautions on overcast summer days—some of the worst cases of sunburn happen on cloudy afternoons when sunblock seems unnecessary. Drink plenty of water and, above all, **limit the amount of time you spend in the sun** until you become acclimated.

The Portuguese man-of-war occasionally visits Bermuda's waters, so **be alert when swimming,** especially in summer or whenever the water is particularly warm. This creature is recognizable by a purple, balloonlike float sack of perhaps 8 inches in diameter, below which dangle 20- to 60-inch tentacles armed with powerful stinging cells. Contact with the stinging cells causes immediate and severe pain. Seek medical attention immediately: a serious sting can send a person into shock. In the meantime—or if getting to a doctor will take a while—treat the affected area liberally with ammonia. Although usually encountered in the water, Portuguese men-of-war may also wash up on shore. If you spot one on the sand, steer clear, as the sting is just as dangerous out of the water.

DIVERS' ALERT
Do not fly within 24 hours of scuba diving.

MEDICAL PLANS
No one plans to get sick while traveling, but it happens, so consider signing up with a medical-assistance company. Members get doctor referrals, emergency evacuation or repatriation, hot lines for medical consultation, cash for emergencies, and other assistance.

➤ **MEDICAL-ASSISTANCE COMPANIES: International SOS Assistance** (8 Neshaminy Interplex, Suite 207, Trevose, PA 19053, tel. 215/245–4707 or 800/523–6586, fax 215/244–9617, www.internationalsos.com; 12 Chemin Riantbosson, 1217 Meyrin 1, Geneva, Switzerland, tel. 4122/785–6464, fax 4122/785–6424, www.internationalsos.com; 331 N. Bridge Rd., 17-00, Odeon Towers, Singapore 188720, tel. 65/338–7800, fax 65/338–7611, www.internationalsos.com).

Holidays

On Sundays and national public holidays, all shops, businesses, and many restaurants in Bermuda close. Buses and ferries run on limited schedules. Most entertainment venues, sights, and sports outfitters remain open. When holidays fall on a Saturday, government and commercial offices close the following Monday, but restaurants and shops remain open. National public holidays are New Year's Day, Good Friday (Mar. 29 in

255

2002), Bermuda Day (May 24), Queen's Birthday (June 10 in 2002), Emancipation Day/Somers Day (Aug. 1–2 in 2002), Labour Day (Sept. 2 in 2002), Remembrance Day (Nov. 11), Christmas, and Boxing Day (Dec. 26).

Mail & Shipping

Allow 7 to 10 days for mail from Bermuda to reach the United States, Canada, or the United Kingdom and about two weeks to arrive in Australia or New Zealand.

OVERNIGHT SERVICES

Overnight courier service is available to or from the continental United States through several companies. Service between Bermuda and Canada takes one or two business days, depending on the part of Canada; between Bermuda and the United Kingdom, generally two business days; and between Bermuda and Australia or New Zealand, usually three.

In Bermuda, rates include pickup from anywhere on the island. Prices for a document up to the first pound range $26–$37 to the United States, $30–$38 to Canada, and $35–$42 to the United Kingdom, Australia, or New Zealand. For the fastest delivery, your pickup request must be made before about 10 AM. Note that pickups (and drop-off locations) are limited on Saturdays, and there is no service on Sunday. Also, packages sent to Bermuda may take a day longer than documents.

➤ **MAJOR SERVICES: Federal Express** (tel. 441/295–3854). **International Bonded Couriers** (tel. 441/295–2467). **Mailboxes Unlimited Ltd.** (tel. 441/292–6563). **United Parcel Service** (tel. 441/295–2467).

POSTAL RATES

Airmail postcards to the United States and Canada cost 60¢, letters 65¢ for the first 10 grams. Postcards to the United Kingdom cost 75¢, letters 80¢ for the first 10 grams. Postcards to Australia and New Zealand cost 85¢, letters 90¢ for the first 10 grams.

SHIPPING PARCELS

Through Parcel Post at Bermuda's post office, you can send packages via either International Data Express (which takes two to five business days to the United States, Canada, the United Kingdom, Australia, and New Zealand) or Air Parcel Post (which takes 5 to 10 business days to the United States, Canada, and the United Kingdom, or two weeks to Australia and New Zealand).

For the first 500 grams, International Data Express rates are $25 to the United States and Canada, $30 to the United Kingdom, and $35 to Australia or New Zealand. Air Parcel Post rates run $7.65 for the first 500 grams to the United States, $9.10 to Canada, $11.95 to the United Kingdom, and $13.95 to Australia or New Zealand.

Most of Bermuda's largest stores offer shipping of purchases. Some may ask you either to buy insurance or to sign a waiver absolving them of any responsibility for potential loss or damage.

➤ **POST OFFICE: International Data Express** (tel. 441/297–7802). **Parcel Post** (tel. 441/297–7876).

Media

E-MAIL

If your hotel doesn't hook you up, you may send and receive e-mail for about $10 per hour at a few places around the island, two of which are also restaurants.

➤ **E-MAIL SERVICES: Freeport Seafood Restaurant** (1 Freeport Rd., Dockyard, Sandys, tel. 441/234–1692). **M. R. Onions Restaurant and Bar** (Par-La-Ville Rd., Hamilton, tel. 441/292–5012, fax 441/292–3122, www.bermuda.bm/onions). **Twice Told Tales Bookstore** (Parliament St., near Reid St., Hamilton, tel. 441/296–1995, fax 441/296–6339).

NEWSPAPERS & MAGAZINES

The *Royal Gazette,* Bermuda's only daily newspaper, is considered the paper of record. Established in 1828, it is published Monday through Saturday and offers a comprehensive mix of international hard news along with sports, business, and features. You can find it on the Web at www.accessbda.bm/gazette.htm. Its weekly sister paper, the *Mid-Ocean News,* is more community oriented, with extensive coverage of local arts, theater, politics, and overseas travel. Published twice a week, the *Bermuda Sun* (www.bermudasun.org) also focuses on local politics, trends, and events.

Appearing monthly in the *Royal Gazette, RG* magazine is a high-quality glossy, with topical features. *The Bermudian,* the island's oldest monthly, is another glossy, showcasing local lifestyles, personalities, history, arts, and social events. Distributed in 80 countries, *Bermuda,* a quarterly, keeps Bermudaphiles up-to-date on local cultural, political, and social trends.

Two quarterlies, *Bottom Line* and *Bermudian Business,* provide comprehensive coverage of local and international money-making, from banking, financial services, and insurance to new technologies.

RADIO & TELEVISION

Dial **Mix 106** (106.1 FM) for calypso, reggae, and soca, plus R&B, adult contemporary, local jazz, and European classical. For country music, listen to **1450 Country** (1450 AM), which also has a midday call-in talk show covering hot local issues. **Z2** (1340 AM) surrounds its talk shows with Billboard Top 100 and country-and-western tunes. You can hear more Top 100 rock, R&B, hip-hop, and reggae on **Power 95** (94.9 FM). Gospel, easy listening, and religious talk are the sounds on **ZFB 1230 AM.** The **Government Emergency Broadcast Station** (100.1 FM) is used in case of a storm.

In addition to a slew of cable television stations (mainly from the United States), Bermudian sets can be tuned in to **ZBM**

("Zed BM"), the CBS affiliate, on TV channel 9 or cable 3; **ZFB** ("Zed FB"), the ABC affiliate, on TV channel 7 or cable 2; and **VSB**, the NBC affiliate, on TV channel 11 or cable 4. Along with the nightly news, local programming, which is interspersed with the networks' offerings, might include a cooking show, a cricket or football (soccer) match, or a program on health awareness.

Money Matters

Since Bermuda imports everything from cars to cardigans, prices are very high. At an upscale restaurant, for example, you're bound to pay as much for a meal as you would in New York, London, or Paris: on average, $60 to $80 per person, $120 with drinks and wine. There are other options, of course; the island is full of coffee shops, where you can eat hamburgers and french fries with locals for about $7. The same meal at a restaurant costs about $15.

A cup of coffee costs between $1.50 and $3; a mixed drink from $4 to $6; a bottle of beer from $2.25 to $6; and a can of soda about $1.50. A 15-minute cab ride will set you back about $25 including tip. A 36-exposure roll of 35mm 100 ASA print film costs $6 to $8. A pack of cigarettes costs between $5 and $7.

Prices throughout this guide are given for adults. Substantially reduced fees are sometimes available for children, students, and senior citizens.

ATMS

ATMs are found all over Bermuda, in shops, arcades, supermarkets, the airport, and two of the island's banks. Both the **Bank of Bermuda** and the **Bank of Butterfield** are affiliated with the Cirrus and Plus networks. Note that the personal identification number (PIN) you use with Bank of Bermuda ATMs must be 4 digits, while Bank of Butterfield ATMs accept PINs with 4 to 16 digits.

CREDIT CARDS

In Bermuda, most shops and restaurants accept credit and debit cards, but some hotels insist on cash or traveler's checks, so **check in advance whether your hotel takes credit cards.** The most widely accepted cards are **MasterCard, Visa,** and **American Express. Discover** and **Diners Club** are welcomed to a much lesser degree.

Throughout this guide, the following abbreviations are used: **AE,** American Express; **DC,** Diners Club; **D,** Discover; **MC,** MasterCard; and **V,** Visa.

➤ **REPORTING LOST CARDS: American Express** (tel. 800/327–1267). **Diners Club** (tel. 702/234–6377 collect). **Discover** (tel. 800/347–2683). **MasterCard** (tel. 800/307–7309). **Visa** (tel. 800/847–2911).

Most 800 numbers still incur a toll when dialing from Bermuda, so you may want to call your company collect.

CURRENCY

The Bermudian dollar is on par with the U.S. dollar, and the two currencies are used interchangeably. (Other non-Bermudian currency must be converted.) You can use American money anywhere, but change is often given in Bermudian currency. Try to **avoid accumulating large amounts of local money,** which is difficult to exchange for U.S. dollars in Bermuda and expensive to exchange in the United States.

CURRENCY EXCHANGE

If you need to exchange Canadian dollars, British pounds, or other currencies, for the most favorable rates **change money through banks.** Although ATM transaction fees may be higher abroad than at home, ATM rates are excellent because they are based on wholesale rates offered only by major banks. You won't do as well at exchange booths in airports or rail and bus stations, in hotels, in restaurants, or in stores.

➤ **EXCHANGE SERVICES: International Currency Express** (tel. 888/278–6628 orders, www.foreignmoney.com). **Thomas Cook Currency Services** (tel. 800/287–7362 telephone orders and retail locations, www.us.thomascook.com).

TRAVELER'S CHECKS

Traveler's checks are widely accepted throughout Bermuda. Lost or stolen, they can usually be replaced within 24 hours. **To ensure a speedy refund, buy your own traveler's checks.** Don't let someone else pay for them, as irregularities like this can cause delays. The person who bought the checks should make the call to request a refund.

Some hotels take personal checks by prior arrangement (a letter from your bank is sometimes requested).

Moped & Scooter Rental

Because car rentals are not allowed in Bermuda, you might decide to get around by moped or scooter. Bermudians routinely use the words "moped" and "scooter" interchangeably, even though they are different. You must pedal to start a moped, and it carries only one person. A scooter, on the other hand, which starts when you put the key in the ignition, is more powerful and holds one or two passengers.

Riding a moped is not without hazards, especially for first-time riders and those not accustomed to driving on the left. Roads are narrow, winding, and full of blind curves. Whether driving cars or scooters, Bermudians tend to be quite cautious around less experienced visiting riders. However, it's still wise to **think twice before renting a moped,** as accidents occur frequently and are occasionally fatal. The best ways to avoid mishaps are to drive defensively, obey the 20-mph (35-kph) speed limit, remember to **stay on the left-hand side of the road**—especially at traffic circles—and avoid riding in the rain and at night.

Helmets are required by law. Mopeds and scooters can be rented from cycle liveries by the hour, the day, or the week. The liveries will show first-time riders how to operate the vehicles. Rates vary, but single-seat mopeds cost about $32 per day or $113 per week (plus the mandatory $15 insurance and repair waiver). The fee includes third-party insurance, breakdown service, pickup and delivery, and a tank of gas. A $20–$50 deposit is required for the lock, key, and helmet, and you must be at least 16 and have a valid driver's license to rent. Major hotels have their own cycle liveries, and all hotels and guest houses will make rental arrangements.

Many gas stations are open daily 7–7, and a few stay open until midnight. The island's only 24-hour gas station is Esso City Auto Market in Hamilton, near the Bank of Butterfield, off Par-La-Ville Road. Gas for cycles runs $3–$4 per liter, but you can cover a great deal of ground on the full tank that comes with the wheels.

➤ **RENTAL COMPANIES: Eve's Cycle Livery** (Middle Rd., Paget, tel. 441/236–6247). **Oleander Cycles** (Valley Rd., Paget, tel. 441/236–5235; Gorham Rd., Hamilton, tel. 441/295–0919; Middle Rd., Southampton, tel. 441/234–0629; Dockyard, Sandys, tel. 441/234–2764). **Wheels Cycles** (117 Front St., Hamilton, tel. 441/292–2245 or 441/295–0112).

Packing

Bermudians dress more formally than most Americans. **Leave your cutoffs, short shorts, and halter tops at home.** In the evening, many restaurants and hotel dining rooms require men to wear a jacket and tie and women to dress comparably, so **bring a few dressy outfits.** Some hotels have begun setting aside one or two nights a week for "smart casual" attire, when jacket-and-tie restrictions are loosened. In this case, women should be fine with tailored slacks and a dressy blouse or sweater (though most Bermudian women wear dresses or skirts and blouses). Bermudian men often wear Bermuda shorts (and proper kneesocks) with a jacket and tie.

During the cooler months, bring lightweight woolens or cottons that you can wear in layers to match vagaries of the weather. A lightweight jacket is always a good idea. Regardless of the season, **pack a swimsuit, a beach-wear cover-up, sunscreen, and sunglasses** as well as a raincoat (umbrellas are typically provided by hotels). Comfortable walking shoes are a must. If you plan to play tennis, be aware that many courts require proper whites and that tennis balls in Bermuda are extremely expensive. **Bring your own tennis balls** if possible.

In your carry-on luggage, **pack an extra pair of eyeglasses or contact lenses** and **enough of any medication you take** to last the entire trip. You may also ask your doctor to write a spare prescription using the drug's generic name, since brand names may vary from country to country. In luggage to be checked, **never pack prescription drugs or valuables.** To avoid customs delays, carry medications in their original packaging. And don't forget to carry with you the addresses of offices that handle refunds of lost traveler's checks.

CHECKING LUGGAGE

In Bermuda you board and deplane via an old-fashioned staircase. Let this be your guide when deciding whether or not to carry on. How many carry-on bags you can bring with you is up to the airline. Most allow two, but not always, so make sure that everything you carry aboard will fit under your seat or in the overhead bin, and get to the gate early.

Bermuda-bound airlines commonly accept golf club bags in lieu of a piece of luggage, but there are fairly stringent guidelines governing the maximum amount of equipment that can be transported without an excess baggage fee. The general rule of thumb is one covered bag containing a maximum of 14 clubs, 12 balls, and one pair of shoes.

Passports & Visas

When traveling internationally, **carry your passport even if you don't need one** (it's always the best form of ID) and **make two photocopies of the data page** (one for someone at home and another for you, carried separately from your passport). If you lose your passport, promptly call the nearest embassy or consulate and the local police.

ENTERING BERMUDA

➤ **U.S. CITIZENS: Bring your passport to ensure quick passage through immigration and customs.** You do not need a passport to enter Bermuda if you plan to stay less than six months, but you must have onward or return tickets and proof of identity (original or certified copy of your birth certificate with raised seal, a U.S. Naturalization Certificate, a U.S. Alien Registration Card, or a U.S. Reentry Permit) and a photo ID.

➤ **CANADIANS: Canadians do not need a passport to enter Bermuda, though a passport is helpful to ensure quick passage through customs and immigration. A birth certificate or a certificate of citizenship is required, along with a photo ID.**

➤ **OTHER CITIZENS: Citizens of the United Kingdom and other countries must have a valid passport to enter Bermuda.**

Safety

Bermuda is a small, fairly affluent country and as a consequence has a low crime rate. Serious crimes against visitors—or anyone, for that matter—are rare. Still, **exercise the usual precautions with wallets, purses, cameras,** and other valuables, particularly at the beach. Always lock your moped or pedal bike, and store valuables in your room or hotel safe. Although an ocean breeze through a screen door is wonderful, **close and lock your hotel room's glass patio door** while you're sleeping or out of your room. Use common-sense precautions as you would in any unfamiliar environment, and be alert while walking at night.

Taxes

Hotels add a 7.25% government tax to the bill, and most add a 10% service charge or a per diem dollar equivalent in lieu of tips. Other extra charges sometimes include a 5% "energy surcharge" (at small guest houses) and a 15% service charge (at most restaurants).

A $20 airport departure tax is built into the price of your ticket.

Taxis

Taxis are the fastest and easiest way around the island—and also the most costly. Four-seater taxis charge $3.12 for the first ¼ mi and 24¢ for each subsequent ¼ mi. Between midnight and 6 AM, and on Sunday, a 25% surcharge is added to the fare. There is a 25¢ charge for each piece of luggage stored in the trunk or on the roof.

For a personalized taxi tour of the island, the minimum duration is three hours, at $30 per hour for one to four people and $42 an hour for five or six, excluding tip.

➤ **CAB COMPANIES: The Bermuda Industrial Union Taxi Co-op** (tel. 441/292–4476). **Bermuda Taxi Operators Company** (tel. 441/292–4175). **Bermuda Taxi Radio Cabs** (tel. 441/295–4141). **Sandys Taxi Service** (tel. 441/234–2344).

Telephones

AREA & COUNTRY CODES

The country code for Bermuda is 441. When dialing a Bermuda number from abroad, drop the initial 0 from the local area code. The country code is 1 for the United States and Canada, 61 for Australia, 64 for New Zealand, and 44 for the United Kingdom.

DIRECTORY & OPERATOR ASSISTANCE

When in Bermuda, call tel. 411 for local phone numbers. To reach directory assistance from outside the country, call tel. 441/555–1212.

INTERNATIONAL CALLS

You can dial direct from anywhere on the island. Most hotels impose a surcharge for long-distance calls, even those made collect or with a phone card or credit card. Many toll-free 800 or 888 numbers in the United States aren't honored in Bermuda— you many want to **consider buying a prepaid local phone card** rather than use your own calling card. Many small guest houses and apartments have no central switchboard. So if you have a phone in your room, it's a private line from which you can make only collect, credit-card, or local calls. Some small hotels have a telephone room or kiosk where you can make long-distance calls.

You'll find specially marked AT&T USADirect phones at the airport, the cruise-ship dock in Hamilton, and King's Square and Ordnance Island in St. George's. You can also make international calls with a calling card from the main post office. You can make prepaid international calls from the Cable & Wireless Office, which also has international telex, cable, and fax services Monday through Saturday 9–5.

To call the United States, Canada, and most Caribbean countries, simply dial 1 (or 0 if you need an operator's assistance), then the area code and the number. For all other countries, dial 011 (or 0 for an operator), the country code, the area code, and the number. Using an operator for an overseas call is more expensive than dialing direct. For calls to the United States, rates are highest from 10 AM to 7 PM and discounted from 7 PM to 11 PM. The lowest rates are from 11 PM to 7 AM. Calls to Alaska and Hawaii are not discounted. Calls to Canada are cheapest from 9 PM to 7 AM; to the United Kingdom, from 6 PM to 7 AM.

➤ **TO OBTAIN ACCESS CODES: AT&T USADirect** (tel. 800/874–4000). **MCI Call USA** (tel. 800/444–4444). **Sprint Express** (tel. 800/793–1153).

➤ **INTERNATIONAL CALLS: Main post office** (Church and Parliament Sts., Hamilton, tel. 441/295–5151). **Cable & Wireless Office** (20 Church St., opposite City Hall, Hamilton, tel. 441/297–7000).

LONG-DISTANCE SERVICES

AT&T, MCI, and Sprint access codes make calling long distance relatively convenient, but you may find the local access number blocked in many hotel rooms. First ask the hotel operator to connect you. If the hotel operator balks, ask for an international operator, or dial the international operator yourself. One way to improve your odds of getting connected to your long-distance carrier is to travel with more than one company's calling card (a hotel may block Sprint, for example, but not MCI). If all else fails, call from a pay phone.

➤ **ACCESS CODES: AT&T Direct** (tel. 800/872–2881). **MCI WorldPhone** (tel. 800/888–8000). **Sprint International Access** (tel. 800/623–0877).

PHONE CARDS

Buy a prepaid a phone card for long distance calls. They can be used with any Touch-Tone phone in Bermuda, although they only be used for calls outside Bermuda. Rates are often significantly lower than dialing direct. For example, Cable & Wireless charges 85 cents per minute for overseas calls; with their calling card, the rate drops to 59 cents per minute. The down side is that some hotels will charge you for making the call to your card's 800 number. Phone cards are available at pharmacies, shops, restaurants, and hotels. Both TeleBermuda and Cable & Wireless sell the cards in denominations of $10, $25, and $50.

You can use any balances remaining on the TeleBermuda cards when you return to the United States, Canada, or the United Kingdom. With Cable & Wireless cards, only balances on Truly Global cards (costing $50, $75, or $100) can be used when you are outside of Bermuda.

➤ **PHONE CARD COMPANIES: Cable & Wireless** (tel. 441/297–7022). **TeleBermuda** (tel. 441/292–7283).

PUBLIC PHONES

You'll find pay phones similar to those in the United States on the streets of Hamilton, St. George's, and Somerset as well as at ferry landings, some bus stops, and public beaches. Deposit 20¢ (U.S. or Bermudian) as soon as your party answers. (You can also deposit a U.S. or Bermudian quarter, but you won't receive the 5¢ change.) Most hotels charge 20¢–$1 for local calls.

Time

Bermuda, in the Atlantic Time Zone, is on Greenwich Mean Time, minus four hours (which means that it is four hours later in London than in Bermuda). Bermuda observes Daylight Saving Time (from the first Sunday in April to the last Sunday in October), so it's always one hour ahead of U.S. Eastern Standard Time. Thus, for instance, when it is 5 PM in Bermuda, it is 4 PM in New York, 3 PM in Chicago, and 1 PM in Los Angeles. Sydney is 14 hours ahead of Bermuda.

Tipping

A service charge of 10% (or an equivalent per diem amount), which covers everything from baggage handling to maid service, is added to your hotel bill. Most restaurants tack on a 15% service charge; if not, a 15% tip is customary (more for exceptional service). Porters at the airport expect about a dollar a bag, while taxi drivers usually receive 15% of the fare.

Travel Agencies

A good travel agent puts your needs first. Look for an agency that has been in business at least five years, emphasizes customer service, and has someone on staff who specializes in your destination. In addition, **make sure the agency belongs to a professional trade organization.** The American Society of Travel Agents (ASTA), with more than 26,000 members in some 170 countries, is the largest and most influential in the field. Operating under the motto "Without a travel agent, you're on your own," it maintains and enforces a strict code of ethics and will step in to help mediate any agent-client disputes if necessary. ASTA also maintains a Web site that includes a directory of agents.

➤ **LOCAL AGENT REFERRALS: American Society of Travel Agents** (ASTA; tel. 800/965–2782 24-hr hot line, fax 703/684–8319, www.astanet.com). **Association of British Travel Agents** (68–71 Newman St., London W1P 4AH, tel. 020/7637–2444, fax 020/7637–0713, www.abtanet.com). **Association of Canadian Travel Agents** (1729 Bank St., Suite 201, Ottawa, Ontario K1V 7Z5, tel. 613/521–0474, fax 613/521–0805). **Australian Federation of Travel Agents** (Level 3, 309 Pitt St., Sydney 2000, tel. 02/9264–3299, fax 02/9264–1085, www.afta.com.au). **Travel Agents' Association of New Zealand** (Box 1888, Wellington 10033, tel. 04/499–0104, fax 04/499–0827).

Visitor Information

➤ **BERMUDA DEPARTMENT OF TOURISM: Hamilton** (Global House, 43 Church St., tel. 441/292–0023; ferry terminal, Front St., tel. 441/295–1480, www.bermudatourism.com). **Canada** (1200 Bay St., Suite 1004, Toronto, Ontario M5R 2A5, tel. 416/923–9600, fax 416/923–4840). **U.K.** (BCB Ltd., 1 Battersea Church Rd., London SW11 3LY, tel. 020/7771–7001, fax 020/7771–7037). **U.S.** (310 Madison Ave., Suite 201, New York, NY 10017-6083, tel. 212/818–9800 or 800/223–6106, fax 212/983–5289).

Web Sites

Do check out the World Wide Web when you're planning. You'll find everything from current weather forecasts to virtual tours of famous cities. Fodor's Web site, www.fodors.com, is a great place to start your on-line travels.

One of the best Bermuda sites is www.bermuda-online.org. It's supported by the *Royal Gazette* and has information on every aspect of Bermuda from local history to transportation. The

Department of Tourism's Web page at www.bermudatourism.com is good for vacation-planning. A popular site is www.bermuda.com—it has a good search engine and links to a number of Bermuda-related Web pages. Another good site is Virtual Bermuda, www.surfbermuda.com, which has a monthly events calendar, links to the Bermuda Yellow Pages, and live streaming video from Front Street, Hamilton.

When to Go

In the summer, Bermuda teems with activity. Hotel barbecues and evening dances complement daytime sightseeing trips, and public beaches never close. The pace slows considerably in the off-season (December–March). A few hotels and restaurants close; some of the sightseeing, dive, snorkeling, and water-skiing boats are dry-docked; and only taxis and the St. George's minibus operate tours of the island. Most hotels remain open, however, and slash their rates by as much as 40%. The weather at this time of year is often perfect for golf and tennis, and you can still rent boats, tour the island, and take advantage of sunny days, shops, restaurants, and walking tours.

CLIMATE

Bermuda has a remarkably mild climate that seldom sees extremes of either heat or cold. In the winter (December–March), temperatures range from around 55°F at night to 70°F in the early afternoon. High, blustery winds can make the air feel cooler, however, as can Bermuda's high humidity. The hottest part of the year is between May and mid-October, when temperatures range from 75°F to 85°F. It's not uncommon for the temperature to reach 90°F in July and August. The summer months are somewhat drier, but rainfall is spread fairly evenly throughout the year. Bermuda depends solely on rain for its supply of fresh water, so residents usually welcome the brief storms. In August and September, hurricanes moving northward from the Caribbean sometimes batter the island and cause flight delays.

Your checklist for a perfect journey

WAY AHEAD
- Devise a trip budget.
- Write down the five things you want most from this trip. Keep this list handy before and during your trip.
- Make plane or train reservations. Book lodging and rental cars.
- Arrange for pet care.
- Check your passport. Apply for a new one if necessary.
- Photocopy important documents and store in a safe place.

A MONTH BEFORE
- Make restaurant reservations and buy theater and concert tickets. Visit fodors.com for links to local events.
- Familiarize yourself with the local language or lingo.

TWO WEEKS BEFORE
- Replenish your supply of medications.
- Create your itinerary.
- Enjoy a book or movie set in your destination to get you in the mood.
- Develop a packing list. Shop for missing essentials. Repair and launder or dry-clean your clothes.

A WEEK BEFORE
- Stop newspaper deliveries. Pay bills.
- Acquire traveler's checks.
- Stock up on film.
- Label your luggage.
- Finalize your packing list— take less than you think you need.
- Create a toiletries kit filled with travel-size essentials.
- Get lots of sleep. Don't get sick before your trip.

A DAY BEFORE
- Drink plenty of water.
- Check your travel documents.
- Get packing!

DURING YOUR TRIP
- Keep a journal/scrapbook.
- Spend time with locals.
- Take time to explore. Don't plan too much.

➤ **FORECASTS: Weather Channel Connection** (tel. 900/932–8437), 95¢ per minute from a Touch-Tone phone.

The following chart lists average daily maximum and minimum temperatures for Bermuda.

Jan.	68F	20C	May	76F	24C	Sept.	85F	29C
	58	14		65	18		72	22
Feb.	68F	20C	June	81F	27C	Oct.	79F	26C
	58	14		70	21		70	21
Mar.	68F	20C	July	85F	29C	Nov.	74F	23C
	58	14		74	23		63	17
Apr.	72F	22C	Aug.	86F	30C	Dec.	70F	21C
	59	15		76	24		61	16

INDEX

A

Addresses, 240

After Hours (restaurant), 172

Airports and transfers, 241–242

Air travel, 240–241, 262

Albuoy's Point, 140

Ambulance service, 250

Angel's Grotto (apartment facility), 214

Annex Toys, 90

Antiques shops, 69–70

A-One Paget (shop), 83

A-One Smith's (shop), 83

Apartments, 212–222

Aquariums, 156

Architecture, 150

Ariel Sands (cottagecolony), 206, 208

Art galleries, 70–73, 153–154

Art House Gallery, 70

Art museums, 142

A. S. Cooper & Son (department store), 67

Ascots (restaurant), 56

Aston & Gunn (shop), 75

Astwood Cove (apartment facility), 215

Astwood Dickinson (shop), 85–86

ATMs, 258

Aunt Nea's Inn, 223

B

Bailey's Ice Cream Parlour & Food D'Lites, 161

Bananas (shop), 76

Bank hours, 244

Barnsdale Guest Apartments, 215

Bars and lounges, 168–171

Beach (restaurant/bar), 32, 168

Beaches, 106–111

Bed and breakfasts, 199, 223–226

Belmont Golf & Country Club, 95–96

Benetton (shop), 77–78

Bermuda Aquarium, Museum, and Zoo, 156

Bermuda Arts Centre at Dockyard, 70, 153–154

Bermuda Biological Station for Research, 157

Bermuda Book Store, 73

Bermuda Civic Ballet, 179

Bermuda Conservatory of Music, 182

Bermuda Department of Tourism, 186, 268

Bermuda Festival, 178

Bermuda Film Festival, 181

Bermuda Folk Club, 173

Bermuda Glassblowing Studio & Show Room, 79

Bermuda Golf Academy and Driving Range, 181–182

Bermuda Jazz Festival, 173

Bermuda Musical & Dramatic Society, 183, 185

Bermuda National Gallery, 142, 183

Bermuda National Library, 182

Bermuda National Trust, 157

Bermuda National Trust Museum at the Globe Hotel, 145, 147

Bermuda Open, 133

Bermuda Perfumery, 89, 157

Bermuda Philharmonic Society, 182–183

Bermuda Public Library, 143

Bermuda Railway, 160

Bermuda Railway Museum, 69

Bermuda School of Russian Ballet, 179

Bermuda shorts, 19–20, 22

Bermuda Society of Arts, 70–71, 142, 179

Bermuda Triangle, 16–17, 19

Bermuda Underwater Exploration Institute, 140

Bicycling, 112

Birdsey Studio, 71

Bird-watching, 112–113

Black Horse Tavern, 60, 163

Bluck's (shop), 81

Blue Juice (restaurant/bar), 43–44, 168

Boating, 113–116

Boat tours, 116

Boat travel, 242–243

Bombay (restaurant), 41–42

Book Cellar, 73

Bookmart, 73

Books about Bermuda, 184

Bookstores, 73–74

Botanical Gardens, 161, 185

Botanic Tea Room, 35

Bowling, 117

Boyle, W. J. & Sons Ltd.(shop), 76

Bridge House Gallery, 71, 147

Brightside Guest Apartments, 215–216

Buds, Beans & Books, 74

Burch's Guest Apartments, 221–222

Burrows Lightbourn (shop), 87

Business hours, 244–245

Bus travel, 243–244

C

Cabinet Building, 141

Cafe Lido, 58

Café on the Terrace, 62

Calypso (shop), 76–77, 78

Calypso clubs, 173

Cambridge Beaches (cottagecolony), 208–209, 229–231

Camden House, 161

Carole Holding Print & Craft Shops, 71

Carriage House (restaurant), 45–46

Car travel, 245

Casey's (bar), 168

Castle Harbour Golf Club, 96–97

Cathedral of the Most Holy Trinity, 141

Caves, 161

Cecile (shop), 78

Cenotaph, 141

Chaplin Bay Beach, 110

Chatham House (shop), 74

Children's attractions, 140, 148, 156, 181–182, 199

Children's Bookshop, 74

China shops, 81

Chopsticks (restaurant), 36

Christ Church, 161

Churches, 141, 149, 151, 154, 161

Cigar shops, 74–75

City Hall (Hamilton), 141–142

City Hall Theatre, 179

Clairfont Apartments, 216

Clayhouse Inn, 173

Clearview Art Gallery, 71–72

Clear View Suites & Villas, 213–214

Climate, 269, 271

Clothing shops, 75–79

Club Azure, 171

Cocktail cruises, 116

Coconut Rock and Yashi Sushi Bar, 40, 168

Coconuts (restaurant), 53–54

Colony Pub, 33

Cooperage Building, 154

Coral Beach & Tennis Club, 127

Cottage colonies, 206–211

Cow Polly (shop), 78

Craft Market, 79, 81

Crafts shops, 79, 81

Credit cards, 259

Cricket, 130, 131

Crisson's (shop), 86

Crown Colony Shop, 78

Cruise travel, 245–246

Crystal Caves, 161

Crystal shops, 81

Cultural activites, 177–188

Currency, 259

Customs, 246–249

D

Dance, 179–180

Dance clubs, 171

Daniel's Head Village, 210–211

Davison's of Bermuda (shop), 76

Dawkins Manor (apartment facility), 216–217

Dennis's Hideaway (restaurant), 60

Dentists, 249

Department stores, 67–69

Dining, 251–253

after hours, 171–172

American/casual, 32

Bermudian, 33, 48–49, 52, 60

British, 33, 35, 45–47, 49, 53

Caribbean, 35–36, 53–54

Chinese, 36

contemporary, 36–37, 40, 47, 54–57, 60–61

French, 40–41, 57–58

Indian, 41–42

Italian, 42–44, 47–48, 49, 58, 61–62

light fare, 62–63, 141, 142, 149, 155, 161, 163

Mexican, 44

price categories, 31–32

seafood, 44–45, 58

steak, 59

sushi, 37, 40

Diving, 117–119, 254

Docksider (restaurant/bar), 35, 169

Doctors, 249

Dorothy's Coffee Shop, 62

Duties, 246–249

E

Eastern parishes

dining, 60–63

sightseeing, 156–164

Edgehill Manor (B&B), 223–224

Elbow Beach, 110–111

Elbow Beach Hotel, 127, 193

Electricity, 249

E-mail services, 256

Emergencies, 249–250

English Sports Shop, 75

Equestrian events, 132

Escape Venue (club), 171

Etiquette, 250–251

Exchanging money, 259–260

F

Fairmont Hamilton Princess(hotel), 193–194

Fairmont Princess Golf Club, 97–98

Fairmont SouthamptonPrincess Hotel, 128, 194

Featherbed Alley Printery, 147

Ferry travel, 242–243

Festival Fringe, 185

Film, 180–181

Fire emergencies, 250

Fisherman's Reef(restaurant), 44–45

Fishing, 119–121

Flanagan's Irish Pub, 169

Flow Sunday readings, 183

Flying Colours atRiihuolma's (shop), 81–82

Folk clubs, 173

Fort Hamilton, 142–143

Fort St. Catherine, 162

Fort Scaur, 154

Fourways Inn, 54, 211

Frangipani (shop), 79

Freeport Gardens(restaurant), 48–49

Fresco's Deli, 62

Fresco's Wine Bar & Restaurant, 37, 169

Frith's Liquors Ltd., 87

Frog & Onion Pub, 49, 170

G

Garden Club of Bermuda, 186

Garden House (apartmentfacility), 217

Gardens, 157, 161

Garden tours, 185–186

Gates Fort, 162

Gay and lesbian travel, 253

Gibbons Co. (departmentstore), 67–68

Gibbs Hill Lighthouse, 162

Gift shops, 81–83

Gilbert & Sullivan Society of Bermuda, 183

Golf, 93–103, 108–109

Gombey dancers, 180

Gosling's (shop), 89

Government Tennis Stadium, 128

Greenbank Cottages, 217–218

Greene's Guest House, 224

Green Lantern (restaurant), 52

Grocery stores, 83–85

Grotto Bay Beach Resort, 128, 195, 198

Gucci (shop), 77

Guest houses, 199, 223–226

H

H. A. & E. Smith's (department store), 68

Hall of Names (shop), 82

Hamilton, 22

dining, 32–45, 141, 142

nightlife, 168–170

numbering of houses, 66

shopping districts, 65–66

sightseeing, 137–144

Hamiltonian Hotel & Island Club, 206

Harbourfront (restaurant), 37

Harley's Bistro, 42

Harmony Club (hotel), 198

Harrington Hundreds Grocery & Liquor Store, 84

Hasty Pudding Theatricals, 185

Health concerns, 253–254

Helmet diving, 119

Henry VIII (restaurant/bar), 53, 170

Heritage House (gallery), 72

Heron Bay Marketplace, 84

Heydon Trust Property, 154

Historical tours, 186–187

Hodge Podge (shop), 82

Hog Penny Pub, 35, 169

Holidays, 254–255

Horizons (restaurant), 54–55

Horizons & Cottages, 209

Horseback riding, 121–122

Horse-drawn carriage tours, 187–188

Horseshoe Bay Beach, 111

Hospitals, 250

Hotels. ☞ See Lodging

Housekeeping cottages, 212–222

House of India (restaurant), 42

Houses, historic, 147, 150–151, 164

Hubie's Bar, 175

I

Ice Queen (restaurant), 171–172

Icons and symbols, 272

Il Palio (restaurant), 49

Irish Linen Shop, 87

J

Jack 'n' Jill's Toy Shop, 91

Jackson School of Performing Arts, 179

Jamaican Grill, 35–36

Jazz clubs, 173–174

Jet-skiing, 122

Jeweler's Warehouse, 86

Jewelry shops, 85–87

Jogging, 122–123

John Smith's Bay, 111

K

Kafu Hair Salon, 72

Kangaroo Pouch (shop), 75

Kayaking, 116–117

Kentucky Fried Chicken, 63

King's Square, 147

L

La Coquille (restaurant), 40

La Trattoria, 43

Le Figaro Bistro & Bar, 41

Liberty Theatre, 181

Libraries, 143, 182

Lighthouses, 162, 163

Lighthouse Tea Room, 53, 163

Lillian's (restaurant), 56

Lindo's Family Foods, 84

Linen shops, 87

Liquor, 87, 89, 252–253

Little Pomander Guest House, 224

Little Theatre, 181

Little Venice (restaurant), 42

Lobster Pot (restaurant), 45

Locomotion (shop), 77

Lodging

cottage colonies, 206–211

guest houses/bed & breakfasts, 199, 223–226

housekeeping cottages and apartments, 212–222

price categories, 191–192

resort hotels, 193–195, 198

small hotels, 198, 200–206

Loft (club), 175

Loughlands Guest House & Cottage, 224–225

Louis Vuitton (shop), 77

Loyalty Inn, 170

M

Magazines, 257

Mail, 255–256

Maritime Museum, 154

Marketplace, 84

Marks & Spencer, 68–69

Marley Beach Cottages, 212

Marula Apartments, 218

Masterworks FoundationGallery, 72

Maximart, 84

Mazarine by the Sea (apartment facility), 218

Media, 256–258

Medical plans, 254

Michael Swan Galleries, 72

Mid Ocean Club, 98–99

Miles Market, 84

Minibus tours, 188

Modern Mart, 84–85

Money, 258–260

Monte Carlo (restaurant), 41

Monty's (restaurant), 33

Moped rentals, 260–261

M. R. Onions (bar), 169–170

Munro Beach Cottages, 213

Museum of the Bermuda Historical Society, 143
Museums, 69, 142, 143, 145, 147, 148–149, 154, 156
Music, 182–183
Music clubs, 172–174

N

Nannini's Häagen-Dazs, 155
National Dance Theatre of Bermuda, 179
Native Adventures, 186
Nea's Alley, 147–148
Neno Letu readings, 183
Neptune Cinema, 181
Newport Room (restaurant), 57–58
Newspapers, 257
Newstead (hotel), 198, 200
Nightlife, 167–174
North Rock Brewing Company, 61
Norwood Room (restaurant), 55

O

Oasis (club), 171
Ocean Terrace (apartmentfacility), 218–219
Ocean View Golf & CountryClub, 99
Old State House, 148
Omax Ceramics Studio, 73
Ordnance Island, 148
Out & About Bermuda, 187
Oxford House (B&B), 225

P

Packing, 261–262
Paradiso Cafe, 32, 142

Paraquet Guest Apartments, 219
Parasailing, 123
Parishes, 21
Parks, 144, 149–150, 163–164
Par-La-Ville Park, 144
Passports, 263
Pasta Basta (restaurant), 44
Pasta Pasta (restaurant), 47–48
Paw-Paws (restaurant), 56–57
Pegasus (shop), 69–70
Peniston-Brown's Perfume Shop, 89
Perfume & Gift Boutique, 89
Perfume factory, 157
Perfume shops, 89
Perot Post Office, 143–144
Pharmacies, 250
Pickled Onion (restaurant/bar), 33, 170
Picnic spots, 52
Pink Beach Club & Cottages, 209–210
Pirate's Port (shop), 79
Playgrounds, 182
Police, 250
Pomander Gate Tennis Club, 128
Pompano Beach Club, 200
Porcelain shops, 81
Portobello (shop), 70
Port O' Call (restaurant), 45
Portofino (restaurant), 43
Port Royal Golf Course, 101, 128
Portuguese men-of-war, 253–254

Price categories
dining, 31–32
lodging, 191–192
Pulp & Circumstance (shop), 82

R
Radio, 257
Readings and talks, 183
Red Carpet (restaurant), 36–37
Reefs (hotel), 200–201
Restaurants. ☞ See Dining
Rib Room (restaurant), 59
Riddell's Bay Golf and Country Club, 102
Rising Sun Shop, 82
Ristorante Primavera and Omakase Sushi Bar, 37, 40
Robin Hood (bar), 170
Robin's Nest (apartment facility), 219–220
Rockfish Grill, 57
Rock Ramblers, 182
Rogers, Tim, 187
Rosa's Cantina, 44
Rosedon (hotel), 203
Rosemont (apartments), 213
Royal Bermuda Yacht Club, 140
Royal Heights Guest House, 225–226
Royal Naval Dockyard, 155
Royal Palms Hotel, 205–206
Rugby, 132
Rum, 88
Running, 122–123, 132–133
Rustico Restaurant, 61–62

S
Safety, 263
Sailing, 113–116
Sail On (shop), 83
St. David's Lighthouse, 163
St. George, 22
dining, 45–48, 149
shopping districts, 66
sightseeing, 144–151
St. George's Club, 210
St. George's Golf Club, 103
St. George's Historica lSociety Museum, 148–149
St. Peter's Church, 149
Salt Kettle House (B&B), 226
Sandpiper Apartments, 220
San Giorgio (restaurant), 47
Scooter rentals, 260–261
Scuba diving, 117–119, 254
Seahorse Grill, 55
Serendipity (apartment facility), 222
Sessions House, 144
Shelly Bay Beach, 106, 110
Shelly Bay Marketplace, 85
Shipping packages, 255–256
Ship's Inn Book Gallery, 74
Shopping
bargains, 80
business hours, 244–245
department stores, 67–69
districts, 65–67
specialty stores, 69–90

Sightseeing
Hamilton, 137–144
the parishes, 156–164
St. George, 144–151
West End, 151–156
Sky Top Cottages, 220–221
Snorkeling, 123–126
Soccer, 133
Solomon's (shop), 86
Somerset Bridge, 155
Somerset Country Squire
(restaurant), 49
Somerset Long Bay, 110
Somerset Marketplace, 85
Somerset Village, 156
Somers Garden, 149–150
Somers Supermarket, 85
Sonesta Beach Resort, 129,
194–195, 231–233
Sound View Cottage, 222
Source (shop), 75
Southside Cinema, 181
Souvenir shops, 81–83
Spanish Rock, 163–164
Spas, 229–233
Speciality Inn, 62
Spittal Pond, 163–164
Sports
participant, 112–130
spectator, 131–134
Spot (restaurant), 141
Spring Garden Restaurant &
Bar, 36
Squash, 126

Stefanel (shop), 79
Stonehole Bay Beach, 110
Stonington Beach Hotel, 201–202
Sunburn and sunstroke, 253
Supermart, 85
Surf Side Beach Club (hotel),
203, 205
Swizzle Inn, 61, 170–171
Syl-Den (apartments), 221
Symbols and icons, 272

T
Take Five (restaurant), 63
Taxes, 264
Taxis, 264
Taxi tours, 188
Tea time, 59
Telephones, 264–267
Television, 257–258
Temptations Cafe, 149
Tennis, 126–129, 133
T.G.I. Freddie's(restaurant),
46–47
Theater, 183, 185
Thistle Gallery, 70
Tienda de Tabacs (shop), 74–75
Time, 267
Tio Pepe (restaurant), 58
Tipping, 267
Toasted Marshmallow & Fireside
Chats, 182
Tobacco Bay Beach, 110
Tom Moore's Tavern, 60–61
Tours, 116, 185–188
Town Hall (St. George), 150

Toy shops, 91

Toys 'n' Stuff, 90

Travel agencies, 267–268

Traveler's checks, 260

Treats (shop), 83

Triangle's (shop), 79

Triathlons, 123

Trimingham's (departmentstore), 69

Tucker House, 150–151

Tuscany (restaurant), 43

U

Unfinished Church, 151

United Dance Productions, 179–180

Upstairs Golf & Tennis Shop, 76

V

Valley Cottages & Apartments, 221

Vera P. Card (shop), 81

Verdmont House, 164

Visas, 263

Visitor information, 268

W

Walker Christopher (shop), 86–87

Walking Club of Bermuda, 187

Warwick Long Bay, 111

Washington Mall Magazine, 74

Water Front Tavern Bar andRestaurant, 47

Waterloo House (hotel/restaurant), 40–41, 202

Waterlot Inn, 55–56

Waterskiing, 129

Weather information, 271

Web sites, 268–269

Weddings and honeymoons, 18

West End, 22

dining, 48–49, 155

shopping districts, 67

sightseeing, 151–156

Western parishes

dining, 52–59

sightseeing, 156–164

Whaler Inn, 58

Wharf Tavern, 171

When to go, 269, 271

White Sands Hotel & Cottages, 202–203

Wickets Brasserie, 57

Wildlife tours, 185–186

Willowbank (hotel), 205

Windjammer Gallery, 73

Windsor Garden (restaurant), 142

Windsurfing, 129–130

Wine, 252

Wine Rack, 89

Wingate, David, 186

Y

Yachting, 133–134

Yankee Store, 77

Yoga, 130

Z

Zoos, 156

FODOR'S POCKET BERMUDA

EDITOR: Melisse J. Gelula

Editorial Contributors: Ron Bernthal, Rachel Christmas Derrick, Kim Dismont Robinson, Karen Smith, Matt Wescott, Lilla Zuill

Editorial Production: Stacey Kulig

Maps: David Lindroth, *cartographer;* Bob Blake and Rebecca Baer, *map editors*

Design: Fabrizio La Rocca, *creative director;* Tigist Getachew, *art director;* Jolie Novak, *senior picture editor;* Melanie Marin, *photo editor*

Production/Manufacturing: Colleen Ziemba

Cover Photograph: Robin Hill/Index Stock (St. David's Parish)

COPYRIGHT

IMPORTANT TIP

Although all prices, opening times, and other details in this book are based on information supplied to us at press time, changes occur all the time in the travel world, and Fodor's cannot accept responsibility for facts that become outdated or for inadvertent errors or omissions. So **always confirm information when it matters,** especially if you're making a detour to visit a specific place.

SPECIAL SALES

Fodor's Travel Publications are available at special discounts for bulk purchases for sales promotions or premiums. Special editions, including personalized covers, excerpts of existing guides, and corporate imprints, can be created in large quantities for special needs. For more information, contact your local bookseller or write to Special Markets, Fodor's, 280 Park Avenue, New York, New York 10017. Inquiries from Canada should be directed to your local Canadian bookseller or sent to Random House of Canada, Ltd., Marketing Department, 2775 Matheson Boulevard East, Mississauga, Ontario L4W 4P7. Inquiries from the United Kingdom should be sent to Fodor's Travel Publications, 20 Vauxhall Bridge Road, London SW1V 2SA, England.